FEB 24

THE GARDENER OF LASHKAR GAH

THE GARDENER OF LASHKAR GAH

A true story of the Afghans who risked everything to fight the Taliban

BY LARISA BROWN

BLOOMSBURY CONTINUUM

LONDON • OXFORD • NEW YORK • NEW DELHI • SYDNEY

BLOOMSBURY CONTINUUM
Bloomsbury Publishing Plc
50 Bedford Square, London, WC1B 3DP, UK
29 Earlsfort Terrace, Dublin 2, Ireland

BLOOMSBURY, BLOOMSBURY CONTINUUM and the Diana logo are trademarks
of Bloomsbury Publishing Plc

First published in Great Britain 2023

A catalogue record for this book is available from the British Library

Library of Congress Cataloging-in-Publication data has been applied for

ISBN: HB: 978-1-3994-1102-8; eBook: 978-1-3994-1099-1; ePDF: 978-1-3994-1097-7

2 4 6 8 10 9 7 5 3 1

Typeset by Deanta Global Publishing Services, Chennai, India
Printed and bound in Great Britain by CPI Group (UK) Ltd, Croydon CR0 4YY

To find out more about our authors and books visit www.bloomsbury.com
and sign up for our newsletters

Dedicated to the 26 Afghan interpreters who died while working with British forces in Afghanistan, to those Afghans still left behind and to David Williams, who never forgot them.

'The lucky ones are here in the UK today, and the others are either dead or left behind'
— Rafi Hottak, former recruiter of
Afghan interpreters, February 2022

Contents

Preface

I was with British troops on their last flight out of Camp Bastion, in October 2014. They were ending their combat mission in Helmand province, Afghanistan, after 13 years of war. The mission was meant to last three years and end without a single shot being fired. Yet by then the military intervention had cost 453 British lives, more than 1,800 US lives and the lives of tens of thousands of Afghan civilians. Some of the northern districts of the country, long fought over, were more deadly than ever. The Afghan National Army (ANA) was suffering losses at an alarming rate. And yet here they were, about to lose their vital air support. On the eve of the pull-out, there were serious security concerns that the Taliban could launch a final attack on the departing troops. Nerves were high, and secrecy was paramount. With a selected group of journalists from the UK's major news organizations, I attended a brief ceremony in which British and US troops stood side by side as the Union Jack and the Stars and Stripes were lowered towards the parched desert floor. Apache attack helicopters provided protection from above. As soldiers paraded to piped American marching tunes, there was a lot to consider. What would be the legacy of the West's intervention? Had it all been worth it? Despite the optimism of some of the officers attending the ceremony, the future, I thought, looked bleak. With NATO's fighting force gone, what would become of the Afghans who had stood shoulder to shoulder with the West, dreaming of a new Afghanistan?

Not long after I arrived back in the UK, it became apparent that the risk to those Afghans who had worked with the British was far greater than had been imagined by the mandarins in Whitehall responsible for drawing up government policy. In August 2015 my colleague David Williams, who had reported from Afghanistan on many occasions, was told of an interpreter, Popal, who had been executed in Iran while trying to reach the West. Popal had been denied refuge in the UK because he failed to meet the relevant criteria outlined in two policies which, in theory, gave Afghans a route to sanctuary in Britain. His case inspired the *Daily Mail*, where I then worked as Defence Correspondent, to launch its Betrayal of the Brave campaign, exposing the dangers faced by interpreters who were coming under attack from the Taliban after serving alongside NATO troops. For the next five years, David and myself did everything we could to highlight the threats locally employed staff faced from the resurgent hard-line Islamist group, with the aim of persuading ministers to allow more Afghans into the UK. Our retelling of their stories of suffering and their abandonment to the Taliban resulted in the government changing its policy towards Afghan interpreters several times. We won Campaign of the Year at the British Journalism Awards in 2018 for securing some of them sanctuary in Britain. But our fight did not end there. As time went on, more and more interpreters and other employees reached out to tell their stories. They all felt they had been left behind at the mercy of the Taliban as the group gained territory across the country. In September 2020, I was invited to Stanford Training Area in Norfolk where Ben Wallace, the Defence Secretary, and Priti Patel, the then Home Secretary, advised me that they would be expanding the existing government criteria for sanctuary to allow more Afghans into the UK.[1] In the book *Escape from Kabul: The Inside Story*, by Levison Wood and Geraint Jones, Ben Wallace credits one of my articles and the wider Daily Mail campaign for persuading him that the policy on Afghan interpreters needed to change. When, in April 2021, President Biden announced the complete withdrawal from Afghanistan by September that year (until then, NATO forces had stayed in the country to train, advise and assist Afghan troops), fears of revenge killings grew. The Afghans who had worked with the British troops were right to be worried. It was not long before the Taliban were seizing province after province and rapidly advancing towards the capital.

I first spoke with Jamal Barak, a former front-line interpreter for British troops, on 1 August 2021, just days before the fall of Kabul to the Taliban. His father, Shaista Gul, was in hiding in Lashkar Gah when it was on the verge of collapse. Shaista had been a gardener at the British military base in his home city for some six years. Jamal, having already made it to the UK through his work as an interpreter, was trying to do everything he could to get Shaista and other members of his family out of the country and to safety. It would be a long, hard struggle, involving significant time and effort by many people from all walks of life, but one that ultimately proved successful. I met Shaista three months later on a bright, sunny day at the Chimney House Hotel, near Crewe, where many Afghan families were staying while the government tried to find them more permanent accommodation. Jamal came along to act as his interpreter because his father spoke little English. We had coffee and Shaista spoke about the flowers he had grown and nurtured back in the garden he tended in Lashkar Gah. I was immediately taken by his warmth and generosity, and that of his whole family. But I was also taken by their plight – the hardships they had endured over the years and the repercussions that Shaista and Jamal's work with the British army had had, and was continuing to have, on each and every one of them. With that in mind, I decided to write this book.

During countless conversations over many months, the Gul family members have tried to piece together the story of their lives to the best of their abilities. Inevitably, precise memories of dates and names of people and places may have sometimes faded over time. Intertwined in Jamal's recollections and those of his parents and siblings are also the stories of other Afghans who worked alongside British forces during the war. A few of them I've known for years, having interviewed them as part of my work for the *Daily Mail*. Some of them made it to Britain as a result of our campaigning. Other Afghans whose stories I tell I initially got to know during the August 2021 evacuation from Kabul airport, by which point I had moved to *The Times* and *Sunday Times*. During that time my phone was flooded with desperate pleas for help, with many Afghans having no clue how to navigate the crowds outside the airport. For some of them, I hope I played a small role in enabling their evacuation, but I know that others are still trying to flee the country.

Some of the names of those whose stories I have told have been changed for their protection.

Behind the Wire: Lashkar Gah, December 2009

It was two days before Christmas, and a grey haze hung over the city's teardrop-shaped military base, home to the headquarters of British forces in Helmand province. Shaista Gul, a local Afghan gardener, was hunched over a bright red rose bush within the compound's walls, gathering fallen leaves.

He closed his ears to the distant crackle of machine-gun fire, and for a brief moment he could forget that his home was in the middle of a war zone. It was easy to forget when he was working in this 80ft-square haven of the world's best-looking poppies, gaudy orange marigolds and hollyhocks that were as tall as the soldiers on the base. The bees swarmed to the white, yellow and purple hollyhocks, supported by wooden sticks pushed into the hard soil by Shaista himself. Some of the flowers, many of which were only recently planted, were blooming, even though it was winter. The splintered bench nearby, normally occupied by soldiers with troubled minds, was empty.

Shaista Gul – a Pashto name meaning 'beautiful flower' – was a willowy man with a short, neatly combed beard and moustache, his skin darkened by hours spent out in the glare of the sun. His dry, cracked hands were etched with the stains of plants and garden soil. Two fading tattoos were visible on his forearm, one inscribed with his own name, the other with that of his favourite brother, Amir. Shaista was only 38, and yet with five daughters, five sons and, for most of his life, barely a penny to his name, he had the wisdom of a man far beyond his years.

Soon it would be lunchtime in Lashkar Gah and, although the air was cold, Shaista could feel a layer of sweat forming on his back from the warmth of the thick waistcoat he was wearing over his washed-out *shalwar*, now the same colour as the earth. He had been working in the garden since shortly after sunrise, following morning prayers, and was tending the plants with an energy he had not felt since his first day at the base more than two years earlier.

As he covered the roses in a plastic sheet, a Chinook helicopter came into view, its blades whirring, causing the flowers to sway violently in its downdraft. Shaista raised his arm to shield his eyes from the powdery dust that swirled in the air. An orange-bellied quail that had been drinking from a small pool of water startled and flew over his head. The arrival of a helicopter was not unusual, Shaista had learned, as senior officers would fly in several times a day from the sprawling British base at Camp Bastion, just ten minutes north-west of here.

Behind a closed door in the labour support office a few metres away from where he was gardening that morning, Shaista's son Jamal was being interviewed by a British officer for a job as an interpreter. Jamal had already been inside for nearly an hour and Shaista was feeling impatient. What were they saying? Was Jamal's English good enough? What if the officer discovered he was lying about his age? The questions raced through Shaista's mind as he walked across the worn path which criss-crossed through the garden, to collect some water from its 300ft-deep well.

As he did so, he passed the pomegranate tree, with its vase-like arching structure, which would soon dangle its leathery, dark red fruit. Shaista liked to take pomegranates home for his wife, Razagulla, who was several years younger than him. She relished eating their fleshy pink seeds, even though they would get stuck in her teeth. Shaista enjoyed making her happy, especially now she was so weary taking care of their toddler, Mohammed Sahil, who seemed to cry more than any of his other children ever did. Shaista knew too that, although she didn't like to talk about it, Razagulla was still mourning the deaths of two of their daughters, one of whom had been stillborn while the other had passed away when she was just six months old. The hospitals were so ill equipped in Lashkar Gah that nobody knew the reason for their daughters' deaths, and probably nobody ever would.

Like many of the women in the city who had lived under the rule of the mujahideen and then the Taliban, Razagulla was uneducated, having never been to school, and spent her days taking care of the home, cooking and raising the children. She did not complain because she had never expected her life to be any different. In fact, Razagulla counted herself lucky compared with many of the other women she knew, as she was Shaista's only wife. Indeed, she and Shaista were envied by people across the city because they had married for love – unlike most couples, who were together because their parents had decided they were a suitable match. And they made a handsome pair: Shaista with his striking brown eyes and charming smile which showed his gleaming white teeth and Razagulla with her glossy jet-black hair and contagious laugh. Together they were kind and keen to welcome any stranger into their family home, no questions asked. Both were Sunni Muslims, like the vast majority of Afghans. They were also Pashtuns from the powerful Barakzai tribe, meaning 'son of Barak' in Pashto – the Barakzai dynasty having ruled Afghanistan for most of the nineteenth and twentieth centuries. The daughter of a relatively rich landowner, Razagulla loved wearing bright colours – pinks and purples – and an abundance of gold bangles. The two of them had suffered many hardships already, but even during the worst of times they had made each other laugh. Shaista would tease Razagulla, saying that even the English food flown out to the military base was better than her cooking at home, much to the hilarity of their children, who knew how much time their mother spent in the kitchen.

Shaista's father had been a gardener, and ever since Shaista had been a child he had loved to be outside among the flowers. He soon became familiar with the names of all the plants, reciting them off by heart. His favourites were the purple and white flowers produced by the basil plants, because they attracted the bees, and jasmine, because of its heavy scent at night.

Razagulla had also grown up in Lashkar Gah and shared Shaista's love of flowers. After they first noticed each other at a wedding in the city, they saw each other nearly every day. Shaista would make up excuses to walk past her house and Razagulla would smile shyly when their eyes met. Encouraged by their son, Shaista's parents eventually arranged a meeting with Razagulla's parents to ask permission for Shaista to marry their daughter. They accepted and everyone was delighted. Razagulla was barely a teenager, but it is common in Afghan culture for girls to marry very young.

Following the birth of Jamal, their second son, in around 1992, Shaista and Razagulla were forced to flee their home in Lashkar Gah to move to Quetta, just over the border in Pakistan. In the early days of their marriage, Shaista had enlisted in the police force, fighting on behalf of the Afghan government, which was then backed by the Soviet Union. In Afghanistan, if you served in the police you could be given a front-line role as if you were in the military. When the mujahideen – who had been financed by Osama bin Laden in the 1980s and then by Washington and Pakistan – took over as the Soviet Union collapsed, Afghanistan was declared an Islamic state. Finding himself on the wrong side of history, Shaista knew that he and his family were in immediate danger. They packed their bags overnight and left the country.

They didn't return to Afghanistan until 2004. By then Lashkar Gah was almost unrecognizable. It had been transformed, with major construction projects under way and new schools and roads being built. 'Who are they?' the 12-year-old Jamal asked his father as he saw armoured vehicles rolling through the streets of the city. 'They are American troops,' Shaista told him.

Shaista's older cousin, Sayed, had been one of the first Afghans to get a job with the British troops after they took over the city's military base from the Americans in early 2006 and turned it into their Main Operating Base – or MOB Lashkar Gah, as it was known by the soldiers. He was employed at the base as a cleaner – by a contractor rather than directly with the army – along with dozens of other Afghans who were given various jobs to do.

When the British troops first arrived, many wore soft berets, rather than the hard camouflage helmets they were to wear later, keen to point out that they would do things differently from the Americans, who had driven around in heavily armoured vehicles. News circulated among the local population that Brigadier Ed Butler, commander of British forces in Afghanistan, had said the UK forces would not go out looking for trouble. Their task was to work on counter-narcotics and reconstruction as part of a NATO-led International Security Assistance Force, and for that they needed the support and cooperation of the locals, although their mission quickly changed from winning over hearts and minds to a shooting war with the Taliban.

The garden in the military compound had initially consisted of just a few flower beds planted by some British civilians. Then Sayed, who was like a brother to Shaista, was spotted watering the plants, rather than focusing on his cleaning duties. Shortly afterwards, with the agreement of his bosses, he took on the job of tending the plants instead. His first task was to turn the dusty ground into fertile soil. This involved Sayed digging channels alongside the flower beds and irrigating them with a network of narrow, open troughs that were home to frogs and toads. The British troops eventually sought to employ two others gardeners, who would each be given their own area to cultivate. Three of Shaista's four brothers – Anargull, Abdul and Amir – were also employed at the base, Anargull and Abdul as chefs and Amir as a labourer (his fourth brother, Bour, was working for a foreign construction firm). Hearing of a vacancy for one of the gardening positions and knowing Shaista's love of plants, they put his name forward. He was offered the job.

Sayed and Shaista had similar features, although Sayed's beard was thicker and fuller, and he wore a black turban – the same colour as those worn by the Taliban – trailing over his shoulder. But they were as ebullient as each other and were now in constant competition over whose bit of garden looked the best. Even so, sometimes they swapped cuttings of the flowers they liked the most. 'My area is still the best,' Shaista would remind Razagulla at least once a month. He was proud of the fact he had grown his garden from nothing.

The income Shaista made from gardening meant he no longer had to borrow from his brothers to pay his rent. (It is fairly common in Afghanistan for families to support each other financially, especially if one family member is earning much more than another.) Shaista had previously struggled to afford the monthly payments on the cramped two-bedroom flat he inhabited with his ever-growing family. The family's sole income at one point had been from his twice-weekly visit to a rich neighbour's garden, where he would tend the flowers for 100 Afghan afghani (about 95p) a day. Now he was earning $450 a month and would be among the wealthiest people in the city.

It hadn't taken long for news of the salaries being offered by the NATO forces to circulate throughout Helmand, a province that grew half of the country's opium poppies. Farmers who had recently seen their poppy fields levelled by government workers seeking to stamp out the burgeoning drug trade had no source of income. A shortage of irrigation during the summer months also constrained their choice of crops, and they had been left with no alternative but to go to Lashkar Gah to find work. Many signed up to work for the British.

The move suited the UK and its partner nations, who wanted to employ more local mechanics, labourers, kitchen staff, cleaners and even cultural advisers, to reduce the number of people they needed to fly out from the UK. The bonus for NATO was that it would also be pouring money into the local economy by giving people jobs, helping to win over the hearts and minds of those they sought to help.

But for the Afghans, working for NATO did not come without risk. Just because the Taliban were no longer in power did not mean they had gone away. Shaista and his brothers all knew how potentially dangerous it was to work with the 'infidels', a term that translates as 'non-believers' and was used by the Taliban as a general term to describe the NATO forces. They were considered 'traitors' or 'spies' for helping them, for which the punishment was most likely a gory death.

As early as 2005 insurgents had begun attacking civilians perceived to be cooperating with the US military. Farmers in Khost province, on the border with Pakistan, were said to have been offered 15,000 Pakistani rupees (US$250) to kill civilians working with the US army.[1] It was common for the Taliban to send *shabnamah*, commonly known as 'night letters', as a method of intimidation for NATO employees like Shaista and his brothers. Some warned of the 'wrath' people would face if they cooperated with US forces, referred to as the 'Christian invaders', or with the government regime of President Hamid Karzai, whom the Taliban regarded as a US puppet. Sometimes these 'night letters' preceded actual attacks, sometimes not.

The threatening messages were also distributed around mosques or schools, some warning against girls' education. People also received them randomly during the night. They were told that, if they dared expose the location of Taliban suicide bombers or insurgents, they would be decapitated. Often the Taliban relied on those who could read to pass on the message to illiterate villagers. They vowed to kill anyone who defied their instructions. Not long after Shaista started working in the garden a Barakzai tribal elder in Helmand told a British commander how the tribe was being targeted by the Taliban. Many Barakzai had joined the ANA or the Afghan National Police, as a result of which many tribal members had been accused of being spies for the British forces.

Yet working with the West seemed to be the only escape from the difficulties many Afghans had been forced to endure. The British troops preferred to recruit Afghans from different towns and villages so the locals could not easily identify those who were going in and out of the base, in case they should inform on them, but it wasn't always practical. It was already well known in Lashkar Gah that Sayed, Shaista and his brothers worked for the UK forces, and at the time none of them thought to hide it.

The first sign of trouble for Shaista had emerged earlier that month when he had received a phone call from an unknown number. It was the Taliban.

'You must leave your job or we will never leave you alone,' a raspy voice had warned him. Feeling confident in the presence of British troops, Shaista had replied quite forcefully: 'I'm just trying to work as a gardener so I can afford my rent and look after my children.'

Then the caller hung up.

The call had shaken Shaista, although he had tried not to let it show when he recounted the conversation later to Razagulla.

In the following days he had just continued gardening as normal, truly believing in his heart that one day the Taliban would be gone.

He was a dedicated, hard-working man and also a creature of habit. He stuck to the same routine every day – six days a week, with the exception of Friday, the day of prayer – watering every inch of the land methodically, worried about the poor soil and harsh weather which had blighted so much of the area. Helmand province was the most fertile region in Afghanistan, yet still in Lashkar Gah, its bustling provincial capital of around 100,000 inhabitants, there was typically only 4 inches of rain a year. Making a living from farming was difficult, and maintaining a garden required dedication and patience in equal measure.

Shaista already felt an affection for the compound garden as if it were his own. As the months passed, he added personal touches to it, and sent Jamal, his most spirited son, off to the bazaar to bring back some local flower seeds. Even when Jamal was only six years old he had been at his father's side, asking to go outside at night to smell the jasmine. This boy had never disappointed Shaista and he never would; he knew that he would take care of his parents as they grew older.

The garden quickly grew into a profusion of flowers, plants and shrubs from areas across Afghanistan, but also from the UK. Much to Shaista's delight, soldiers stationed at the base began to ask relatives to pack seeds in the parcels they sent. Others brought packets back with them from leave and then asked Shaista for some seeds of native Afghan flowers to take home with them. In fact, when Shaista arrived at the base it was the first time he had seen an English rose. Some of the flowers from the UK struggled to survive because they could not cope with the heat. Their leaves would burn in the smouldering sun. Yet by bringing the seeds, the soldiers and other officials working there brought a little slice of Britain to the base 4,000 miles from home. Shaista often daydreamed about the cuttings from the plants he could take, should he ever be able to afford a bigger house with a garden.

Where he and the family now lived was only a short walk from the base, but Shaista always left plenty of time to get to work. He was never late arriving, and never early leaving. Life outside was an incongruous contrast to the patch of garden paradise inside. In winter, the desert sand turned into a thick grey mud that clung to your shoes like clay. The smell of freshly baked naan mixed with the odours of livestock being taken to market, the high-pitched chatter of children going to school, the muezzin's call to prayer on the loudspeaker mounted on the minaret at the mosque – all served as comforting reminders that the fighting had not reached the centre of Lashkar Gah.

In the mornings, the elders would sit outside on flimsy plastic chairs and dip warm, freshly baked bread in glasses of boiled tea leaves. Shaista could barely walk a few steps without bumping into someone he had known for most of his life and entering into a lengthy conversation. Everybody wanted to know what it was like to work behind the heavily fortified blast wall lined with razor wire that encircled the base.

As local Afghans approached the compound, they could make out a fully manned sentry post constructed out of concrete at the main entrance point and similar positions around the perimeter, but they couldn't see any further inside. Troops manned the posts day and night. They always worked in pairs, one armed with an SA-80 rifle and the other with a general-purpose machine gun. The British weren't taking any chances – and with reason. There were concerns insurgents could attempt to ram a car packed with explosives into the base, as had been attempted elsewhere. There was also the risk of a lone sniper taking pot shots from a nearby window.

When Shaista got close to his work, he always made sure to slow his pace, in case he was mistaken for an insurgent. Having exchanged pleasantries with the guards, he was searched from head to toe before being allowed inside. At first, the process had felt quite uncomfortable; however, the soldiers had become slightly more relaxed as they got to know him. As the months went by, they no longer searched him quite so vigorously.

The presence of British troops in his city had not felt as strange to Shaista as it had to younger Afghans who had never seen Westerners before. When he was born, in the early 1970s, Lashkar Gah – which is Persian for 'army barracks' – was relatively peaceful and, as strange as it seemed to its inhabitants now, there had once been Americans living there in harmony with the locals.[2]

From the 1950s it had become the centre of a major American project to turn the barren Helmand desert into an agricultural oasis of dams and crops. Those behind the project hoped it would showcase the virtues of the Western world and the fruits of modernization, while weaning the Afghans away from Soviet influence. Lashkar Gah itself, where Shaista's family had lived for generations, was transformed from a small Afghan village on the banks of the placid River Helmand into a model city housing both Americans and Afghans employed by the same US engineering firm that had helped build the Hoover Dam.

Back then, Shaista remembered, some parts of the city had looked like an American suburb, with well-built white stucco houses and long lawns, a tennis court, a cinema and even a swimming pool. The American children went to a different school from Shaista and his brothers – the only one in Afghanistan where boys and girls could study together – and they listened to Elvis Presley records and drank lemonade. Afghans christened it 'Little America', and the project became the largest development programme in the country's history.[3] It led to the building of two huge dams – the Kajaki dam and the Dahla dam – as well as 300 miles of irrigation canals and 1,200 miles of gravel roads.

Yet, despite the huge ambitions of the project, it was doomed from the start because nobody had carried out proper water and soil surveys. The dams were never completed to the height that had been set out, they lacked certain crucial equipment and only a third of the projected land was irrigated. The soil in the Helmand valley quickly became waterlogged and the salts moved to the surface. And then, in a sign that it was no longer fertile, the ground began to sparkle. The project, which consumed vast amounts of US aid money, ultimately failed to produce the wheat yields envisaged, and Washington finally pulled its people out in the late 1970s as the Soviets invaded, when Shaista was about eight years old.

Now, decades on, with rows of pine trees still lining some streets, Lashkar Gah felt like a besieged frontier city as the Western forces had moved in, militarized the area and taken on the Taliban in the towns and villages that surrounded it. Shaista never had any reason to leave the city, but he knew that those who entered it from the bleak stretch of unforgiving desert that lay beyond it were greeted by two British army Land Rovers marking a checkpoint.

All of Britain's war-fighting operations in Helmand were commanded from the MOB, which had earned the nickname LashVegas, not because soldiers could drink alcohol or gamble there but because the food, much of it fresh, was considered the finest in all the NATO bases. Hundreds of soldiers were stationed there at any one point, mainly from Britain but also from other NATO countries such as Estonia and Denmark. Some were part of a provincial reconstruction team and others worked with the Afghan police. To the north-east was the town of Sangin, beyond which were Musa Qala and Kajaki, while to the north-west was Nad Ali, straddling the strategic centre of Helmand. It was widely believed that whoever controlled Lashkar Gah controlled Helmand itself.

Over time the purpose-built military base of Camp Bastion, to the north-west of Lashkar Gah, had massively expanded to accommodate 14,500 troops, of whom almost 3,500 were British. By May 2010, thousands more would arrive too. It served as a sign to both the Afghan civilians and the Taliban that the Western forces were there to stay.

Shaista had also heard of the huge field hospital there, storing hundreds of units of blood, to cope with the never-ending stream of trauma patients being flown in from across the province. Helicopters flew between the MOB and Camp Bastion day and night.

For as long as Shaista had been there, the base at Lashkar Gah had been 'locked down', in military speak, which meant the UK troops were not allowed outside because of the threat of attack. They were facing regular attacks from a resurgent Taliban, and in 2009 alone at least 100 soldiers had already been killed in the fighting. Troops could only leave if they were driving in armoured vehicles on a 'road move' or going out on foot patrol, which by now meant wearing body armour and helmets.

Although the base felt relatively safe compared to the small forward operating bases (FOBs) and patrol bases out in the valley, the soldiers and senior officers stationed there were always aware of the imminent danger. Those inside the MOB's operations room were in charge of the fight on the front line. One of the screens showed footage of the battlefield from a drone overhead. A red light would turn on whenever soldiers had come into contact with the Taliban and someone had been injured. It was turning on more and more frequently, making the room feel increasingly claustrophobic to those who worked there.

Shaista was not allowed inside the room, but he had learned to sense when something wasn't right. There would be the sound of the explosions as they travelled down the valley, sometimes so vivid the rocket blasts sounded like the screech of nearby tyres. Military jets roared overhead more frequently than in the periods of relative calm, helicopters flew in and out more often and the mood would turn sour and the atmosphere tense. Then there would be a heavy stream of soldiers coming into the garden for cigarette breaks, either sitting on the benches closer to Shaista or, for more sociable encounters, under a wooden pergola.

Some soldiers came to the garden with their colleagues simply to talk and unload. But for others it seemed to offer something more. These men just sat in silence, taking calm and deliberate inhalations of breath. The different shades of green stood out from everything else in the compound, covered in sand, dust and, in the winter months, mud. It seemed to make them feel at ease. A couple of minutes in the garden was often enough to recharge even the most anxious soldier's emotional batteries. Sitting there took one officer back to his grandparents' garden which he visited often when he was a little boy. Some troops compared it to a walled garden in an English stately home – and thought of a life far away from the bloody war around them.

The brains behind the pergola was Brigadier John Lorimer, who had been deployed to Afghanistan in April 2007 as commander of Task Force Helmand, as the British operation was known. As the most senior British officer at the base, John enjoyed the garden even more than most, as his tent opened directly out on to the flowers. His daily routine began shortly after 6 a.m., when he would set up his foldable chair amid the greenery and read through newspaper cuttings and intelligence files from the previous day while Shaista pottered around watering the flowers. On the quieter mornings he would have time to read letters from his wife and family back in England. For him, that first hour or so early in the morning was sacrosanct. He would stand there with his first cigarette of the day and a giant mug of coffee; it was the only time when no one would disturb him and he could gather his thoughts for the day ahead. He felt a huge responsibility for the men under his command, and it weighed heavily on his mind.

John's only communication during those early hours would be with Shaista, whom he greeted with *as-salamu alaykum* ('Peace be upon you' in Arabic). Sometimes they would shake hands. He often wondered whether Shaista slept at the base because he always seemed to be in the garden, smiling whenever their eyes met. At a minute before 8 a.m. John would leave to go to his first meeting of the day.

During the summer months, when it was roasting hot outside but the air conditioning unit in his command tent never seemed to work properly, John preferred holding meetings in the garden, where, if he was lucky, there would be a light breeze. Somehow, for John, the garden felt like neutral territory when he met up with local leaders. It wasn't in his office or in a green army tent; it also had the added advantage of having no visible maps or sensitive documents pinned up on the wall. And that was when he came up with the idea of the pergola – somewhere for the troops to sit outside in the shade. Like any task given to the army, it was built quickly, with the leftover wood used to build a small table.

Since 2007 it had been used more and more, with troops often sitting outside. Shaista made sure to communicate with those who still came there with hand gestures and smiles. Sometimes they would point with appreciation to the spring onions, lettuce, okra, spinach and radishes that he had started to grow.

Shaista could never understand what the soldiers were talking about because he could barely speak a word of English. He hadn't needed to before the British troops first drove into his town in their soft-topped Snatch Land Rovers in 2006, although he did remember how Jamal, then aged about 14, had run up to them shouting 'Hello' and 'How are you?' as they patrolled past the bazaars. Ever since he had encountered some Americans several years earlier, Jamal had always been intrigued by the foreigners, and one afternoon he had returned home breathless and beaming as he told his father how the soldiers had spoken back to him and shaken his hand. Following this encounter, he announced to the family that he was going to study English and become an interpreter.

Shaista, who used his savings from his gardening to pay for private English classes for Jamal, was so proud that his son had picked up the language so quickly and that he wanted to make a career of it. Yet he also knew what being an interpreter would entail: his son would be expected to go into battle with the British against the Taliban. And when he thought of Jamal on the battlefield, where British casualties were in the dozens and where many civilian interpreters had already died, he felt a knot of anxiety in the pit of his stomach.

But now, in December 2009, here he was, waiting for Jamal as he was being interviewed for a job as an interpreter. Jamal not only spoke Pashto, but also Dari (the most widely spoken language in Afghanistan) and Urdu. Shaista knew that his son had to be at least 18 years old before the British would allow him to go to the front line, but Jamal, who wasn't sure if he was even 17 yet (no one in Afghanistan celebrates, or even recognizes, birthdays), had refused to wait that long. He had applied for a job three months earlier but, much to his disappointment, had been turned away. 'You are too young, wait until you are 18,' the British officer had told him.

However another chance had opened up in the last few weeks, as the battalions rotated. There was now a new officer in charge of the recruitment of interpreters, and Jamal told his father he would try again. Shaista didn't feel able to stop him. Jamal's plan – which he had laid out to his parents in detail the previous night – was to change his date of birth on his application. Nobody would know, he claimed, because the birth certification process in Afghanistan was so vague it was easy to forge such documents. The British troops were also unlikely to question it too much because they desperately needed interpreters on the front line.

When Shaista and Razagulla initially protested at their son's choice, Jamal told them, 'I have to do this.' Shaista could not understand – after all, as a gardener at the base he was now earning enough money to support the whole family. 'Dad, I have to get to this place one day,' Jamal replied, adamantly. It wasn't just about the money for Jamal, though, it was what came after that; he was as sure as he could be that he was destined to go to England.

Lying in bed that night, unable to sleep, Razagulla told Shaista that she doubted the plan would work. 'He looks so young, they'll never believe him,' she whispered, worried that Jamal would hear them in the communal room where they all slept. Jamal, like most boys of his age, had a thick head of longish hair that fell over his ears, but no beard or moustache. It was difficult to believe he could pass for 18. His English was much improved, but Razagulla wondered what use he would be on the battlefield when bullets were flying and bombs going off. That morning she prayed for her son and his safety, but then pushed aside her worries and helped Jamal pick out his best grey *shalwar* and his best shoes, the red sandals with the German label on them.

And now it was 4 p.m., the time when Shaista usually packed up for the day. There was still no sign of Jamal; he had been inside for almost five hours. He stopped concentrating on his garden and began to worry.

Meanwhile, Jamal was coming to the end of his interview, which had included an English test. 'You've passed, Jamal. Well done. I'm sending you to Musa Qala,' the British officer told him, pausing to allow the news to sink in. 'Now this could be risky – you could die, you understand?' he added. Musa Qala was a town that had been captured from the Taliban two years previously. Jamal was unfazed, thinking only happy thoughts about how he would at long last be working alongside the soldiers he so revered. 'Send me to the most dangerous place,' he replied, feeling brave. He wouldn't die, he was invincible, he thought to himself, knowing then that this was one of the greatest moments in his life.

The officer told him he needed to be ready to leave on 25 December, in two days' time.

Jamal couldn't wait to tell his father, who he knew would be anxiously looking at the time. Escorted by a soldier because he did not have a security pass, he was led outside to where he saw Shaista crouched down, pretending to trim one of the bushes. Before Jamal uttered a word his father, could tell by the expression on his face what he was going to say.

'I passed the test. I'm going to be an interpreter now,' Jamal told him, grinning. Shaista stood up and started laughing, hugging his son. He couldn't believe that Jamal's plan had actually worked. But his joy was coloured by the knowledge that the British troops needed interpreters on the front line as soon as possible and it would only be a matter of days before his son left. Jamal had less than 48 hours to pack his things and say his goodbyes.

That evening Razagulla prepared her best dish – the Kabuli pulao, a heavenly mixture of fluffy rice, lamb and caramelized carrots spiced with garam masala, cinnamon, cumin and cardamom pods. As she added the final touches, Jamal came into the kitchen. 'Mum, I don't need that many clothes, I'm going to be in uniform,' he said, having seen the bulging bag that she had already packed for him. He wasn't sure he would even need any traditional Afghan dress where he was going. 'Jamal, just take them, you don't know what you'll need when you are there,' she insisted. It was at that moment that Jamal realized how much he would miss her. He had never been away from his mother before, not even for a night. Now he was heading to the battlefield with hundreds of soldiers he had never met, speaking a language he barely knew.

The news of more deaths of soldiers which had trickled through recently also weighed heavily on Jamal's mind. This year, 2009, had been Britain's bloodiest year to date in Afghanistan, with 102 troops already dead. In the most recent attack, a few days earlier, two soldiers had been killed in a suicide bomb blast while on patrol at a checkpoint on a route into central Sangin, less than 20 miles south of where he was going, Musa Qala.[4]

Two years previously, in 2007, more than 1,000 British troops, including some Royal Marines in 40 Commando, had, along with some American and Afghan forces, seized Musa Qala after a brutal five-day battle with the Taliban. There were rumoured to be as many as 2,000 Taliban fighters in the town who had apparently beefed up its defences with hundreds of mines. But four days after the troops moved in on the town, the Taliban had withdrawn their forces northwards into the mountains. Many locals had fled the fighting, but those who stayed behind reportedly cheered as they saw the NATO forces. It was unclear exactly how many Taliban and civilians had been killed in the operation, code-named Operation Snakebite, but it left two British soldiers dead.

The mission – overseen from the MOB in Lashkar Gah – had been the first major test of the newly NATO-trained ANA, and at the time it was largely viewed as a success – testimony to the use of careful and intelligent planning over brute force. The victory was symbolic too, because the previous year (2006) the town had been handed over to a council of tribal elders in a widely criticized British-led initiative, only for it to be taken by the Taliban months later.

Since its recapture in 2007, the Americans believed that the British had made limited progress.[5] They had established front lines some 12 miles around the centre – their so-called 'ring of steel' – but everything beyond that was insurgent country. A circle of a dozen small patrol bases, manned by both British and Afghan troops, were battling attacks from the Taliban from every direction. 'Welcome to Stalingrad,' said a home-made wooden sign at one of the bases.[6] Although the bazaar in the centre of the town was bustling again and a school, a mosque and a clinic were also up and running, reconstruction efforts were slow. The town's grand mosque, which was destroyed in the 2007 military operation but was meant to have been rebuilt, was still a giant hole in the ground.[7]

Jamal had no idea what awaited him in Musa Qala, nor how soon he would be deployed there, but the impression left by one British officer with a journalist two months earlier suggested that, without further troops and reconstruction, the Brits had found themselves in a virtual stalemate with the Taliban.[8] And yet Musa Qala was strategically important because it dominated much of the fertile land of northern Helmand and was crucial to the drugs trade, as it sat astride key trafficking routes. It was also close to the key British-held strongholds of Sangin, Nowzad and Kajaki. Although Jamal didn't know it yet, in the coming months responsibility for the dusty town would be handed over to the Americans.

Jamal left home as planned on Christmas Day. He had tried his hardest not to cry as he hugged his mother at the doorstep. When he got to the military base, the soldiers were wearing Santa hats, and seeing them all dressed up and jovial gave him a moment of light relief. He walked over to the sandy-coloured accommodation blocks – which had flowers interspersed around them. His father would be pleased to see those, he thought. One of the soldiers handed him his new military uniform all neatly folded, a rucksack, a pair of camouflage army socks and heavy desert boots and body armour that was almost too heavy to carry. The camel-coloured combat fatigues felt tight on his body compared with his loose-fitting Afghan clothes, which he took off and scrunched into his bag.

As he waited for the Chinook helicopter to transport him to Camp Bastion (his next stop before the front line) he said goodbye to Shaista, who had left his garden to walk to the helicopter landing zone to see him off. They shook hands as the RAF pilot started up the helicopter, and Jamal watched how to put on his helmet, ear defenders to muffle the noise of the engine, and goggles, which he thought looked pretty cool. Then he was guided across the runway – avoiding the rotating blades – along with a group of other people bound for Bastion. His breathing became faster as he struggled under the weight of the rucksack and the armour, which dug into his side.

At the last moment, before stepping on the helicopter, he looked over his shoulder and saw his father wave. There was no going back.

2

Preparing for Battle: Camp Bastion, Christmas Day 2009

A wide-eyed Jamal thought he had stepped on to foreign soil when he first arrived at Camp Bastion, a teeming military metropolis of shipping containers and earth-filled bags dropped in the red Helmand desert, like the first city on Mars. The veritable fortress, with its radar towers, aircraft hangars and cream-coloured buildings that looked like motels, seemed out of place in the arid, treeless landscape. A casualty on a stretcher was being wheeled into a single-storey white block, the busiest trauma hospital in the world.

It all suddenly seemed very real. Jamal felt very scared and very young. 'I've never been away from my mum and dad before,' he cried to the Afghan supervisor who greeted him – an unusual display of emotion at a base full of macho military types ready for war. His phone had been taken from him before he boarded the flight so that he couldn't be tracked – or use it to communicate with the enemy. The British were taking every precaution to make sure they hadn't allowed spies – or, worse, fully-fledged militants – into their base. But without his phone Jamal couldn't call his parents to reassure them he had arrived safely either. He knew his mother would be worried.

'Don't cry, you should be fine. You'll get used to it,' the Afghan supervisor told him when they were alone, handing him the standard Afghan offering of green tea with sugar. There was an uncomfortable emphasis on the word 'should', and as Jamal wiped his wet cheeks with the back of his hand he wondered what use an inexperienced teenager would be to the well-trained British troops on the battlefield.

There were two things Jamal learned in his first few hours as he was given an elementary tour of the base, known by some as a 'tent city' because of the long rows of sandy-coloured canvas tents that squeezed in dozens of weary soldiers every night. First, there was no escaping the thick, treacly mud that had formed as the winter rain mixed with the film of dust and sand coating the ground. His newly issued combat boots already looked like they had endured months of hardship before he had even set foot outside the barbed wire and blast blocks. And yet he was told that the summer months at Bastion were far worse, when mini-dust whirlwinds created a layer of powder a foot deep. The dust, coupled with the unrelenting heat of the desert climate, sapped the energy from the soldiers, who had to constantly clean their weapon systems in case of attack. But aside from the dirt, the base was considered relatively comfortable compared with the front line – which, surprisingly to Jamal, many of the soldiers were itching to get to. There, he was told, troops were eating the same packaged ration packs every few days and living in holes with only sandbags on top for protection. Also out there, in the unknown, the temperatures could dip to as low as −10 °C at night and the rainwater could leave the soldiers ankle-deep in mud. It was not uncommon to see snow either, although Jamal much preferred snow to the summer heat.

The second thing that Jamal learned was that, unlike the troops – who were keen to get out there and put their training into practice – many of the Afghan workers didn't want to venture outside of Bastion at all, even to go home on leave. This was for one simple reason: they were too afraid. The Taliban were stepping up their attacks on anyone connected with the Western troops. Caterers, mechanics, interpreters, labourers – all were considered targets. Travelling by road to go home – often the only choice for those living and working at the base – was considered particularly dangerous. And with reason: the previous year the body of a young worker called Shafiqullah had been found in a nearby canal.[1]

After listening to a security briefing and checking out the shower facilities, Jamal dragged himself to dinner, despite feeling painfully shy. He watched others in front of him wash their hands with alcohol gel and did the same before joining a queue for food. As he saw the slabs of meat in front of him on the cookhouse counter, he panicked. One of the trays looked like it contained pork – which as a Muslim he was forbidden to eat. No, it was OK, it was turkey. (It is not uncommon to eat turkey in Afghanistan, where there is an abundance of the birds.)

When he sat down with his tray and plastic knife and fork, he covered part of his face, painfully aware of how young he looked. Would the soldiers realize? He picked at a plate of roast potatoes, carrots, turkey and, a first for him, Brussels sprouts (which he loved). Surrounded by party poppers and balloons, he watched as the British troops piled their plates high with meat and all the trimmings. Enormous in Jamal's eyes. Embarrassed by his comparatively small helping, he thought about going back for seconds, but then another wave of soldiers arrived to join the queue. That first night he barely talked to anyone – except briefly with some fellow Afghans – worried that his English wasn't up to scratch. Suddenly he felt overwhelmed and left the canteen by the back door.

At this time, more than three years after it was first built, it didn't take long to walk from one part of the camp to the other, although it was to grow rapidly over the coming months. There were no street lights or pavements, so the British soldiers had brought with them head torches to navigate the camp at night. But for Jamal, who had come unprepared and wouldn't have had a clue where to get a head torch anyway, making the journey back to his tent in the dark was very difficult. The huge accommodation tents all looked the same, and he had to circle the camp several times before he found where he was sleeping. Nearby was a toilet block with its unseemly bright lights. He made a mental note of it so that it would be easier to find his tent the next time.

Inside the tent, used by both British and Afghan forces, there were a few dozen folding military beds, known as cot beds. Other tents would have bunk beds. As the last in, Jamal had the one closest to the draughty exit. Resting on the side of the tent was a cardboard cut-out of a woman in a gold bikini. He averted his eyes, embarrassed even to look at it. As he put on extra layers of clothing in order to try and keep warm, he half-listened to the faint sound of Christmas songs, interspersed with laughter, coming from outside the NAAFI (the name given to the local shop on military bases). Although it was only a ten-minute helicopter ride back home, Jamal felt like a stranger in his own land. The temperatures had dipped close to freezing, and as he shivered in his sleeping bag, he cried.

MUSA QALA, LATE DECEMBER 2009 – JANUARY 2010

A few days later Jamal flew to Musa Qala, Helmand province's northernmost major town, sitting aside a wide, gravelly wadi. Now was a relatively quiet period there, he had been assured, presumably because neither side appeared to be making much headway.

'Oh my God,' he exclaimed as they landed in a helicopter, although the whirring of the blades was so loud nobody heard him. Soldiers with their fatigues drenched in blood ran towards the landing pad carrying casualties who were groaning in pain. They were presumably being sent back to the hospital at Camp Bastion, where everyone knew they had some of the finest doctors and best medical equipment in the world. 'So much for quiet,' Jamal murmured to himself.

Beside the dry patch of ground where the helicopter landed was the district centre – or DC, as it was referred to. The army had set up camp in a bombed-out hotel built by the Russians in the 1980s. Before UK troops moved in, it had been the Taliban's headquarters in the town, earning it the nickname of the 'Taliban Hotel'. It was also rumoured to have been a large opium market, serving as a sleeping quarters for addicts. This wasn't surprising: Musa Qala, like many areas in Helmand, was long known to have been plagued by its out-of-control opium poppy economy. Jamal walked past the hotel's concrete walls, where he spotted intricate drawings of rockets and men with guns. One of them especially caught his eye. It showed three soldiers, presumably from NATO, surrendering to Taliban fighters wearing their distinct black turbans. The soldiers had their hands above their heads and were carrying rifles. A couple of the Talibs were carrying rocket-propelled grenades (RPGs) – weapons not to be underestimated, Jamal had been warned by another Afghan interpreter. The drawings appeared to have been the Taliban's attack plan – unsurprising, given that most of the insurgents were illiterate. There was something unsettling about seeing their murderous plots so vividly displayed in front of him. Jamal didn't like to think what would be the fate of those they captured.

There were a handful of rooms for the locally employed staff, among them interpreters like Jamal. As he walked into one of the rooms he overheard the end of a conversation between a group of young Afghans sitting cross-legged on the floor. 'He was killed, another injured. They are dangerous,' one was saying to the others in a low voice. He stopped talking as soon as he noticed the eyes of his colleagues darting towards the open door. He turned around and stood up to welcome Jamal. 'Brother, *as-salamu alaykum*,' he said, exchanging formal greetings with the newcomer. The others followed. 'There's nothing to worry about,' interjected another man, sensing Jamal's anxiety. Yet his voice sounded unconvincingly bland. Jamal fidgeted nervously, the blood drained from his face, unsure of what to say or how to react. Who had been killed? How? Was this his fate too? He chose not to confide his fears.

It didn't take him long to find out what they had been talking about. Fourteen interpreters were already dead, seven of them killed in 2009 alone. Many more had been injured.[2] One of them, a man named Mohammed, had been blown up in 2007 in a mine strike at Kajaki, a village a few hours to the east of Musa Qala. The incident had happened in the middle of the night when soldiers from 2 Yorks and their ANA patrol were travelling at speed down a dry riverbed to meet up with the Royal Marines for an operation. For reasons not fully understood by those on the ground, Mohammed had run straight past the soldiers as they waited for the area to be swept for mines, stepped on a mine himself and was blown up. His injuries were ghastly – his left hand was blown off, and he had a hole in his chin so they couldn't even give him mouth-to-mouth. One of the soldiers who tried to save him remarked that, if the same had happened to him, he wouldn't have wanted to make it either.

Although Jamal joined too late to appreciate the difference, other interpreters before him had been given body armour by the British that they believed did not give them sufficient protection. Unlike the soldiers, many of theirs had consisted of just a small ceramic plate that covered only their hearts. To make matters worse, most of them wore just civilian clothes and shoes under the armour. Jamal was lucky to have been issued with a full military uniform. The Taliban had also worked out long ago that, if they could identify the interpreter, they could pick out the most senior soldier on the ground, as they were almost always accompanied by one. One of the interpreters, Rafi Hottak (known as Raf to some British troops, who seized any opportunity to shorten a name), had learned the hard way how vulnerable that made them. A few years earlier he had been out on a foot patrol in Sangin, south of where Jamal now was, when he heard cries of 'Allahu Akhbar' ('God is Great') seconds before he was blown up. Rafi, only in his early twenties and with a wife and baby daughter waiting for him at home, was thrown 15 metres. Bleeding from what felt like every crevice of his body and with his vision a blur, he tried to stand up, only to collapse again to the ground. His left hand, torn apart by pieces of shrapnel, was almost dangling off. But he survived. It was the captain he had been walking beside who had been the prime target. Rafi, who had a moustache and piercing green eyes, had been interpreting Taliban conversations over the radio for him. All that was left of the captain's body was a small piece of his chest, protected by the armour.

Rafi had been easily identifiable as an interpreter because of his civilian-grade helmet, scruffy trainers, jeans and T-shirt. Not until later – after months of protesting by Rafi (who, unable to continue on front-line duties because of his injuries, was sent to Kabul to head up the recruitment of interpreters) – were all interpreters given full body armour and military-issued kit.

Jamal, like the rest of them, had also been given no training at all: not even basic survival skills or first-aid training. He had no idea how to survive an ambush or what to do if he came under fire out on patrol. That meant he was less prepared for the front line than the foreign journalists who accompanied the British troops out on the ground. At least they had had hostile environment training back in the UK before being allowed anywhere near the front. He was also unarmed: other interpreters before him had begged to be given weapons so that they could defend themselves, only to have their pleas rejected.

There was no waiting around in Musa Qala HQ. The following morning the platoon Jamal was assigned to drive through the desert in armoured vehicles. It was dangerous travelling over land because the few roads and bridges that existed were the favoured targets of the Taliban, who had become increasingly adept at laying roadside bombs. To add to the platoon's problems, there appeared to be an unusual amount of rainfall.

Jamal was one of only two interpreters for almost 30 British soldiers, all desperate to know what the Taliban were talking about on their radios. Most locals, including Jamal, mistook the infantry fighting vehicles for tanks because they had similar guns and tracks. Yet these Warriors had much smaller guns and were used primarily as 'battle taxis' to carry soldiers to the front line, whereas the tank is designed to destroy enemy tanks (which the Taliban did not have). Intrigued – having never been inside one before – Jamal strained his head to take a look at the camera feed which the troops were using to navigate through the endless wadis. The route they took was already worn, bomb disposal experts having searched the ground a few days before for explosives. There were old Soviet mines to watch out for, as well as the Taliban's freshly laid ones, targeted at Western troops.

Jamal quickly learned that the Taliban had a way of marking the ground to warn other insurgents of the dangers ahead. A marker could be something as simple as a red or yellow stone facing a certain way. Another sign to watch out for was disturbance to the ground, such as smoothed-over sand or soil. Sometimes the troops missed the signs and the Taliban got lucky. If you were in a Warrior, though, you had a much better chance of survival than most. Its interior stank of diesel, grease and sweat, but it was one of the most mobile vehicles the British army had there, and the best-protected against explosives. If you were hit by one of the home-made bombs in one of these, the chances were that the bottom of the vehicle would be mangled but that you would survive. And yet, even so, that summer a young soldier from the Welsh borders had been blown up at the wheel of a Warrior while out on patrol near Musa Qala.[3]

Today's mission was to patrol the local area before setting up camp for the night at a base a few miles away. It was going to be cold – the temperature was already near freezing, with patches of ice glistening on the vehicles. Each platoon in Musa Qala had a different task, with some stationed in overwatch positions and others going out on patrol. Those in overwatch were positioned on the higher ground, keeping an eye on any movements on the main road in and out of the town. The aim was to keep the roads open, just as insurgents were trying to achieve the opposite. The insurgents had long known they were there – that much was clear from the conversations they were having over their insecure radios – but with the Taliban only recently having been pushed out of the town, patrols into the remote villages and rural communities of peasant farms on Musa Qala's outskirts were vital for getting a sense of how supportive the locals were. One of the hardest tasks for the British was distinguishing between a local civilian going about their ordinary business and an insurgent. That's where Jamal came in. For it was only really the interpreters, who could both communicate with the villagers and pick up subtle signs, who could make that initial assessment. Yet even if the locals seemed happy to see the foreign troops, the Brits knew that the threat of violence was never too far away.

They passed flat-roofed houses of mud and straw – indistinguishable in their features – before coming to a village on the side of a canal. They got out of the vehicle purposefully, taking in every inch of their surroundings. One of the soldiers spotted a man by the water washing his face and hands. Jamal knew he was preparing to pray, a common sight in Afghanistan. 'Jamal, go and ask him what he is doing,' said one of the senior soldiers, suspiciously. Jamal kept his thoughts to himself as he walked over to the man, whose weathered face and unkempt, matted beard spoke of someone who had lived his whole life outdoors. 'I live here,

I'm a farmer. This is my land,' the man replied, slightly taken aback by the direct questioning. Having exchanged a few more words, Jamal returned to the soldiers. He thought the man was telling the truth. And yet, as he explained to them, a local might be a farmer one day and pick up a weapon the next. They would have to let him pass. A farmer was not a legitimate target of warfare, and treating him as such could see them ending up in the dock back in the UK on trial for murder. Also, all the insurgents needed was for the Western forces mistakenly to shoot a handful of civilians and their actions would see another five or six Afghans join their cause.

As they drove away, the soldiers passed a young boy walking along barefoot, despite the frozen ground. Behind him was a cow that he was presumably taking to market. This was not an unusual sight in the outskirts of Musa Qala. Yet it made it easy to see why some Afghans might be persuaded to take up the cause with the promise of some cash or debt write-offs. Jamal made a mental note to have some biscuits ready in his pocket for the children on the next patrol.

Further along the bumpy, uneven road the patrol came to the next village. Now Jamal's translation skills would really be tested. The soldiers were greeted by some tribal elders (respected figures within the community who were key to solving local grievances), who invited them to sit down and drink tea. Jamal was fidgeting with nerves. The commander looked to him, with his uncovered face, and began his introductions. 'We are here to help. We are here to bring security and peace. I know there is no water pump here and we have a team that can provide that. We can get you water and we can get you electricity,' he said, slowly, having already sussed out that Jamal's own understanding of English was quite limited. But the meeting seemed to go well.

Although Jamal was so desperate to please his bosses that he didn't care at the time, leaving his face exposed when he had no idea where these men's sympathies really lay had made him instantly vulnerable. A local from Musa Qala could identify the accent of a man from Lashkar Gah, meaning it was not implausible that Jamal could one day be tracked down to his family home. Other more experienced interpreters preferred to cover their faces with a scarf at such meetings, knowing that they would be dead men walking if they were recognized by the Taliban further down the line. And yet not all of them had a choice, with some British soldiers asking them to remove the scarves because they believed it would make communication with the villagers easier. At that time it was hard for the gung-ho Western forces, intent on delivering promises of a better future, to envisage the insurgents ever taking back control of the land they were there to liberate.

As the British navigated their way further south to their base for the night, it began to get dark and drivers turned off their vehicle lights to prevent detection by the Taliban. Although it was pitch black, with a thermal imaging system they could make out what was in front of them for quite some distance. Surprise would give them an advantage. The Taliban had no such technology.

But the lashing rain turned the mud into thick clay, and the heavily armoured vehicle that Jamal was in became stuck in a ditch full of water. It was all hands on deck, although Jamal was not sure how much use he could be. It should have been no problem. The soldiers were well trained for such an eventuality – given it happened fairly regularly – and every platoon had with them well-qualified engineers ready to fix almost any issue. Yet that night it was different, and for reasons Jamal did not fully understand they would have to wait. That wait meant the soldiers would be sitting ducks until just before sunrise, when some other vehicles were due to arrive to pull them out.

It was a long night for Jamal, who, used to sleeping undisturbed, was struggling to get comfortable in his sleeping bag. He also sensed that the others were on edge, so he was alert too, listening out in case the radio picked up any noise from approaching insurgents. If Jamal mistranslated something crucial, he became suddenly aware, it could be the difference between life and death.

He didn't want to go out into the cold, but when he could hold out no longer, he clambered out of the vehicle to go and relieve himself. There was no privacy even at the back, as the soldiers maintained a round-the-clock lookout for the enemy from every direction. Jamal took a moment to soak up the rare moment of silence. The skies had cleared and the stars bathed the distant grey-pink mountains in their light. To the west were some cliffs. To the east was the hulking form of the mountain the soldiers apparently called 'Mount Doom', in reference to the forbidding volcano in the *Lord of the Rings* trilogy – although this was lost on Jamal, who only watched Bollywood films at home. He wondered how far away the Taliban were and whether they were watching them.

And then, as he clambered back inside the vehicle again, he heard it. The staccato sound of AK-47 gunfire. As the noise got louder the bullets started ricocheting off the vehicle. 'Contact rear, contact rear,' came the shout over the radio. Jamal was in a frenzy of fear. Should he get out? Stay in? Try to hide? He looked around to see what the others were doing.

It was common at that time for the insurgents to try to take a pop at the Western forces with their rusty AK-47s and other small arms. Sometimes a lone fighter would try his luck, although it would more often than not end up worse for him than for the heavily armed troops. This time there seemed to be quite a few insurgents out there.

A few seconds later Jamal was lying on the ground outside in the darkness as around him soldiers fired back with their rifles. The senior soldiers barked orders as they pushed the less experienced troops into positions and guided their fire on to targets. 'What are they saying, Jamal?' shouted the commander over the din. He strained his ears to try and make out their thick Pashto accents over the radio. Again and again the voices repeated the same phrase. He didn't really understand it. 'Be careful, the flies are coming,' he translated, shakily. They must mean helicopters, he guessed, although he had no idea whether there were any close by. More chatter. The fighters had nicknames for each other which made no sense to Jamal. 'Keep going, keep going. They are infidels! We are strong!' shouted one man who appeared, from his commands, to be in charge of the operation. Jamal translated into English. He was so worried about getting the translation wrong that any concern that he could be killed at any moment was pushed to the back of his mind. And then the enemy fell silent. Yet in the darkness, and not knowing who else was out there, none of the soldiers dared go and assess the fallout.

Then they moved to a base on a hillside not far from the river. Many of the bases were named after the battle honours of the unit that had set them up, and sometimes two or more bases even had the same name, which added to the confusion. This one was largely constructed from Hesco barriers – collapsible mesh boxes with heavy-duty fabric liners. These were filled with dirt and gravel to provide a layer of protection to the troops camped behind them. The technique has been in use since the First World War, so it was nothing special. As was also standard, there were ditches around the barriers, which proved to be a nightmare to negotiate in the dark but which, should they come under fire, the soldiers would be grateful for. The platoon commander and the gunner would often sleep inside the vehicles, which offered more protection from both the enemy and the elements. The soldiers – and Jamal – slept outside. They used a sheet of plastic tied to the edges of the Hesco barriers to try and keep out the wind. Yet as the night-time temperatures dipped to well below freezing, even their thick military-issue sleeping bags did little to ward off the cold. By morning, the gallons of water they had brought with them had turned to ice.

The first mistake Jamal made was when he awoke at around 5 a.m. to pray. He changed into his Afghan clothes, found what little water he could to wash and then stepped out of the compound. He had no idea that where he was going was a forbidden area. The next thing he knew he triggered some sort of alarm by stepping on a thin cable running along the ground. For a split second Jamal thought he had trodden on a bomb. His heart stopped. 'What the fuck are you doing, you fucking terp?' screeched one of the soldiers on watch, using the shortened version of 'interpreter'. Jamal was lucky he recognized his face, otherwise he might have had his head blown off.

Some days the troops went out on patrol on foot – often through poppy fields – which Jamal thought to be a safer alternative than the vehicles because it was easier for them to spot the improvised explosive devices (IEDs) hidden beneath the ground. One quiet day, not long after they arrived at the base on the hill, Jamal made his second mistake. He changed into his Afghan clothes and simply walked out from the base alone. He wandered down the hill to one of the fields where he had seen a group of locals when out on a previous patrol. It could have gone horribly wrong. Yet, instead of shooting him – as many would have feared – they invited him in for a cup of tea. 'Since the foreigners arrived we are more happy – they have helped us. We didn't have a water pump in our village and now we do. We hope they don't leave,' said one of the younger-looking men jubilantly. The positive exchange made Jamal feel braver. And so the following day, having been goaded on by some hungry soldiers fed up with their ration-pack diet of cold beef and chicken, Jamal left the camp again and went to a local shop to buy some potatoes. When he arrived back, the soldiers were delighted and started a fire to make chips. But his unsanctioned outings were short-lived.

'Can you come to my room please, Jamal,' said the captain, although by 'room' he meant a small area that was kept separate from the rest of the troops by a cloth hanging. Jamal blushed. 'How and why did you go out?' the captain quizzed him, although he already knew the answer. Jamal started to speak, but the captain cut him off.

'What happens if the Taliban kill you? Then we are in trouble,' he added.

'I'm sorry, I should not have done that,' replied Jamal meekly.

The captain gave him a warning and told him not to do it again. He certainly wouldn't.

It wasn't the first time an interpreter had been shouted at for overstepping his duties. In another patrol in Musa Qala several years earlier an exuberant interpreter had tried to solve single-handedly a problem the soldiers were having with their radios. The commander was trying to make contact with a vehicle at the rear so that they could rebalance some of their ammunition but was struggling to establish communication.

The interpreter jumped out and ran across the ground with an anti-tank weapon strapped to his back. He was well and truly scolded for running around in the middle of a battlefield. The message was clear: interpreters should not be used for anything other than interpreting. Sadly, some of the British contingents that came later did not get the memo and tried to make interpreters carry out all sorts of menial tasks, which some of them refused to do. This would have grave consequences further down the line.

The next time Jamal went out on a foot patrol they were ambushed. The first sign of danger had been five words that he had picked up over the radio. 'Be ready, they are close,' a zealous-sounding voice had yelled in Pashto. Jamal warned the patrol and they all dropped to the ground. Less than a minute later they came under heavy fire from the direction of some thick bushes by the canal. Had Jamal missed the message, some of the soldiers with him would have already been dead. He did not dare to move as the bullets whizzed back and forth over his head for over ten minutes. And then, to his relief, an Apache attack helicopter came into view, the beat of its rotors getting louder by the second. That scared away however many Taliban fighters remained. There were no casualties on the British side, but it was hard to tell if they had successfully hit any Talibs because by the time they got to their positions the insurgents had disappeared along a series of well-dug-in trenches.

In the short time he was there Jamal also experienced another tense moment. It was not uncommon at the time for the soldiers to be handed information about the whereabouts of the Taliban by poor, hungry locals, who expected a small amount of cash in return. Trying to work out whether the intelligence was accurate was difficult, and it was up to the senior officers to decide whether to act upon it or not. One of these local informants came by one morning to meet with the commander. His son-in-law worked with the Taliban, so what he was doing was highly dangerous. If the son-in-law found out what he was doing, he would undoubtedly be killed. Jamal was to translate the conversation. The platoon commander got out a map of the battlefield and splayed it out over a makeshift table. 'They are placing bombs there, there, there. They also plan to put them here,' said the old man, confidently. He looked around the same age as Jamal's father, although much poorer. Jamal, who prided himself on being a good reader of faces, couldn't tell if he was there for the money or because he disagreed with what his son-in-law was doing. Suddenly the base came under fire. Jamal watched as the soldiers darted around getting into position. He ran for cover, and as he did so he saw the man jump into an empty Hesco container. Jamal blocked out the noise, certain it would be short-lived. Half an hour later, after the attackers had run away, he emerged to find the man still there, trembling with fear. The incident really brought home to Jamal how much some Afghans were prepared to risk for very little.

Jamal and the soldiers carried out similar missions for days. For Jamal especially this meant very little sleep, as he had been given the 24-hour-a-day job of listening out for any Taliban chatter over the radio. This was the front line in Helmand, and for Jamal it would become the new normal.

3

Taking Bullets: Nad Ali, February 2010

Jamal's toughest encounter as an interpreter came very quickly after this. In a mission code-named Operation Moshtarak – which means 'together' in Dari – around 15,000 British, American and Afghan troops prepared to carry out the biggest military offensive of the nine-year war, for which they would need plenty of interpreters. The plan was to launch simultaneous attacks on Taliban strongholds across the province in an attempt to crush the insurgents and stamp out the narcotics trade once and for all. The battle plan mapped out by senior commanders focused on the town of Marja, situated in the opium-rich district of Nad Ali, about an hour west of Lashkar Gah. The area was a hotbed of Taliban insurgency, with the ANA having almost no presence.

Military planners believed the offensive would cause hundreds, if not thousands, of civilians, fearing retribution by the Taliban, to flee to Lashkar Gah. In the days leading up to the official start of the offensive, Jamal was told that he would be sent on a daring operation to the village of Sayedabad in Nad Ali, where he would be needed most. Unlike Musa Qala, the land around Nad Ali was as flat as a billiards table, and the presence of a series of canals and ditches in every direction was defining the way in which the war was fought. Sayedabad itself was well known for its Hazara community, a largely Shia minority who have a long history of being persecuted. The village was built around a school, but attendance had been banned by the Taliban since they had captured it years previously. The Qur'an was only to be studied in the mosque. Many of the 500 or so villagers had long since fled, fearing execution.

For this deployment, Jamal was actually given a brief bit of training. Another interpreter, Sayed Wafa, who he would hear of again years later, told him how to work with the platoon commander and how to be careful on the ground – the basics, really. After that, they left together for a flight.

'We are going to have to jump. If the helicopter lands, we are all dead,' shouted one of the soldiers over the screaming of the rotors as the Chinook's ramp was lowered, allowing a violent gush of cold air into the helicopter rammed full of troops. They were a few metres off the ground and the threat of bombs hidden beneath the sand meant it was too risky for the helicopter to land. Jamal's feeling of nausea from standing on the steel deck and breathing in the stench of aviation fuel disappeared momentarily. The operation, planned down to the last detail, was really happening. He grabbed hold of his rucksack, almost bursting with enough food and water for a week, and jumped. As soon as he hit the ground, he, like the rest of the unit, ran for cover. It was 2 a.m.

A few miles away a second Chinook had dropped off another unit. They were headed to the rugged area of Shin Kalay – or 'green village' in English – in what was to be a coordinated operation to push out the Taliban from the area.

For this mission Jamal was one of a handful of interpreters for around a hundred British troops, plus more than a dozen members of the ANA, who had been training at Camp Bastion the day before. There was a palpable nervousness among the British soldiers, who were fully alert to the possibility that a Talib could have inveigled his way into the Afghan army's ranks. In November three Grenadier Guards and two members of the Royal Military Police had been shot dead by a rogue policeman who had opened fire at a checkpoint not too far away from where they were now. The soldiers had been living and working at the checkpoint as they mentored the Afghan National Police, and nobody had seen it coming.

The ANA had problems. The life of an Afghan soldier was very different from that of a British soldier, with junior ranks sometimes deployed to the front line for as long as four years with hardly a break. Pay was erratic, and seeing family members was by no means a given. Inevitably, such treatment had led to problems with desertion and had also bred resentment. Even if the British army went so far as to control the Afghan army vetting procedure in an attempt to weed out possible insurgents, there would always be a threat from the enemy within.

'Everybody stand still. Do not move,' shouted a member of the bomb disposal team. A couple of these specialist troops had positioned themselves at the front of the unit to search for explosives using the best tools they had available to them, metal-detectors. At that time there were some concerns that either not all of them worked or that the Taliban were managing to create bombs that had so little metal content in them that they were virtually impossible to detect. Jamal watched with interest as they used a fluorescent liquid to mark a safe pathway in the darkness. The others followed their every move. One missed device or one wrong step and their legs could be blown off in an instant. Unlike the British soldiers, the interpreters were not given night-vision goggles, as there had been a shortage of them for over two years. Even with the liquid and the moonlight to guide him, the journey ahead felt almost impossible to Jamal.

They were at least a mile out from Sayedabad and what ought to have been a short walk felt like forever as they crossed the sandy ground with eyes wide, searching for IEDs. As the weapon of choice for the Taliban, partly because they were cheap and easy to make, these could kill in at least two ways. If the explosive was big enough, they could blow the target – in this case, the British soldiers or Jamal – instantly to pieces. Yet a smaller explosive could also be lethal, ripping a soldier's body in half and leaving him or her to die slowly in agonizing pain. Even those who survived sometimes, perhaps only for a brief period, wished they hadn't. Legs torn off, mangled body parts and genital mutilation were commonplace.

British troops were typically finding bombs as small as 5 kg or as big as 15 kg – enough to cause what would be deemed back home a major tragedy. When they first started being deployed on the battlefield, they were crudely crafted devices made up of locally available parts, but over time they were slowly evolving to become more sophisticated and more destructive. The insurgents were relying on them to kill and maim British and American troops in preference to gun battles, which were proving costly in both equipment and men. The IEDs were built in a number of ways. Some were detonated remotely by a transmitter such as a cheap mobile phone or a basic hand-held radio. But those ones required time and dedication, as the insurgents would have to be on the lookout for vehicles or patrols going past before setting them off. Others just exploded when someone – anyone

– stepped on a trip wire or pressure plate. These could be kept buried under the earth for weeks, waiting to claim their victim. It was feared that there were thousands of them lying in the ground in Helmand and that, unless the troops had Taliban informants to point out their locations, everyone was at risk nearly all of the time.

Jamal should have been more worried than he was, but he was still recovering from the sickness he felt while being forced to stand in the helicopter. He wiped the beads of sweat off his forehead. Although the day had only just begun, he was already struggling to keep up with the professional soldiers, who had had years of training carrying heavy loads on their backs. Jamal had certainly put on weight and built up strength since he had signed up a few weeks previously, but in comparison to them he was still just a scrawny boy.

After they had been walking for around ten minutes, a mud-brick settlement came into view. Its inhabitants appeared to be sleeping, but the soldiers knew that the Taliban were out there somewhere. It was some comfort to know that there were also a couple of Chinooks close by, should they be needed.

Jamal jumped involuntarily in the darkness. Suddenly: 'They are here! Get ready. We must be quick!' screeched a panicked Talib fighter over the radio in Pashto. He translated. They must have heard the helicopters. Shots were fired in quick succession into the air, in the direction of the choppers. It was difficult for those on the ground to see where they were coming from. But it didn't matter. A few seconds later the gunner on the helicopter fired back. Then silence.

The troops on the ground moved further in. Jamal worried there were more Taliban lurking inside the village. The fact he could barely see in the pitch darkness merely added to his anxiety. The British commander whispered to him to go and knock on the front door of what appeared to be the main house. No response. There was also no one to be seen. The commander was becoming agitated: his troops were out in the open and he felt exposed.

'Jamal, you need to tell them to open the door. Tell them they must leave the house and we will pay them money,' the commander instructed his young interpreter, who was starting to feel faint from the heaviness of his body armour. It may have offered him some protection, but it was like wearing a thermal blanket. 'You need to open the door,' Jamal shouted in Pashto as one of the soldiers started climbing up a rotten ladder at the side of the compound to see if he could take a closer look.

A few minutes later an old man opened the door, with his tousled-haired son standing next to him. 'Who are you?' asked the old man, frostily. There was no time for pleasantries. 'You need to leave, we will pay you. We need to carry out an operation here,' Jamal told him, trying to sound authoritative. But the old man didn't want to move. He was adamant. 'It's the middle of the night. What about my animals?' he said. 'I'm not leaving my animals.' Eventually Jamal persuaded him to send his wife and children away, but he got his wish and stayed behind with his animals. He also refused to take any money.

Dozens of weary soldiers piled into the compound, and although it was huge by local standards, with at least six rooms, it was barely big enough to fit them all in. Jamal felt suffocated as soon as he stepped inside. What if the Taliban were already moving in and had them surrounded? They would never be able to escape. He tried to calm his nerves by chewing on a flattened oatmeal biscuit from his ration pack. After checking out every room and realizing they were all practically the same, he made his way to the far corner of one with a window in it that had a marginally less pungent smell of sweat, grateful for the rug to sit on. Nobody was allowed to remove their body armour in case they came under attack.

Jamal sensed something bad was about to happen. The Taliban had gone quiet, but there was no way they could have been pushed back that easily, even if the British did have helicopters hovering above.

Still more alert than ever, some of the soldiers began to fill the giant bags they had brought with them with sand and clumps of dirt and carried them up to the rooftop. They needed to have a high vantage point so they could spot the Taliban coming and the sand-filled bags would protect them from bullets. Although, with their night-vision goggles and their superior weaponry, the impending firefight was set in their favour, in the next hour someone missed a trick.

As dawn broke, a soldier cautiously opened the door of what had been transformed overnight into a makeshift military base. Before he even managed to breathe in the cold morning air, he was shot in the leg by a Taliban sniper. As his injured body was dragged to safety, all hell broke loose. Rockets ripped through the sky, sending reverberations throughout the compound. Bullets ricocheted off the walls as the soldiers fired towards the building where the shots were coming from. Jamal's ears were ringing, his hands were trembling. Without a gun, he felt defenceless; there was nothing he could do but listen to the radio. Anything that would point to the Taliban's next moves, location and numbers could help them win the battle.

The firefight went on for hours. During a brief lull a helicopter was able to get close enough to air lift the injured soldier to hospital. And every time it subsided momentarily, one of the troops volunteered to get some water from the pump by the front of the door. But then they were fired upon again. They were quickly running out of water, and it was becoming a problem.

A while later, the soldiers edged out of the building, with Jamal following on behind them. More bullets came their way. Jamal instinctively ran to a pomegranate tree for cover. Just when the British thought they had wounded one fighter, another one popped up. It was like every insurgent in the district was descending on the village. The troops eventually had no choice but to go back inside the old man's house. Two Chinooks thundered overhead in an attempt to take out the apparently increasing number of enemy fighters. There was incomprehensible shouting over the radio. They are really scared now, thought Jamal. 'Are you OK?' said one voice, shortly answered by another: 'No! I've lost five men.' They said they were bringing in vehicles to take away the wounded, Jamal told the commander. He never found out if they managed to get away in time because at that point they seemed to get spooked by one of the helicopters. Overpowered by the air support for the British troops, the Taliban retreated.

By the time he returned to the compound, Jamal hadn't slept for 36 hours. His clothes were drenched in sweat from wearing the body armour and helmet. Although he was desperate to take them off, he knew that to do so would be suicide. In the early hours of the following morning, and unable to sleep, Jamal overheard that the soldiers who had been sent to Shin Kalay were facing an even tougher time. Having withdrawn, the unit, who were a few men down already, would be arriving at Sayedabad imminently. Sending a helicopter to take them back to Camp Bastion had been ruled out because of the likelihood of explosives in the area. Instead, they were making their way on foot to Sayedabad, using the cover of darkness for protection. They would have to sleep on top of each other, Jamal thought.

Deflated and tired, the soldiers in Jamal's unit carried on as ordered and, as the sun started to rise, lighting up the sky with a vivid red and orange, they went out on a foot patrol. They passed apricot trees and the abandoned school, from which earthen pathways diverged through fields of crops: wheat, corn, opium poppies, depending on which direction you took. As usual, Jamal went with them, never straying too far away from the commander on the ground.

They had barely left the village when Jamal spotted a man with a wiry grey beard and black jacket emerge from a narrow dusty path. He didn't appear to have any weapons, but one of the soldiers, clearly on edge, got ready to open fire. 'Come here, take your jacket off!' shouted Jamal to the man, as instructed. They all wondered whether he was hiding a suicide vest. It would only take a split second for him to detonate it and they would all be dead. No reply. The man ran in the direction of a cluster of bushes. He returned with what looked like a machine gun. 'He's shooting at us!' screamed Jamal. But before they were hit, the soldier to his left fired a volley of bullets in the insurgent's direction, leaving the man's body smouldering on the ground.

They moved on, taking the route across the poppy field. Around this time of year, just as the plants were starting to sprout, farmers were usually to be found weeding the fields so the poppies would grow faster and stronger, and in the end produce more opium. It was unusually quiet. They had only gone a few hundred metres away from the village when Jamal saw another man, wearing an Afghan shawl, darting through the trees in the distance. Then he spotted another compound positioned slightly back from the trees that had not been visible at first. As the soldiers slowly moved closer, a couple of shots were fired in their direction. Jamal dropped to the ground. AK-47 rifle rounds cracked over his head. That's when he saw it. There was soil pouring from one of the compound walls. In a panic, the insurgents were desperately trying to make a hole to stick their rifles through. 'Look! They're going to shoot us,' Jamal told the soldier next to him, frantically waving his arms towards the wall. He felt a rush of adrenaline through his veins. The soldier got on the radio to inform the troops waiting on the roof back at the old man's house. They needed back-up. They couldn't move forward but they couldn't go back either because of fears they were being surrounded. On the roof of the compound was a small cache of Javelin missiles, ready to be fired once the call came in. Launched from the shoulder, these potent missiles were highly sought after by many of the Western units in Afghanistan. Their main downside was that they were quite heavy to lug around on foot patrol. However, they were especially useful when deployed against immovable positions such as bunkers and buildings. It only took a few seconds from when the call was made for the missile to roar up into the sky then come screaming down, blasting a hole in the compound wall. How many insurgents were killed was anyone's guess.

After some five hours of fighting, at around four o'clock that afternoon, Jamal was shot twice. The first bullet went into his right arm. At first he felt a numbness, followed by an intense burning sensation like someone had put a red-hot poker to his body. Was the Talib firing at random or targeting him? There was no way of knowing and no time to react before the second bullet hit him on the right side of his chest (where there was a gap in his body armour). Jamal gasped for air, struggling to breathe. Four other bullets narrowly missed his torso. So preoccupied were all the soldiers that it took a while for anyone to notice he had been wounded. Jamal eventually reached out his hand to touch the leg of the soldier next to him and muttered weakly, 'I got shot.' The soldier looked at the pool of blood beside Jamal, horrified, and alerted the others. 'The interpreter has been shot,' he shouted on the radio. As the blood poured out of Jamal's body and he could feel himself staring into the jaws of death, the world around him became silent.

The next thing he knew he was being carried in the direction of the base on a makeshift stretcher. But then he suddenly crashed to the ground again, the pain reverberating across his whole body. The Taliban had shot one of the soldiers who was carrying Jamal to safety. And yet, in what seemed like a miracle, they eventually made it back to base at the old man's house, where another soldier hurriedly tore Jamal's clothes. His body was checked for any other injuries and a medic tried to stem the blood flow with bandages. He was given some water as the old man watched on silently from the corner. A helicopter was requested to take Jamal and two other injured soldiers back to Camp Bastion, but it was not able to land in case it became a target. 'You want me to die? Why are you not taking me to hospital?' Jamal cried out to those around him. He knew there must be Chinooks close by and ready to fly a team of medics to him. They were so well equipped by that point that Jamal had heard they could transfuse blood while still in the air.

As he lay there in agony, he thought about what his family would say when they found out he was dead. They should get around $10,000, at least – a small fortune to his father, even with his gardener's salary. But was it worth it? Another Afghan had spoken of how, when an interpreter had been shot on duty, his father had sat in the British officer's office a few weeks later, wearing shoes so worn his toes were hanging out, and cried. Nobody in their village had shown any sympathy for the family. The locals had refused to allow his son to be buried, saying that he was a slave of the infidels. 'Some day your family will understand why your son died,' the officer told him, which was of little comfort to the grieving man.

After what seemed to Jamal like several long hours, he was carried outside into the fast fading light, at which point he blacked out. When he opened his eyes 24 hours later, he was in a hospital bed. 'What am I doing here?' he asked the military nurse, disoriented. He looked up at the sanitized white walls, the bright lights and then the machines he was attached to. But as he tried to get up and leave, he felt shooting pains across his chest and suddenly light-headed. The nurse helped him to lie down again. Only then did he notice the others. On one bed was a soldier with no legs, covered almost head to toe in bandages; another had lost one of his hands. The man behind him appeared to have been shot in the back. And there were at least a dozen others, all suffering similar injuries. Doctors and nurses – some reservists who had paused their jobs back home with the NHS to help in Helmand – were buzzing around the patients, trying to conceal their exhaustion. Jamal wanted to vomit. He reached for some water on the table next to him. And then he noticed for the first time the bullet wound in his arm. It was all too much for him to take in.

He found out later that the raid he had been caught up in had lasted several more days – but the old man had survived, along with his animals. What remained of his home was now covered in pockmarks. And he had accepted the money from the British troops.

Three others had apparently been wounded in the operation, and when he heard that, Jamal felt lucky to be alive. The British casualty rate across the district was going up almost every day. This was about as dangerous as it would get in Helmand.

Back in Lashkar Gah, Shaista broke down as a soldier told him that his son had been shot. At that time Jamal was still in hospital and unable to get up even for meals. Desperate to see him, Shaista asked for a flight to Bastion. He was promised one, but it never happened.

When Jamal was feeling stronger, he asked for a phone to call his family. The first person he got through to was his uncle Abdul, one of the chefs working for the British troops. Jamal could hear the relief in his voice. 'Yes, Jamal, your dad has been really struggling. As soon as he heard what happened to you he ran to the office next to the garden and begged to come and see you. They've said as soon as you're transferred from the ward to your room then he can come – or maybe they will send you back here before then.' Jamal, still only a teenager, wanted nothing more than to leave the hospital and see his parents; it had been months since he had hugged them. But he was learning fast, and in reality he knew that the British would never fly his father to the base. There was too much going on elsewhere across the province.

While he was still resting in bed, he was given the news that another soldier, Lance Sergeant David Walker, whom he briefly remembered meeting at Camp Bastion, had been killed out on patrol. It had happened when Walker and his team had come under fire as they left another base in Nad Ali. He had been shouting for his men to take cover, telling them to keep as low as possible, when he had been shot in the head. He was killed instantly. Aged just 36, he had five children back at home in Lancashire. Although Jamal had barely known David, his death was a reminder to him, if any were needed, of how fragile life was out here.

There were miracle stories that swirled around the hospital too. According to one legendary story, a Chinook pilot had recently survived a Taliban bullet that had hit his helmet just above his eyes.[1] He had been on standby at Camp Bastion in January when a call for help came through. The next thing he knew he was flying into a fierce gun battle to rescue casualties from the US Marines and the ANA. The firing was so intense that he had to circle for nearly an hour before he could land. The crew were eventually able to pick up the casualties, but a volley of bullets from a hidden machine-gun nest hit the chopper. One of them hit the pilot. He escaped death by an inch. It was stories like that that kept the men and women on the front line going.

During his time in hospital Jamal was moved to another ward, for reasons he never understood. This one was full of Afghans, including women and children. Their injuries were hard to stomach. Some had lost their legs and hands after stumbling across home-made bombs. The children were the most vulnerable because, like all children across the world, they liked to go out and play. And if they saw something shiny, they wanted to pick it up. But, unlike in other countries, in Helmand province that shiny object was likely to explode in their hands. Jamal couldn't stop looking at one little girl who had particularly ghastly scars. He was told that the British and Americans had been engaged in a firefight with the Taliban, who were hiding inside her compound, when, in order to protect their forces on the ground, their pilots carried out an air strike on the hideout, killing and injuring women and children in the process. The girl, who must have only been about three years old, was hit by pieces of shrapnel that had torn across her tiny body. Seeing her still manage a smile was heartbreaking for Jamal. Yet he knew that this was not the first time that ordinary Afghan civilians had been caught up in the war, and nor would it be the last. In May of the previous year, 2009, as many as 140 civilians had been killed in US air raids on the village of Granai, in the province of Farah, around five hours' drive north-west of Lashkar Gah. Everybody had heard about it. Facing pressure from both inside and out, an internal US military investigation eventually found that one of its aircraft had been cleared to attack the insurgents but had then had to circle back, thereby losing several minutes. The aircraft apparently then didn't, as it was supposed to do, reconfirm the target before it dropped its weapons, raising the possibility that by that point civilians had entered the area.[2]

Even though the British were known to have stricter rules of engagement than the Americans, both on the ground and in the air, that didn't stop them killing civilians by accident too. In the same month but further east, in the Nawa district of Helmand, eight members of the same Afghan family were killed in a coalition air strike on a village. The British government would later pay out the equivalent of £7,205 in compensation to a man for the deaths of his nephew, his nephew's two wives and their five children.[3] A few months later, NATO forces carried out air strikes on two oil tankers hijacked by the Taliban near the city of Kunduz, in the north. The air strikes caused a fireball that killed 95 people, including dozens of civilians. According to reports, most of those who perished were burned to death.[4] Many of them could not be identified. Behind the scenes, Hamid Karzai, the Afghan president, was repeatedly warning the Americans that civilian deaths from air strikes were merely playing into the hands of the Taliban.[5] By the summer, the Americans claimed to have changed their policy, saying the use of air strikes would only be allowed to prevent Western forces from being overrun.[6]

There were so many casualties flying in and out of Camp Bastion every day that the Afghan children typically only remained there until they were well enough to be moved to a local hospital. Many of the British medics treating them had never seen such young children with gunshot wounds before. They were also reliant on a small team of interpreters so they could tell the scared children what was happening to them.

As well as Afghan civilians, the hospital also treated members of the ANA, police and even suspected Taliban fighters themselves. Although the militants were guarded at all times and nursed behind screens, recovering soldiers understandably complained about being treated at the same place as those who had sought to kill them. On occasion, they were even treated on the same ward.[7] In its defence, the Ministry of Defence (MoD) said that everyone had to be treated the same under the Geneva Convention.

While Jamal was still in the ward with the Afghan women and children, an interpreter working at the base came to visit him, giving him the chilling news that the Taliban had deliberately targeted him, having identified him as an interpreter because he carried no weapon. Although Jamal had not been aware of it at the time, one interpreter told him that the Talibs had been heard over the radio saying something like 'Kill the massive infidel, the eyes of the British soldiers.' Even though they only confirmed what he already knew, Jamal found hearing those words deeply unsettling. The Taliban were hell-bent on killing any Afghans they saw as traitors for working with the coalition forces.

Unable to go back to front-line duties any time soon, Jamal was told he would be sent back to Lashkar Gah, where they would find him a job near his family home. He would be working with the Afghan police, which he knew some of the troops saw more as tribal militias than as any kind of effective national crime-fighting force. Jamal didn't disagree. They may have worn the uniform, but there was no doubt they were corrupt. They would arrest the local criminals and members of the Taliban but then ask for money to release them. Jamal believed they were working for their pockets, rather than their country. But nevertheless, he would be happy to be away from the battlefield while still, he hoped, doing something useful.

As Shaista waited for his son's return, they had a surprise visitor in Lashkar Gah. The Prince of Wales secretly flew in by helicopter, becoming the most senior member of the royal family to visit Afghanistan. He was given a tour of the base, with the officers delicately navigating his route away from the posters of page 3 models dotted around the compound. Much to the embarrassment of those on the ground, as the prince got ready to leave there was a problem with his helicopter, so he had to wait. Realizing it could take as long as two hours to rectify the issue, the most senior officer on the base took him to the wooden pergola in the garden for a coffee. Shaista was oblivious to the older-looking gentleman and had no idea what all the fuss was about. Little did he know that the future king spent that time talking about his and Sayed's flowers.

After weeks of some of the world's best treatment, Jamal returned home by helicopter. He had still not fully recovered and was wincing in pain from carrying his heavy bags on and off the aircraft. But his mood lifted immediately when he saw his father and uncles come to greet him.

Shaista hadn't been able to believe that Jamal was alive until he saw him for himself. As soon as he landed, Shaista wept. It was the first time Jamal had seen his father cry.

4

The Prison: Camp Bastion, 2014

Four years on, in 2014, Jamal still bore the scars, both physical and mental, of the incident. He kept waking up in the middle of the night replaying the moment he was shot. Although he did not know it, he was showing signs of post-traumatic stress disorder. His flashbacks were not helped by the fact that, although the NATO operation in Nad Ali was initially deemed successful, the international forces and the Afghans were unable to set up a properly working government in Marja, leading to a resurgence of the Taliban. Several months later, British troops, along with Afghan forces, were back in Sayedabad trying to clear out insurgents and stop them using the area as a base to launch attacks. Had it all been for nothing? US Army General Stanley McChrystal, the top allied military commander in Afghanistan at the time, referred to the battle to oust Taliban fighters from their long-time stronghold as the 'bleeding ulcer'. Although by now Jamal had been in the thick of a firefight on several occasions, the Nad Ali operation was the one he struggled most to forget.

Nowhere felt safe to him any more, not even the house in Lashkar Gah. When home on leave two years earlier, he had received a phone call in the middle of the night. 'We have your picture. You were in a white car,' the voice had said threateningly. 'Stop working with the British.' And then, around a year after that, Jamal was heading home in the same white car from the police headquarters in Lashkar Gah, where he was then working as an interpreter at the Operational Coordination Centre for Afghan security forces in Helmand province. It was getting dark when he stopped at the pharmacy for some medicine. As he was driving away and slowed down to go over some speed bumps he noticed a shabby-looking motorbike in his rear-view mirror. On it were two men, both wearing traditional Afghan blankets covering the top halves of their bodies.

At that time, rumours abounded that the Taliban were assassinating locals on a regular basis for cooperating with the British and the Americans: soldiers, policemen, intelligence officers, labourers – anyone regarded as collaborating with the infidels. They used motorbikes because they could shoot their targets and then zoom down narrow alleyways and disappear through the bustling markets of the city before anyone could see or catch them. Jamal's Afghan supervisor, Dawari, had been informed repeatedly that intelligence gathered by the Afghans was suggesting that locally employed staff at the compound were at risk. He had told them to keep changing the routes to and from work and to travel at irregular times. Some of them had been urged to change their phone numbers too, although not all of them took the warnings seriously. Jamal, especially, thought Dawari was very bossy.

Jamal sensed straight away that the two men were following him. They started to speed up. The man driving the motorbike was taller than the one sitting behind him, and even from this distance Jamal could make out his crooked, yellow-stained teeth. He pressed his foot firmly on the accelerator. He needed backup. While keeping one hand firmly on the wheel, he used his other to call the commander at one of the local police stations. The line was busy. It was too late. The bullets hit his car – one into the back of the vehicle and another into a side door. Jamal threw the phone down on to the seat next to him and drove as fast as he could. It seemed that the motorbike was trying to overtake him so that the two Talibs could fire through the window and kill him. But Jamal wasn't ready to die that day. As he got closer to his house, he managed to lose the motorbike. Perhaps they had just wanted to scare him. It worked.

When he arrived home, the police commander called him back. Jamal told him everything. Later that night the commander came round with an AK-47 rifle. 'Keep that in your house. If anyone asks, tell them to come to me,' he told him. It was not unusual for Afghans to keep rifles in their homes for protection, but it posed the risk of them being mistaken by the Western forces for insurgents. After Jamal recounted the story again the following day at work, another senior Afghan police officer authorized him to carry around a pistol. He had no clue how to use either weapon, but it felt comforting to know that they were there should he need them. Ever since then Jamal had tried to push both incidents to the back of his mind, but he never stopped worrying about his family's safety.

By now, Britain's mission in Helmand province was drawing to a close and all the Afghans who worked at the base were being made redundant. The decision to leave the province followed a commitment made by US President Barack Obama in 2012 to end America's combat presence in the country by 2014. David Cameron, the British

Prime Minister, even travelled to Camp Bastion, where he said troops could come home knowing it was 'mission accomplished', a phrase that would stay with him long into his premiership. Yet a much-reduced coalition force would remain in the country under the banner of the NATO-led Resolute Support mission, which would focus on training, advice and assistance to the ANA. It wasn't clear how long it would be there for.

Shaista had been made redundant by February 2014. As part of his redundancy package, he had been given 18 months' salary by the UK government, which he could withdraw in bits every month – and for which he would be forever grateful. Though still only in his early forties, he resigned himself to a life sitting at home with his family and tending to his much-loved quails in his garden. (Keeping quails is a Pashtun tradition said to be thousands of years old.) Jamal, meanwhile, had been told he would be eligible for sanctuary in the UK because he had served in a front-line role. It seemed as if his dream of going to Britain – one of the reasons why he had become an interpreter in the first place – might at last come true.

But there were many other Afghans who were not happy with the British offer. The drivers, cooks, cleaners and others who were employed at bases across the province were not granted a British visa, among them Shaista. They were told they could either take the extra salary, as Shaista had done, or receive training or education funded by the UK government for up to five years. The problem was that many of them didn't see a life for themselves in Afghanistan and they, especially the younger ones, believed getting to Britain was their only way of escape. Even the interpreters, who were often the ones most exposed to the Taliban, had to meet strict criteria. Jamal was among several hundred who did so, but thousands did not. For instance, those who had not spent an entire year out on the front line with British troops and had not been serving on an arbitrary date in December 2012 were not eligible for a visa. That automatically ruled out interpreters who had spent nine months risking their lives on the battlefield in Helmand during some of the most dangerous years of the war. Interpreters who had quit their jobs or had had their contracts terminated were not eligible either. In one case an interpreter claimed to have gone on leave to look after his mother, who was dying of cancer, only to be told when he returned that he did not have a job. An administrator promised to call him about it, but he waited for five months and after that gave up. As he had only served for ten months, he didn't make the cut. Others told the British Army they had been forced to quit out of fear for themselves and their families when they started receiving death threats from the Taliban. Why shouldn't they be allowed into Britain?

Yet more were furious that, having been sacked for 'minor misdemeanours' such as being found with a mobile phone or a SIM card, they were also not eligible. One interpreter was said to have been dismissed for having headphones. It seemed so cruel that these men were having their futures decided on the basis of a small mistake. To make matters worse, they had no right of appeal, and some of them never fully understood the reason for their termination. There were other, more serious cases, of course. Some had apparently lied about keeping weapons at home or carrying bullets that should never have been in their possession in the first place. But the government view was that, if the troops couldn't trust them out in Afghanistan, then it was too great a risk to allow them into Britain.

A second government scheme, which had been revised in 2013, gave hope to some of those who had failed to meet the criteria of the first. If they could prove that they were being 'intimidated' by the Taliban because of their work with British forces, then they would be allowed into the UK. How they would be able to prove that was anyone's guess, and as the years went by interpreters who claimed they were shot at, had family members killed and/or received death threats had their cases rejected because they were not believed.

So Jamal was one of the lucky ones. He had finished working in Lashkar Gah in April 2014 and knew he would be allowed into the UK. But before he could fly to Britain he had one final brief mission, one that the troops didn't like to talk about. He had been given the job as an interpreter at a secret prison within Camp Bastion, where he was told 37 Taliban fighters were being held, apparently indefinitely, by UK forces. The job required coming face-to-face with the *doshman* – the Pashto word for 'enemy' – who had been trying to kill them on the battlefield. Any interpreter who entered the prison faced a barrage of death threats. However, despite the high stakes involved, they were paid much less to work in the prison than on the front line, as they were supposedly in less physical danger. Outside the base, Jamal was paid $1,300 a month. Inside Camp Bastion, his pay dropped by almost half, to $699.

When he was first told about the job in the prison, he refused to take it. 'I don't want to do the job any more,' he told a British officer overseeing his employment. By that point he knew he was going to the UK and he couldn't wait to get out. Some of his friends, also eligible, had started to pack their bags already. 'You have to do it because the prison needs someone, a very trusted interpreter,' the officer told him. Flattered, but also unsure about what would happen if he declined, Jamal reluctantly gave in.

He knew other interpreters who had requested to work there because it was away from the front line, but their requests had been denied, due to the sensitivity of the place. Jamal was different. He had glowing recommendations from the officers he had worked with in his most recent job at the police headquarters. They didn't want to see him go – one officer described him as 'one of the most valuable interpreters' at the centre, where he earned the nickname *Jamal khana* ('the little king' in Pashto). He was also incredibly well connected, having interpreted multiple conversations between the most senior Afghans on the ground and the British troops. The officer, an army captain, also liked Jamal and thought him funny – a rarity amid so much misery – and believed that without interpreters like him the army's mission in the city would be 'significantly constrained'.

Most of the British officers could not believe how young he looked – they thought he was still in his teens – but nonetheless regarded him as an 'important guy'. For the Afghan police officers he was a crucial link to the Brits, who had the resources, weaponry and equipment they needed. He told them what the British were planning, and the Afghan officers who were involved in counter-terrorism provided vital information about possible attacks by the Taliban in return for the goods they wanted. In Afghan society, youth is often not regarded as an advantage, as it is usually the older people, the ones with the grey beards, who are the decision-makers. Yet Jamal, rare as it was, exerted a lot of influence. There was a running joke among the British that Jamal knew what was going on in the area before the coalition forces even had a clue that the bang had happened.

On one occasion that would long be remembered by the British soldiers who worked with him, Jamal was called by a senior officer in the Afghan police who told him they had just arrested a known individual who had been recruiting suicide bombers. It was a big deal. The man's role was to go to Pakistan, to the madrasas (Islamic religious schools), and select and groom particularly desperate or fanatical young males. He would then hand them over to technical specialists who would provide them with the bombs. Jamal was straight on the phone to the British officer – Captain Rich, as he called him. Remarkably handsome, some senior members of the Afghan police knew him as the 'very cute' one. Jamal knew that within hours the man would have enough influential backers in the province to secure his release. He urged the British team to intervene. A few phone calls later and the commander of the International Security Assistance Force (ISAF), the name given to the overall NATO mission in the country, was informed. The military chief was able to exert pressure on the Afghans not to release him.

By this time Jamal had endured the terrifying madness of the front line, but, despite displaying unbelievable maturity in other ways, he still bore some of the characteristics of a teenager. He would get stroppy if something didn't go his way and, like teenagers the world over, would grasp any opportunity for a quick nap. He suffered from acne and would ask the British soldiers who went back to the UK to return with bottles of 'Clean and Clear' face wash because it soothed his skin. But the British often relied on him to pick up what was happening on the streets. They knew that some of the Afghans working with them were doing dodgy things – such as stealing large drug hauls that they had seized from insurgents, having told Jamal that they were burning them – but there was little they could do about it. And they relied on Jamal to keep the channels open.

The troops Jamal worked with in Lashkar Gah were, by the end, the sole remaining British unit operating outside Camp Bastion. There were only 13 of them, living inside a safe house inside the Afghan-run headquarters, but they were armed to the teeth with a cache of grenades, shotguns, pistols and rifles – enough weapons to start a small war. In the event of an attack, the drill was that they would withdraw behind reinforced steel doors and wait to be rescued by special forces in a helicopter. Their main job was to know what was happening on the ground and report intelligence back to senior British officers. Which was where Jamal came in. The information he provided could prove crucial to an operation.

For Jamal, this meant spending a lot of time sitting on tacky leather sofas sipping Afghan tea while waiting for thick-bellied senior police officers to finish speaking to a long line of locals who had come to them with their various grievances, although the tea usually came with pistachio nuts, fudge and Iranian sweets, much to his delight. Jamal found it amusing how horrified the British were to find the tea boiled in a pot with a curled piece of metal on a rod connected to exposed wires precariously pushed into a plug socket. Such was everyday life in Afghanistan. Although this role was meant to be away from the front line, Jamal often found himself accompanying officers to meetings with community elders and leaders in dangerous areas where the fighting raged.

On the other, considerably more dull, days Jamal would be given piles of documents to translate. After every shift he drove out of the gates of the headquarters in full view of passers-by. Before he bought his car, he either hitched a ride on a passing motorbike or walked home. The British soldiers must have known how exposed that made him. There was no doubt that so-called 'dickers' – British army slang for look-outs – would be watching everyone who came in and out. They would sometimes be seen on mobile phones, presumably calling the Taliban to inform them of any movements. Jamal was very vulnerable.

It was also extremely dangerous inside the Camp Bastion prison. Its official name was the 'temporary holding facility', although to those who worked there it was clearly a prison. Around the perimeter were towering walls made out of Hesco barriers stacked high and topped with razor wire. Once you made it past the first layer, there were more layers of barbed wire, each as impenetrable as the last. Security cameras covered every inch. At its peak there were as many as 90 detainees at the prison, holed up inside converted shipping containers. Many of them had been brought to Camp Bastion 1, the main headquarters of the camp, a short distance away from the airport, from patrol bases across the region.

Working inside the camp was not for the faint-hearted, especially if you were Afghan. On Jamal's first day, the confident, happy-go-lucky 20-something was shaken by how frightened the prisoners made him. He commented to others how 'scary looking' they were with their long beards and unkempt, matted hair. This was heightened by the fact that they kept hurling questions at him, all eager to know who the baby-faced newcomer was. Where are you from? What's your name? How long are you going to work here for?

Sensing his alarm at the circumstances, another of the other interpreters, who was, like Jamal, highly trusted by the British troops, passed on his wisdom. 'Don't get close to them. Don't build any relationship with them, and especially do not trust them,' he warned. As they walked around the facility – Jamal staying closely by his side – he pointed out who the worst ones were. Some of them seemed harmless enough, but still they were angry at being locked up. The unlucky interpreters frequently had faeces thrown in their direction.

Jamal tried to cover his face as much as possible, fearing they would be able to identify him should they ever escape. He told them his name was Fareed and that he had been sent to Afghanistan from the UK to interpret, even though he knew they probably didn't believe him.

Interpreters who worked with the prisoners before him had already come face to face with the suspected insurgents. In the early days, one Pashto interpreter employed by the counter-intelligence team at Camp Bastion to help carry out interviews was asked if he wanted the suspected insurgent to be blindfolded while they spoke. There were obvious concerns that if he didn't have his eyes covered he could recognize the interpreter further down the line. Yet the interpreter, Ahmad, declined, leaving himself fully exposed and therefore at greater risk when he left the camp. In those days it was assumed by many Afghans that, now that the Western troops were there protecting them, the Taliban would never return.

Yet back at Ahmad's home in Logar province his brother, a farmer, started receiving threatening calls and letters. The Taliban named Ahmad, even though he had never used his real name inside Camp Bastion, and accused him of being a spy. They wanted money. From then on Ahmad's brother was forced to buy the Taliban motorbikes to save his life.

Another interpreter, too frightened to be identified, entered the facility a few years later to see a tall man with a long black beard and wearing a long black 'Helmandi' dress of a style typical in the province. He was being allowed fresh air outside, in an open cell (which was similar in appearance to a metal cage). He was not blindfolded and he was breathing noisily, having been angered by something. The interpreter bore the brunt of his rage. 'You are the servant of the infidel. I will remember your face when I am out of here, I will see you. It is because of you people I am here,' he snarled. The British officer next to him asked for a translation. 'We've got your back, don't worry,' he assured the interpreter, who could still recall the incident in around 2010 with a shudder like it was yesterday.

Even if the interpreters covered themselves up inside the prison, the Taliban were also believed to have spies inside the camp. So, as well as interviewing the prisoners, Ahmad's job was to root out suspected insurgents who were applying to be locally employed staff – or, in some cases, were already among them. This was a big job as he was interviewing some 50 applicants a day: the pay was good, and for many people that seemed worth the risk. Ahmad had a jolly, round face and pearly white teeth, and wore a black scarf loosely around his neck even when the days were warm. One day he was approached by a contractor who was working there as a labourer. He gave Ahmad a warning. 'You are a very good man. But you work for the British army. It will be better for you to leave this job,' he told him under his breath. After that, when Ahmad tried to file a complaint about the man, he was told that he had gone on holiday. He never saw him again, but the threat remained with him.

A few days into the job it was Jamal's turn to feel the wrath of the Taliban. 'When I get released, if I catch you I'm going to cut your head off and drink your blood,' one of them spluttered to Jamal as he walked with the man back to his cell. The prisoner had been allowed out to Skype his family in his home village. Jamal was under strict instructions to make sure that this prisoner, as with other prisoners, did not reveal any information about his whereabouts or the length of time he expected to be there. To Jamal, this was beginning to feel like the least of his problems.

The British forces had no means to prosecute any of the prisoners and so, once they finished their investigations, the men were supposed, in theory, to be either released without charge or handed over to the Afghan government to face trial. Yet it was not always as simple as that. The UK government did not believe it could legally hand prisoners over to the Afghan forces in cases where they feared they would be tortured or subjected to degrading treatment in contravention of the Geneva Convention. And so most of them were held at the camp indefinitely, in a kind of legal limbo – too dangerous to be released but unable to be prosecuted. Only in a few cases, where the British had been given assurances that they would be treated fairly and put on trial, were prisoners transferred to the Afghan authorities. Years later, the decision by the British to hold prisoners for more than 96 hours, the maximum length of detention as stipulated by guidelines agreed by NATO, would be pored over in the Supreme Court.[1]

If given the choice, Jamal preferred interpreting for those brief moments when the prisoners spoke to their relatives, rather than when they were allowed out for exercise. The British troops would watch on carefully as the suspected insurgents played football on a small playground area. As an interpreter, it seemed to Jamal that he was expected to kick the ball around with them too. It was then that he felt most exposed of all, his senses heightened, as he felt waves of emotions from fear to hate to sometimes – but rarely – pity.

By 2014 it was apparently decreed that the prisoners were allowed to wear a *shalwar*, traditional Afghan clothing, which the troops would wash for them regularly (before then, some had been seen in prison uniform). They were given fresh halal food for breakfast, lunch and dinner and were allowed to have showers. They also had a place for worship. Although Jamal, like many of the interpreters, believed the prisoners were lucky to be treated so well – much better than the Taliban had ever treated any of their own prisoners – some of them went on hunger strike, often not eating for days. At that point an army doctor was brought in, with Jamal having to go along to interpret. The doctor would threaten to transfer them to the camp hospital to be force-fed if they did not start eating. Jamal got used to being sworn and shouted at. Sometimes they would try and attack him, only to be held back by soldiers. He only managed to get through the days by dreaming about what life would be like when this was all over and he had moved to Britain.

There was one prisoner at the facility that Jamal feared above all others. He was known as Mullah Ahmed. He was allegedly a senior member of the Taliban who, Jamal had been told on his first day, had been imprisoned by the Allies for several years, although others said it was only just over a year. Jamal heard he had been detained by the Americans years earlier but had been released, before being caught again by British soldiers. As he was considered so dangerous he had extra security, but even so, when Jamal had to interpret for him, his heart raced to the extent he found it hard to breathe in his company. What if he worked out who Jamal was? What if he was let out again? It didn't bear thinking about.

Not everyone held at the camp was dangerous, though, and it was the job of some of the interpreters to help decide whether they were or not. A few years before Jamal arrived there had been a case when the British had arrested a man outside the military base amid suspicions that he was about to target British troops with a bomb. When he was later quizzed by an interpreter, he said that he was a shepherd tending to his animals. The interpreter, who understood the local culture much better than the British, was adamant that he was not a Talib and they took his word, releasing him. He was right. As well as intuition there were also physical indications. If there were red marks on one of his shoulders that could have been a sign that he had been carrying an AK-47. The suspects' hands were also examined by the military, although it was never obvious to the interpreters what they were looking for. There were so many people coming in and out of the camp that everyone was deemed a security risk, but it was also almost impossible to catch everybody. Around the same time as the shepherd was detained, a suicide bomber, posing as a delivery driver, set off his vest outside the base. His target had been a queue of locals waiting to get inside – 'collaborators', as the Taliban called them. An interpreter was severely wounded in the blast. He told one of his friends afterwards that his lasting memory had been of a piece of human flesh stuck on his lips.

Every day at the prison was different. As it got closer to the British troops' withdrawal date, there was more and more interest in it from outside the camp. Jamal was told an Afghan delegation would be coming, made up of senior judges, officials and anyone else who had an interest in the prosecutions. The visit would also include representatives of the president himself. 'They want to see how we treat the prisoners and how many we've got,' Jamal was told. It seemed not everybody was happy with the way they were being held. There were also questions being raised about how long they had been there for – one of the detainees had apparently been there for 31 months but had no case file.[2] Although the main interpreter for the visit would be a much more experienced man who had worked at the prison for a long time, Jamal was told he would need to be present for the visit – just in case.

On the day of the visit, and keen to impress, Jamal made sure his military uniform was pristine, his boots polished and his hair neatly combed. A long convoy of vehicles arrived, presumably some carrying security guards, and suddenly the atmosphere became tense. The British were as keen as Jamal was to satisfy their inquisitive guests. Before the delegation was shown around the facility, he stayed back and yet close enough to be within earshot of the conversation. They started off exchanging pleasantries. Clearly nervous, the other, more experienced interpreter was mixing up his words and so changing the meaning of some of the conversations between the British officers and the Afghans. Jamal bit his tongue until it got too much for him to listen to. 'His translation is wrong,' he told the British commander, retranslating what one of the Afghan officials was saying. There were a few hushed words between the British, unsure how to handle the situation. In the end, given the importance of the visit, any niceties were pushed aside and Jamal was told to take over the interpreting. Although he tried not to show it, he was secretly delighted he would be able to show off his skills in front of some of the most important people in the land.

Jamal's main task was to translate for the senior British officer, whom he understood to be a general. 'We have 37 prisoners here and we will allow you to see each of them. The only person you cannot see is Ahmed. We've spoken to President Karzai about this. We will either release him when we leave Afghanistan or we might hand him over to the Afghan government. We can't allow you to see him.' Jamal fed this back to the Afghans. They were not happy. Their eyes shifted to one another as their suspicions intensified. Jamal didn't need to translate anything. The British general sensed their displeasure and filled the silence. 'He's a very senior person. If we release him, we might lose in Afghanistan,' he added, somewhat hyperbolically. When they reached the waiting prisoners – the part the guests had been waiting for – the British general slipped up. 'Jamal, could you please ask him ...', he said, before recoiling in horror at his mistake. Jamal was called Fareed behind the prison walls. 'I'm sorry, I mean ...', he garbled to his young interpreter, who was ashen-faced. It was too late. All Jamal could do was hope the prisoners hadn't been listening.

A few hours later, after the guests had left and Jamal had gone back to his room, one of the men from the Labour Support Unit, responsible for the employment contracts and salaries of locally employed staff, came to him. The officer in charge wanted to see him.

'The British general told us what happened this afternoon. He apologizes for using your real name in front of the prisoners,' said the officer – a stocky, well-spoken man – from behind a desk. 'You still want to go to the UK?' Jamal told him that he did, after which the officer asked if he would consider staying on a bit longer to work for the general. But Jamal had had enough. He just wanted to get out of the country before anything else happened or the British changed their mind about his visa. The officer tried again, but again he refused. Now that they had potentially risked his life by exposing his identity to senior Taliban fighters they had to follow through on their promises.

One night, some days later, Jamal was woken up in his bed by another interpreter. 'Jamal, we need you. Hurry up!'

He had been deeply asleep and it took him a while to realize what was happening. He rushed to the prison, having barely had time to get dressed. A solicitor had arrived from the UK (from the MoD, he thought) to speak to Mullah Ahmed, and the Brits wanted Jamal to translate the conversation. It wasn't clear to him what the urgency was or why they wanted the interview to be carried out in the middle of the night. 'What are you doing here, Jamal? I'm here,' said the night shift interpreter to him, fuming at the intrusion. 'I'm sorry, it's nothing to do with me. They came and told me to come and do the translation,' Jamal replied, apologetically.

Everything was recorded. There were three cameras, one each placed in front of Jamal, the solicitor and Ahmed, who sat on the far side of the room. Jamal was told the translation would also be sent to the UK, where it would be checked for errors. Ahmed was, in fact, an excellent English-speaker, although he spoke to the solicitor in Pashto. Jamal had been told previously that he had been receiving English lessons every day while in prison, from the 'lady with a computer' (a woman who walked around the base with a laptop) – although he didn't believe it until he first heard him speak. The lawyer told Ahmed that the British officials had decided he would be handed over to the Afghans when they pulled out later in the year. Ahmed interrupted, incredulous that they could change their minds in this way.

'You told me six months ago there were two options – either you would hand me over to the Afghans or you would release me when you left. I told you to release me. Now you change your mind,' he spluttered.

The lawyer remained calm. 'I'm sorry, it's not for me to decide. I know you've been here a long time but it's not my decision,' he replied.

'If I am handed to the Afghan government I'll be here for another five to ten years. You've already kept me here without any proof.'

There was a long pause. The solicitor spoke up. 'If we release you, what are you going to do?' he asked. It was not clear why he was asking that question now, except for his own curiosity, given that the decision had apparently already been made to hand him over.

'I want to be a teacher and teach English to people,' replied Ahmed.

To this the lawyer responded by telling him the story of how they had detained a district governor who they suspected was a member of the Taliban. When they released him, they followed him back to his village, where he was given a hero's welcome. He had joined the fight again. And with that, the conversation was over.

Shortly after the visit, rumours began swirling around the prison that Ahmed was going to be released. They had no proof that he had done anything wrong and, so Jamal gathered, he was due to receive millions of pounds in compensation. Jamal didn't stay long enough to find out whether Ahmed ever got the money, but he did hear that he had been moved to Bagram airfield, the US base known locally as Afghanistan's Guantánamo, such was its reputation for the mistreatment of prisoners.

Eventually, at the end of the summer, the prison was closed for good. Meanwhile, back home in Lashkar Gah once more, Jamal waited anxiously for details of his flight to the UK.

5

A Proposal: Lashkar Gah, January 2015

A fat pigeon pecked at rubbish strewn on the ground outside the former British military base, which was now under the control of the Afghan security forces. It had been split into two sections – one the locals believed was being used as a base for special forces and the other as a health clinic. No trace of the UK soldiers remained. The flags of the NATO countries were long discarded, the benches, tables, chairs and cables used for communications presumably looted by locals. Even the trees had been cut down. The earth had become so dry without Shaista and the other gardeners watering it every day that the flowers had all died.

On his last day at the base the previous year Shaista had used his limited English to say goodbye to the handful of British officers he liked the most before walking away from his precious flowers with tears in his eyes. He had been through so much since he had first started and it had been hard to stomach the reality that he had lost his job and he would never go back. Over the years he had been promoted from a simple gardener to a more specialist position which also involved teaching local farmers the best way to grow alternative crops, a position he had loved. Although it had been inevitable that his work would come to an end at some point, given that it was widely known that British combat troops would soon be pulling out of Helmand province, somehow he never believed that it would actually happen. He assumed a new leader would get into power in the USA and would decide that they should stay after all. The first thought that crossed his mind when he was told he was being made redundant was who would water the flowers. It seemed silly, especially when so much else was going on, but somehow also important.

In recent years Shaista had been made to feel like a mini-celebrity at the base, with soldiers coming to take photographs of themselves with him or of him while he was hard at work. Sometimes he asked them to send him the pictures, despite knowing that they would never actually do it (and even if they tried, the postal system in Lashkar Gah was so basic, they would never arrive). He wondered where those photos ended up. Were they on the walls of their family homes? At their workplace? What did people think of him back in England, the clothes he wore, his awkward expression? One year an officer proposed to his girlfriend while they were sitting underneath the pergola. Their photograph ended up in a newspaper. Were they still together? What were they doing now? More than one year on Shaista longed for the comforting sounds of the soldiers laughing and chatting as they grilled lamb and chicken on the barbecue during periods of relative calm. He missed his morning greetings with the British as they went off to breakfast and the excitement, fear and anxiety of what the day would hold, all at the same time.

Shaista had seen so many people pass through his garden over the years: generals, royalty, the ordinary officers and soldiers who had been deployed thousands of miles away from home to fight a war that would never be won. Some of those he had smiled at would have died out there on the battlefield. Others would still be trying to recover from what they had seen, but never could. And many of them would have since moved on, bought a house, got married, had babies. For them, Afghanistan was just a small if significant chapter in their long lives. Names and places forgotten, Afghan faces merging into one. Yet if you asked them if they remembered the garden in Lashkar Gah there would be only one answer: yes.

These days Shaista walked past the base often, almost as if he was in mourning. Today was no different, and as he peered inside through a gap in one of the walls he thought back to the day the last British flight had left the city, in early 2014. He had been standing outside, watching the aircraft flying higher and higher until it disappeared from view. Later that night his stomach had ached from the stress. For Shaista it felt as if a dark cloud had hung over the city ever since.

As soon as the troops left, the violence increased.

Now it was only January, but the people of Lashkar Gah were bracing themselves for the spring offensive – the term given to the surge in violence that always came with the warmer weather, typically following the harvesting of the opium crops. The Taliban controlled two of Helmand's 15 districts, including the desert district of Dishu in the south, near the Pakistani border, a long-time base for drug trafficking. They also controlled the desolate mountainous region of Baghran in the north. They had managed to keep hold of these two districts effectively since 2001. To Shaista, who was sceptical about how effective the ANA would be without support from its Western allies, it felt like only a matter of time before they would sweep across other areas.

He also worried for his own personal safety, and that of his family, as anyone in his position would. People in the city liked to gossip, and he knew that ever since the British troops had left, the risk to them had increased. At night, when the house was quiet and everyone else was asleep, he lay awake wondering if the Taliban would come in and kill them in revenge for collaborating with the Westerners.

Shaista ambled back to his house in time to prepare some plastic bags full of aubergines, radishes, tomatoes and okra. He had so many vegetables growing in his garden that he gave most of them away for free. He had always been a charitable man, but now, with his savings from his time working with the British, he felt he could afford to be particularly generous. He also had little else to spend the money on other than his house and his children – of whom there were now twelve: seven boys and five girls.

From his years of working on the front line with the British, Jamal had managed to save a sizeable chunk of money, which was enough to move the entire family out of their cramped rented two-bedroom flat into a six-bedroomed house with its own garden and which was even closer to the military base – only a couple of minutes on foot. At the front was an apple tree and a pomegranate tree, while at the back Shaista grew mostly vegetables, but also some flowers.

For Shaista, the garden was becoming everything he had ever wanted as he and Razagulla worked together on it. He planted the seeds and Razagulla watered them, also giving him ideas on how best to arrange the flowers they grew. Indeed, Razagulla loved gardening almost as much as her husband did. And by now it had got to the point that people from outside the city had heard of Shaista and his garden and would make regular stops there on their way to or from the bazaars on market day.

Jamal, now in his early twenties, had been at home for several months after leaving Camp Bastion in the autumn of the previous year. He had no work and so spent most of his days reading – poetry, mainly. Many of the poems were about Afghanistan and the beauty of his country. He had longed to explore it properly, but all he had ever known in his adult years was war. His father loved having him around, as did his mother, who no longer tossed and turned until the early hours worrying about him, Shaista noticed. They both knew, however, that one day soon their son would leave them again, only this time it could be for ever.

The next morning there was a thin dusting of snow on the ground. Razagulla had woken up early to prepare their best clothes. She had picked out her most brightly coloured *shalwar kameez*, an emerald green, with gold patterns around its hem, and loose trousers to match. She was choosing the most appropriate colour for Shaista's outfit when Jamal emerged, looking anxious. He started pacing around the room. 'She is a good person for me, Mum, I know it,' he told Razagulla, who loved her potential daughter-in-law like she was her own daughter. Yet she couldn't help but think how lucky she would be to marry her son, who would soon be living in England. 'I know, son, I know. Of course they will say yes,' she responded, although she too was worried about what would happen next.

Jamal had never expected to marry Spozhmai, a young woman who lived less than 15 metres away from the Gul house. But when it was first suggested to him, after one of his sisters, Naz, who was bubbly and shorter than the others, married Spozhmai's stepbrother, he happily agreed. (In Afghan culture it is common to keep marriages within the wider family.) Spozhmai had spotted Jamal long before he had noticed her, though – from across the room at her stepbrother's wedding. Salma, Jamal's eldest sister, must have noticed her fluttering glances in his direction when she thought no one else was looking as the women danced: 'We want you for our brother,' she told her, determinedly. Spozhmai blushed. She knew her secret. They had known each other since they were young girls and had become good friends. But in Afghan culture it wasn't common to discuss matters of the heart too openly. Jamal, on the other hand, had not noticed her and so had no idea even what Spozhmai looked like when the discussions about his future were first taking place (his defence later would be that there had been more than 200 other women at the wedding). He would be pleasantly surprised.

Spozhmai had dark brown teddy-bear eyes, jet-black hair, thick neat eyebrows and a roundish face that was perfectly in proportion to her features. She dressed prettily, with dangly earrings, bracelets and colourful dresses. Although it was still quite rare for women to go to school in Helmand, Spozhmai was well educated – her brothers had made sure of that. She was also funny, which is why she got on so well with Jamal's mother (who spent a lot of time at their family home), although Jamal wouldn't discover that until much later. Spozhmai knew how popular he was with the women in Lashkar Gah – she had been told how flirty he could be – and so when it looked like the marriage would go ahead, she secretly felt very lucky.

Shaista and his brothers had arranged that morning to go to Spozhmai's house to ask her brothers if they would allow her to take Jamal's hand in marriage. Normally they would have waited, as Jamal had spent all his money on the house and had barely anything left to pay for the actual marriage, but he could be leaving for the UK any time now and his parents did not want him going there without having a wife lined up first.

In Afghan culture it is customary for the groom's family to initiate the marriage proposal. If the bride's family agrees, then the financial negotiations begin. It is also traditional for the father of the bride – or, in his absence, her oldest brother – to specify how much money her family requires. This is based on the education, skills and beauty of the bride. The groom is expected to raise the money for the wedding, which could easily reach US$10,000 in Kabul, and not much less in the provinces. In Helmand province, drugs were – and still are – considered the best currency. It is not unusual for wealthy families, in preparation for a proposal, to stash a large block of heroin wrapped up in cling film in a hole dug under their house.

Jamal and Spozhmai were not madly in love – at least, not yet – but they had told their families that they wanted to marry. Spozhmai's father had died when she was only two years old, so today's meeting was about persuading her brothers to agree to an engagement, with no set date for a wedding. Jamal would have to save up a small fortune before they could have the ceremony and he planned to go to England to work and to find a house for them both to live in. Razagulla already knew Spozhmai was keen for the marriage to go ahead because she had asked her directly a few days previously, so perhaps that would help?

'We will not leave until we have your approval that your sister can marry my son,' Shaista teased her brothers once the formalities were over and they were sitting having tea. Like Razagulla, he too was already very fond of Spozhmai and was keen for the marriage to go ahead. Her brothers accepted the proposal quickly. Spozhmai, who had been waiting in the guest house, wearing her favourite white dress to mark the occasion, was delighted.

Spozhmai had no memory of her father, but he had been a very rich man. Back in the 1990s, he had been head of the counter-narcotics department in the ANA and was well respected by everyone, in particular for the speed with which he could catch criminals. Yet his high profile also meant that he was a target for warlords. Whenever he left the house he was escorted by five to seven cars of security guards, all for his protection. But it was not the criminals that killed him. On the day he died he was driving a Land Cruiser towards a suspected gang of drug smugglers and he just lost control and crashed the car, dying instantly.

After he died, his seven houses were left to Spozhmai's 17 brothers and stepbrothers. Most of them now lived together in one giant house in Lashkar Gah, along with all four of his wives and some of his daughters, including Spozhmai. With four floors and up to six bedrooms on each floor, it was one of the biggest houses in the city. Everybody knew who the family was and how important their father had been. Often passers-by would stop to admire it, envious of its size and beauty. His wives had spent more than a decade cooking together, eating together, praying together, and so now they regarded each other as family (in Afghanistan, it is not common for women to remarry if their husband dies). Spozhmai's mother was fairly young when her husband died, although by then she already had three sons and three daughters. However, she was a strong woman; she felt she was supported by the other wives and she would do her best to look after the best interests of her daughter.

After the engagement Jamal saw his future wife for the first time. Not properly (in his eyes) – she still had to wear a headscarf to cover her hair – but enough to know he was happy with his decision. They started talking on the phone, too embarrassed to meet each other under the conspicuous stares of their families. Sometimes they would get to see each other through the windows of their respective houses. Spozhmai would have goosebumps. It felt strange, even to her and Jamal, but they both accepted that they would have to wait until they were married before they could be alone together.

Most of their chats on the phone were about their future. What job would Jamal get? When would they see each other again? 'I'm going to be here alone. Why can't you take me now?' Spozhmai asked, repeatedly, when he talked about his plans to go to the UK. She could not understand why they had to be married before she could join him in Britain. Jamal assured her that it would not be long before they would be together and that there would be no problem in her coming to the UK once they were married. She told him how it was her dream to have a huge wedding – 'one of the best weddings in the whole of Helmand province', as she described it. They would invite everyone they knew and she would wear the biggest white dress she could find. Jamal agreed. He had many friends in high places and he relished the opportunity to show off his good fortune. All he needed to do in the meantime was to stay safe and not get killed. Every day that went by he felt relieved that he had not been targeted by the Taliban.

Unlike Jamal, some of the Afghans employed by the British had already made the decision to leave the country and go to the UK – illegally, believing it was too dangerous to stay. Others were simply ahead of Jamal in the visa queue. One of those was Rafi, the interpreter who had been blown up while on patrol with British forces in 2007, who had left the country back in 2011. After the incident he had been employed at Camp Souter, a heavily fortified military base in the shadow of the Kabul mountains named after Captain John Souter, one of the few survivors of a disastrous retreat made by the British during the first Anglo-Afghan war of 1839–42, the first time a Western power had invaded Afghanistan. Some locals had found the choice of name suspicious.[1]

His body now covered in deep, unsightly scars, Rafi became involved in highly sensitive work which made him a prime target for many hostile groups almost immediately. And much of his work, which he was not allowed to talk about, meant he left the base in his car very late at night, putting him even more at risk. In the most brazen attack, Rafi was grabbed and punched in front of the gate to the camp by two unidentifiable men. They attempted to drag him into their car but he got away. There were other attacks too. He was driving to work on the main highway in broad daylight when two cars started following him. One pulled in front of him to try and block his way, while the other came up alongside. Between them they managed to ram his car into a ditch on the side of the road. They left him alone, though – this time. He was shaken, but tried to push the incidents to the back of his mind.

And then came the kidnapping threat. Rafi was told by one of his contacts in the north of the country that there were plans under way by a criminal mafia group to kidnap him. 'You have to be careful. They are planning something to pick you up,' his contact told him. The group was well known in the area for arranging kidnappings and it was worrying that they had picked Rafi as one of their targets. He started to take precautions and stopped travelling alone.

After that was the most alarming incident of all. He received a menacing phone call from a number that was traced back to the mountainous region of Tora Bora, an area dotted with caves along the country's border with Pakistan and teeming with Taliban and Al-Qaeda operatives. The voice down the end of the crackly line told him that they knew what he was up to and they knew where his family lived. As a result Rafi was told that he must live at the base because it was too dangerous for him to go home. His father and brothers, who were attending the local school, also started taking precautions. But by 2011 the threats from the Taliban had become so intense that he knew the only way he would be safe was to quit his job, leave his pregnant wife and two young daughters and smuggle himself to Britain (at that time there was no specific scheme in place to enable him to get there legally). It was a heartbreaking decision to make, as it would be for any father. He flew to Turkey and used up most of his savings from working as an interpreter – $16,000 – to pay smugglers along the route to the UK. From Turkey to Italy he survived five days and nights at sea in a small inflatable dinghy packed full of some 60 asylum seekers, mostly from Syria and Iran. Then he took a train from Italy to France before making his final journey in the back of a lorry across the Channel. Once he arrived in the UK, just over a month after he left Kabul, he walked into a central London police station and made his claim for asylum. Now, almost four years later, he was still fighting deportation back to Afghanistan. He had never met his youngest child, Mudasir. On the bad days he questioned whether it had all been worth it, but he knew for sure that he did not want his children to grow up to be orphans.

Then there was Dawari, Jamal's former supervisor from back when he was working at the police headquarters in Lashkar Gah. Like Jamal, he was eligible to live in the UK and, much to his relief, had recently been told that his visa had been granted. He would soon be flown to Glasgow with his wife and two small children. Although he could not wait to be out of Afghanistan, his only regret was that he could not take his parents and brothers with him. His father was employed by the Afghan government, making him an obvious target immediately, and Dawari had also often allowed his younger brothers to accompany him in his work. Any spies watching the police headquarters would have noticed them coming in or out. He worried they would become targets instead of him once he left.

Dawari was not taking any chances with his family: he stayed at home and did not talk to anyone until he was on a flight to Kabul. He too had been chased by a man on a motorbike who seemed determined to send him some sort of message. He had managed to lose him in the busy traffic, but one interpreter he knew had not been so lucky. Naqebullah had been shot dead some 300 metres from his home. Dawari, who continued to work at the police headquarters until 2014, was passed intelligence that he had been deliberately targeted because of his work with the West. Naqebullah's death gave Dawari another reason to be cautious. Months later Dawari and the family got out.

If Jamal had turned down the job at Camp Bastion, he would have been out of the country at the same time. Yet it would take a while longer before he could join his friend.

A few months after the engagement, in late spring, Jamal was sitting inside the house while his father was outside gardening when the message he had been waiting for came through. 'Your visa has been approved,' said the text from the International Organization for Migration, which was dealing with his application. Before reading any further he ran outside to tell his father, who had taken a break from watering the plants and was sitting in a chair in the shade. 'I'll miss you, son,' he said wistfully, while at the same time congratulating him. It was a bittersweet moment for both of them. Shaista knew in his heart of hearts that Jamal had to leave. 'It's not safe for you to stay here all your life,' he quickly added, wanting to reassure his son that he was definitely making the right decision. But had it been the right decision to let Jamal join the British army all those years ago? He was no longer sure.

A couple of days later Jamal left the house for his flight to Kabul. From there he would go to the British embassy to collect his visa, carry out his medical tests and then be flown to Britain, along with some other eligible Afghans he had not yet met.

'I just don't know how difficult it will be there, Spozhmai. It's better you come later on,' he reassured his fiancée as they said their goodbyes. By this point she had moved in with Jamal's family, as was the custom, with the intention that she would stay there until she got to Britain. They shook hands, mainly out of shyness; they still didn't really know each other. As Jamal walked away from the house he waved and smiled. He would later find out that after they said their goodbyes, Spozhmai was so upset that she fasted for two days. Razagulla, meanwhile, was inconsolable. She wept at the doorstep as if she was in mourning. Jamal's sisters tried to console her but they were crying too. Even Shaista had a tear running down his face.

Jamal saved his most emotional farewell for one of his younger brothers, Mohmood Khan, whom he knew was prone to be more daring than the others. 'Do not go out of the house, don't even go out with your friends. You know it's not safe for you,' he told him. Jamal was afraid that Mohmood would try and join the Afghan forces. He was also very aware that Mohmood had served as an interpreter inside the same base as Jamal, although for a private foreign company, and that made him a target. It was now the 'fighting season', and the Taliban were on the march across the province. But Jamal's warning fell on deaf ears.

When he arrived at Kabul airport, Jamal met another former interpreter, Abdullah Abdul, who would be on the same flight. They had much in common. They had the same boyish humour, they were about the same age, and both had lied about their age in order to work as interpreters for the British. Neither had been to Europe before. From that moment on they were inseparable.

Abdullah had started working on the front line for the coalition forces in 2010, a couple of years after Jamal. When he first signed up as an interpreter – in his case for the Americans – he was 17 and still studying. He knew his family was struggling for money, so he changed his age on his ID document and the Americans let him in. His first mission was in Kandahar, where the US army was trying to drive out the Taliban, but with little success. People there were poor, many of them without clean water and electricity, and their poverty was fuelling the insurgency. Teenagers were being paid to plant roadside bombs and keep watch on the US and Afghan troops. Even low-level government workers such as police officers were being targeted for assassination.[2] Abdullah only lasted five months. His parents realized how dangerous it was and begged him to come home and finish school instead. He initially agreed, but after a few weeks at home he was missing the big salary. So when he turned 18 he went and joined the British. By then it was towards the end of 2010 and already dozens of British soldiers had been killed across Helmand province that year. Abdullah was posted to Gereshk District, east of Nad Ali, where the ANA, supported by the British, was trying to drive a wedge through the heart of the Taliban operations. After that, he was posted to Camp Bastion. And then, having risked his life on the front line, he was made redundant. But with the redundancy came the promise of a visa to Britain.

Abdullah had spent the last few months living in a private room in Kabul because he was so afraid he would be killed if he stayed in Logar province, where he came from, just south of the capital. It had been among the country's most insecure provinces for years. Around the time Abdullah was made redundant, rumours were circulating that, as well as the Taliban, there was a group of Islamic State supporters operating in the region. Abdullah's family had suffered repeated threats and they were desperate for a quiet life. There would be a knock at the door, typically around midnight. They never answered, but they all knew who it was. It was a cruel way of intimidating them as it kept them constantly on edge. The women felt especially vulnerable as Abdullah's father also spent a lot of time away from home, helping with the transport convoys that shipped goods from Kabul to Helmand for the British army.

When Abdullah was initially made redundant, he returned to Logar to see what life would be like there for him. But he soon realized that he could not stay, even for a short time. Everyone in the village knew he had been away working with the British army, and so there was no point trying to pretend anything different. He sensed immediately that the attitude among the villagers had changed. Some of them tried to hide their displeasure, but others were more open. And then he knew he had to leave when he went into the shop of a neighbour – a man he had known for years – for a chat and to watch the cricket on television. He often went there, along with the other men, to gather and gossip, especially in the late afternoon. But that day a group of men turned up whom Abdullah had never seen before. They singled him out immediately. 'You betrayed your people by working with the British army. You deserve to die,' spat out one of them. Word that he had worked with the 'infidels' had clearly spread further than just the immediate neighbourhood. Abdullah wanted to defend himself but then thought about his family's safety and decided to keep his mouth shut and leave. Following a couple of similar incidents he knew that he could not stay. He used all his savings to rent the room in Kabul and waited. When his visa eventually came through, he had been on the brink of joining the ANA just to make enough money to survive.

The flight to Birmingham was long and tiresome (they had to change twice, in Dubai and Amsterdam), but at least Jamal and Abdullah were seated together. They had been allocated a house with two other Afghan men in Coventry. They had no idea where that even was, but they were too excited to care. With their English skills, they should be able to get good jobs and meet lots of other Afghans. Over time their families would join them and it would feel just like home. For both, this was going to be the fulfilment of their wildest dreams, they just knew it.

6

Taliban Revenge: Coventry, November 2015

The family had kept the secret from Jamal long enough. Shaista would make the call. When the phone rang, Jamal was sitting on the sofa in the terraced house he was now sharing with three fellow former interpreters in a run-down area of Coventry. 'Your brother Mohmood has been shot,' his father blurted out. 'Three months ago,' he added, before Jamal could ask any questions.

But he was still alive.

He had been shot 14 times in his legs and stomach by the Taliban. Nobody had wanted to worry Jamal when he was all alone, thousands of miles away. He had enough to think about. But now Mohmood was a bit better, they thought it was best he knew.

Because Mohmood had been employed by a private contractor as an interpreter, and not directly by the British government like Jamal, he had not been entitled to sanctuary in the UK. It seemed so unfair, especially as they had both worked at the same police headquarters in Lashkar Gah, they had both carried out jobs for the British and had seen each other every day for nearly two years. Mohmood had worked for a foreign construction company that was mainly focused on laying cables underground and helping to build accommodation. Most of its employees were British or American, although the company also employed 20 to 30 local members of staff. Mohmood's job was to interpret conversations between the locals, who needed help with access to the base each morning, and their foreign bosses. The project ended when the British withdrew from Lashkar Gah and Mohmood was asked if he wanted to go and work with the firm at Camp Bastion for a final few months. It had been tempting – the pay was good – but after much thought he decided he would prefer to stay at home and continue with his studies. He used some of his savings to enrol on an English and computer studies course at a private college in the city. But life seemed hard. Now that the foreigners had gone, there were few opportunities for young men like him in Lashkar Gah.

The brothers were close in age, and Jamal had always looked out for Mohmood. They had the same neatly trimmed beards and moustaches. But that was where their physical similarities ended. Mohmood was slimmer than Jamal, with a prominent jawline, and his skin much darker from the sun. Some people didn't believe they were brothers. But they were both clever and exuded confidence. Perhaps that was why they got on so well.

It had been Jamal's regret that he had not succeeded in getting Mohmood a job directly with the British forces. Several years previously, in around 2011, he had tried by using his British army connections in Kabul. But when Mohmood travelled to Camp Souter in the hope of being offered a job, he was told to come back another day. With hardly any money, he couldn't afford to pay for somewhere to stay in the city and so returned home. The brothers' plan never came off. If it had, Mohmood would have been living in Coventry with Jamal.

Now Shaista was explaining to Jamal how Mohmood had been riding his motorbike at the time, on his way back from an English class at the private university in the mid-afternoon. But Mohmood, who had been sitting next to his father as he spoke, grabbed the phone from him, wanting to tell Jamal the rest of the story himself. There had been no warning sign, no threats in the days leading up to the attack, he told his brother. Indeed, it had started out like any other day. His classes had been uneventful, as had lunch, and then he set off back home. 'I was on my motorbike and had nearly got home when I knew something wasn't right. I looked back and I saw that two people on motorbikes were following me. I started to go faster and I could see in my mirror that one of them had covered himself with a blanket and had a rifle to his side. Then he just fired at me.' He didn't remember anything after that. When quizzed a few days later about the incident, he told the police that his assailants had their faces covered with scarves. The two men would be impossible to identify, just as they would have hoped.

'They thought they'd killed him, they left him for dead. People in the village heard the sounds and came running. They took him to hospital. He was a mess,' continued Shaista. Mohmood's body was ridden with bullet holes. There had been so much blood it was hard to know where it was coming from. Nobody knew who the locals were that rang the ambulance to take him to hospital, but the family would be eternally grateful that they got him out of there so quickly. Any longer and he might not have survived.

When he heard that his son had been shot, Shaista rushed straight over to the emergency department, but they wouldn't let him in. He contacted one of his son-in-laws, who was a doctor, who tried to persuade the nurses to let Shaista see his son. But it was a firm 'No'. Shaista was told that the doctor who was looking after him would explain his son's injuries to him over the phone, as he would with any other relative. Their insistence made Shaista suspicious. Although he knew there were strict visiting hours at the hospital, he thought having a son covered in bullet wounds would be reason enough to let him inside. Driven mad with worry, he started to question whether Mohmood was even still alive. Had something gone wrong? Were they biding their time because they didn't want to tell him he was dead? He waited outside the hospital, not wanting to leave in case they suddenly changed their minds and opened the door.

The doctor eventually called to say Mohmood had been shot in the legs, hand and stomach and seven times in the chest. 'I said, "That's it, he's gone,"' Shaista told Jamal, believing there would be no way he could recover from such injuries. His concerns only got worse with every hour he was left waiting outside, with no idea as to how they were treating him. Was Mohmood conscious? Did he even know what had happened to him? Shaista dreaded to think what was going through his mind as he lay there alone in the hospital bed.

Mohmood spent six days in hospital before he realized he had been shot. Floating in and out of consciousness, he didn't have the mental capacity to understand what was going on. On the sixth day he opened his eyes and thought he was dreaming. Then, when he tried to move, he saw the extent of his injuries. He could hardly remember anything – how they shot him or how painful it had been. It was as though his brain had blocked the incident from his memory because it had been so traumatic.

Listening to his brother's account, Jamal was teary-eyed, knowing exactly how Mohmood felt. The conversation brought back emotions he had long tried to bury. He was suddenly taken back to his own time in hospital at Camp Bastion and the shock he felt when he discovered what had happened to him. Sitting on the sofa in Coventry, he felt very alone and a very long way from home.

In the end Mohmood was hospitalized for weeks. The family had wanted to send him to India for proper treatment, to save his leg, but they couldn't afford the fees. Although the treatment in Lashkar Gah was poor by comparison, Mohmood's leg was eventually saved. However, the doctors told him he would never walk properly again. Having spent eight weeks in hospital, he was discharged. He was told that he would need at least six months of specialist care.

Mohmood was lucky to have survived. Others didn't. A few months previously another interpreter, who had been wounded in Helmand, several years earlier, while serving with the Parachute Regiment, had been murdered while trying to reach Germany.[1] Popal, as he was known as by the British soldiers he worked with, had fled Kabul after his brother, who had also worked with the UK troops, had been killed by the Taliban. Popal himself had faced repeated death threats but the British government had rejected his pleas for help, claiming that there was insufficient evidence that his life was at risk. This was not unusual, as officials had dismissed all claims they had received for the intimidation scheme so far. Popal made it as far as Iran, but then they caught up with him. A friend reported that he had been 'executed' near the city of Mashhad, hundreds of miles across the border. His body was returned to his family home in Kandahar.

At that time, many Afghan interpreters were so fearful for their lives that they were considering fleeing their country illegally, as Rafi had done four years earlier. It was either that or stay and risk the wrath of the Taliban, who were on a relentless march across the country.

Ahmad, known as 'Chris' by the British troops who had worked with him, was one of them. His hellish story began when he started working for the British military in October 2008, when he was around 18. Similarly to Jamal, the job was all he had ever wanted to do ever since he had seen American troops on patrol in his town years earlier. He would ride his bicycle next to their convoys, holding up his English books and shouting that he wanted to be an interpreter for them. However, he eventually chose to work for the British because his grandfather, who seemed to know a lot about the UK, told him that they were the best people to work for. He did not question why. (In Afghani culture, the older generation are always right.) He was first posted to Kandahar and then to Musa Qala, like Jamal, just before the British handed control of the town over to the Americans as part of a 'rebalancing' of UK forces in the region. He was super-smart and quick to develop his English, frequently picking up colloquialisms such as 'mate'. Among the visitors he interpreted for was Gordon Brown, the then Labour Prime Minister, although this meant little to him at the time.

One day Ahmad was about to jump on a helicopter at Kandahar Airfield when he was spotted by a group of truck drivers transporting some equipment for NATO troops. They were from his home village in Khost, south-eastern Afghanistan. They recognized him and shouted his real name – loudly, so everyone could hear. He ignored them, terrified of the consequences. Perhaps if he stayed silent they would think they were mistaken? He was angry at himself for not covering his face, as he always did when he was out on patrol.

Back in his village, where he had told everyone that he was working for a small electronics company in Kabul, the word spread quickly that he was in fact working for the British as an interpreter. Not long after, the Taliban turned up at his family house. Khost province straddles an important transport corridor to nearby Pakistan, and its porous border was then being used by both locals and insurgents, making it a primary spot for infiltration. The Talibs' warning was clear. They told his father that his son had to stop working for the British army. 'Otherwise he will be killed,' one of the men told him, matter-of-factly. It was a threat his father had heard issued many times before. 'My son will not listen to me. He is a grown-up. He does whatever he wants,' he replied, trying to sound unafraid. Ahmad got the message a few days later. It was enough to make him return home immediately. He relocated his wife and son to another house temporarily while he assessed the risk to their lives.

A few months later, having heard nothing since the knock at the door, Ahmad returned to Helmand to continue working with the military. He went on to carry out daring operations with British special forces in both the Special Air Service (SAS) and the Special Boat Service (SBS), the most highly trained of all the British military units. Around that time he spent almost half a year interpreting for Sergeant Danny Nightingale, the SAS soldier who was later put in military detention back in the UK for hiding a Glock 9 mm pistol and 338 rounds of ammunition in a rented house he shared with another soldier near the SAS headquarters in Hereford. Nightingale had served all over the world, having joined the SAS in 2001, and Ahmad had liked him a lot.

Soon after, Ahmad realized he had underestimated the Taliban and their desire to carry through on their threats. The next time he was home, he was walking near his village with his brother and cousin when they spotted a group of insurgents some 300 metres away. A man who appeared to be the commander signalled for Ahmad to come over. Ahmad knew that he had a wad of US dollars stuffed in his pocket and that would immediately arouse suspicion. So the three of them ran for it, bullets flying at them from every direction. The sound was deafening. Luckily for them, they all missed. Some Taliban fighters were poorly trained and used old rifles with mismatched ammunition that were prone to mistakes; fortunately, that seemed to be the case today. Ahmad wondered later whether they were there to kidnap him or to kill him.

Afterwards he told the British military what had happened, but they said there was nothing they could do to help him because he didn't know who the men were. He felt he had no choice but to resign from his job simply to protect his family. But that didn't stop the attacks.

The next time Ahmad was shot at he was not so lucky.

It was dusk one day in December 2014 and he had decided to go out for a stroll with his son, who was then around two years old. His wife stayed inside to prepare dinner for them and the rest of the family. As he walked out of the gate of the family compound he saw two men wearing black masks standing waiting for him across the path. One of them told Ahmad to come over but he refused. Nothing good could come of any discussion. Within seconds they got out their rifles and fired at him. Ahmad pushed his son under his chest to protect him from the gunfire as they both fell to the ground. A bullet pierced Ahmad's right leg. Blood trickled down his son's nose and forehead where he had grazed his head under the weight of his father's body. Ahmad ignored his own pain, only caring about whether his son had been hit. But it was fine – the pool of blood his son was now lying in was not his own but Ahmad's. The boy wasn't crying. He couldn't even talk. The memories of that day would haunt the child for ever.

The sound of gunshots had been heard throughout the neighbourhood. Ahmad's parents and wife ran out to see what had happened. As soon as they saw them, the insurgents ran away towards the mountains. His wife, who was pregnant at the time, was so distressed by what had happened that everyone feared she would lose the baby. Ahmad spent six weeks in hospital being treated for his injuries, although thankfully the doctors said his son's injuries were only superficial. When he left hospital, Ahmad contacted the British army again to tell them what had happened. They interviewed him multiple times and in the end gave him $1,600 to cover his family's costs while he got better. They also offered him a safe house within one of the military camps. But his wife, who came from a conservative Muslim family, didn't want to go because it would have been deemed culturally inappropriate for her to live among so many men.

The insurgents wouldn't give up and continued to make life hell for Ahmad. One day he was driving to Kabul on one of his journeys to be interviewed by British troops with another of his brothers-in-law when they noticed they were being followed. They were on winding, uneven roads carved into the rugged mountainside where there were no police checkpoints – the whole area was considered to be hostile territory. As they sped up, the driver in the vehicle behind them started honking his horn, clearly indicating to them to stop. He had a passenger. Who were they? What did they want? Ahmad and his brother-in-law calculated it was not worth the risk of stopping. They sped up. Bullets shattered the glass in the rear window of the car and pierced the chassis. They were almost out of the mountain path and knew there was a police station not far up ahead. So too did the insurgents, who disappeared out of view.

When Ahmad reported what had happened to the police, they did nothing. Too traumatized to continue the rest of the journey, he never made it to the interview. He suffered from mental health problems after that, believing without any doubt that the Taliban were targeting him because of his work with the British. In the following months he changed location many times, taking his wife and now two children to Kabul, to the eastern city of Jalalabad and to different houses across the province. The family was getting tired of life on the run. Ahmad hated having to hide inside, but he knew the Taliban would not stop until they had killed him. By then, although he knew of the risks involved, he was starting to believe he had no choice but to try to get to England.

Niz, whom Jamal would meet later in Coventry, was another interpreter facing death threats and considering paying smugglers to get him out of the country. Having first joined the British military in 2009, he spent nearly six months on the front line in Helmand, listening in on Taliban conversations, before getting a more senior position with the British Foreign Office. They sent him to a US Marine base not too far from Lashkar Gah, where military personnel were bringing in captured suspected Taliban fighters straight from the battlefield for interrogation. Niz, a stocky, unassuming character, known for his fancy watches and hearty laugh, was acting not only as an interpreter at that point but also as an adviser. His key role, however, was to be there for the interrogations. Over the course of two years he came face to face with some 200 detainees. But Niz decided not to cover his face during that time, and for two reasons. First, he was from Kunar province, a place of lush, green mountains and flowing rivers nestled against the Pakistan border. It was far away from Helmand and he didn't think it possible that he would be recognized from back home. Second, he, like so many Afghans, thought the Western forces were building a new Afghanistan, one where he and his family would be free. He never thought for a moment that the Western forces would abandon his country and that the Taliban would eventually take over again.

Under policy agreed by NATO, the captured Talibs could in theory only stay at the Marine base for less than 96 hours before a decision needed to be made between the Afghans, the British and the Americans as to whether there was enough evidence to charge them and send them for trial in Kabul. Yet it was unclear at this time which rules applied. Sometimes, during the interrogation, the detainees would hurl abuse at Niz, accusing him of being an 'infidel'. Most of them had been brought in on terrorism charges, having been caught laying roadside bombs. Others were there on suspicion of smuggling opium for lots of money – money which, it was feared, was being used to help fund the Taliban's resurgence. If the evidence was too flimsy, they would be allowed to walk. If it wasn't, they would be moved on. But even if it was decided that they could be charged, getting them to the capital was a logistical nightmare. They couldn't travel by road because of the risk of the convoy being intercepted by other insurgents. The only option was to fly the captured Talibs by helicopter, which meant taking up valuable resources. Niz was good at his job and highly respected. But suddenly, out of nowhere, in the spring of 2012 he was made redundant. The Americans and the British were withdrawing from the base where Niz worked so he was no longer needed. The timing had been crucial. If it had been six months later, in December 2012, he would have been eligible under the arbitrary timings rule to apply for the British interpreter scheme that would have led him to safety in the UK.

That was when everything started to go badly for Niz. But mistakes had already been made over the years that had put his life at even greater risk than most. The biggest one had been made way back when he had started out as an interpreter. He had been deployed to the town of Babaji, north of Lashkar Gah, where 3,000 British soldiers were engaged in a bloody five-week offensive known as Operation Panther's Claw. The aim of the mission was to clear this former Taliban stronghold to make it safe for voters to go to the polls. There were heavy losses, with ten British soldiers dying in the operation.[2] Niz had been tasked with helping a British military team that was compensating villagers who had had their houses damaged during the fighting. He was both interpreting and helping the villagers to fill out the paperwork. The team were accompanied by an international television crew, who filmed Niz in their footage. He raised his concerns with the British afterwards, although by then it was too late. His face was forever to be seen in that clip.

In Helmand, Niz also spent a lot of time working with the ANA, in which there were soldiers who were also from Kunar province. People gossiped, and Niz knew that it was only a matter of time before everyone in his home village knew that he worked for the British. Lastly, when he was made redundant from the British forces, he signed up with the Americans. They sent him back to Kunar province. Niz accepted this because he was unemployed and recently married. He needed the money to support his family, and his only option was to work with the Americans. Yet it added further to the risk.

In Niz's case, initially the Taliban went after his loved ones. On one occasion his brother was stopped in the street by some Talibs and quizzed about what Niz was doing. When they didn't like the answer, they beat him up. Then came the phone calls from untraceable numbers. This time the threats went directly to Niz. The voices down the line would tell him that they knew who he was and they knew that he worked for the infidels. They were after him, he was told. He kept changing his phone number, but somehow they always managed to track him down.

When Niz's work with the Americans ended, he enrolled on a university course in Asadabad, the capital of Kunar province. Sometimes, when he was feeling particularly anxious, he stayed overnight in a hotel. It was harder for the Taliban to get him there because it was under the control of the Afghan government. By chance, one of the nights he stayed over, the Taliban came knocking at his family house. His father answered. There was a big group of them, all armed. 'Where is he?' they demanded, to which his father simply replied that Niz wasn't at home. One of the Talibs hit him on the back with his rifle butt. He fell to the ground, struggling to breathe. Niz's brother-in-law tried to intervene, but they whacked him too. They started searching the property, turning boxes upside down, rummaging through piles of papers and leaving them scattered across the floor. Then one of them picked something up and showed it to the others, who nodded. They had got what they came for. It was a certificate from Niz's British army days. The Taliban knew how important such documents were to those who had served with the UK forces. For many it was their ticket out of there because it proved their employment.

After that, Niz started emailing everyone he had ever worked with, begging for help – including the British, who told him he didn't have enough evidence to prove he was under threat. As he was no longer working, he didn't have the money to take his family away from the house and bring them to Kabul. Things had got so bad that he spent most of the time agonizing over whether to leave his wife and children and try to go to Europe by himself. When he was there, he thought, he could get a job without worrying about being attacked, and his family could follow later. Then another voice in his head told him it was a bad idea. What if he never saw them again? Earlier in 2015, when he was only about 26, the Taliban launched an ambush near his home, attacking a white vehicle that was identical to his. They killed two innocent men and injured a third. The men, all mechanics, had been coming home from working at night along the same road Niz used to travel home from university, and at around the same time. But that evening he had been persuaded to stay in the city because some friends were having a party. It was all too much of a coincidence. He knew that it should have been him in that car.

In the end, he decided not to risk the journey. Three years later, in 2018, Gavin Williamson, the then Defence Secretary, changed the rules on who was eligible, to enable those who had served prior to 2012 and been made redundant to come to Britain. He brought about the change after three years of pressure from the Daily Mail's Betrayal of the Brave campaign which was highlighting the dangers Afghan interpreters were facing as a result of their work with the British troops and making the case for them to be allowed to enter the UK. Although his move was well intentioned, it only seemed to benefit two Afghan interpreters – one of whom was Niz. In 2019 he made it to Britain legally with his family.

Elsewhere in the country the security situation seemed to be getting worse. The fighting season between the Taliban and Afghan security forces had started off as one of the bloodiest on record since 2001.[3] Without the air power that the Western troops brought with them, the Afghans were taking large numbers of casualties. It wasn't clear how long they could sustain such losses. Civilian deaths also shot up. But the Taliban were showing no signs of letting up. Such news made the interpreters even more anxious.

By now it was 2014, and the Western forces were limited to the area in and around Kabul on what was deemed a purely non-combat mission, under the NATO banner of the Resolute Support Mission. This meant that they were no longer engaged in the actual fighting, but were instead focusing on training, advising and assisting Afghan forces, as well as advising the country's government on other security-related matters. For Britain, that meant building up its multi-million pound 'Sandhurst in the Sand' military academy, officially known as the Afghan National Army Officer Academy (ANAOA), in a place called Qargha, on the outskirts of the capital. Seen as central to Britain's legacy following their withdrawal of combat troops, it was designed to be a replica of the world-renowned Royal Military Academy in Berkshire, which had been turning out officers for the British army since 1741. The academy was training both young men and women in how to be soldiers on the front line, in the hope that this would strengthen the Afghan military. But the MoD hired no new interpreters for the academy, or indeed any other role they needed filling. Instead, they recruited them via third parties. A cynic might suggest that, by doing so, the MoD reduced the chances of having to give them a new life in Britain when they had finished. Left with the only option but to escape the country via illegal means, those Afghans might end up contemplating the same way out Niz and Ahmad had considered.

Later that evening, having recovered from the initial shock of the news of his brother's attack, Jamal phoned Shaista back. 'Do you know why they targeted him?' he asked, dreading that it had something to do with him. He knew the stories about interpreters and their families being targeted.

'It could have been anything, but you know what he is like. He had been telling everyone how his brother had gone to the UK and how he was an interpreter who had worked in the MOB. He's so proud of you, Jamal, he couldn't help it.' Mohmood had always been the same, ever since he was born, around a year after Jamal. He looked up to him more than any other of his siblings, and so of course, after Jamal got a job as an interpreter, Mohmood had wanted to become one too. Perhaps they would all have been better off if the boys had stayed in school, Shaista thought to himself. It was a constant doubt troubling his mind.

What Shaista didn't tell Jamal was that soon after he had left Lashkar Gah he had started to receive more threatening phone calls. The voices down the other end of the line would mention his 'sons who worked for the UK government' and demand money, which they had yet to hand over. Although Shaista tried not to take the threats too seriously – nobody had actually visited the house – he was so worried about his family's future that he was barely sleeping.

Mohmood had a different theory on the shooting from his father. He thought the attackers must have recognized his face from going in and out of the police base. It wouldn't have been difficult. There were new people coming in and out of the compound every day. Some of them were employees who worked for a couple of weeks and then never showed up again. Any one of them could have been a spy for the Taliban. Maybe they had his photograph? Maybe the Taliban had him on a list of targets? The possibilities were endless. And Mohmood desperately wanted to reassure his brother that it was not his fault.

After the shooting, however, Mohmood changed. He was in a wheelchair and needed help even to go to the toilet. He felt embarrassed. Ever since he had returned home, Shaista had remarked to Razagulla how reserved he had become. He rarely engaged in conversation with anyone outside the family, and even then the conversations always seemed like hard work. It was difficult for Shaista to watch his son become so introverted when he knew he had much more in life to give. But listening to him now talking so animatedly to Jamal, who knew more than most how he must be feeling, made him feel encouraged, for a brief moment, that his son would eventually become again the sunny young man he had once been.

That night Jamal struggled to sleep, wondering if he should have left them all behind. Despite what Mohmood said, he couldn't help but think he was to blame for the attack and worried that someone else in the family could be targeted because of him. He also felt guilty, for the truth was that he was starting to enjoy himself in England.

His first few months in Coventry had been a struggle, undoubtedly. Like the other interpreters newly arrived in the UK, he had been reliant on government handouts and was desperate to find work so that he could send some money back to Afghanistan. Although he felt uncomfortable doing it, he traipsed around from shop to shop with his passport and visa asking for work. But there seemed to be few jobs to be had, and those that were available got snapped up quickly. It was much harder to settle than he had envisaged, despite the fact that Coventry has a long tradition of welcoming refugees and asylum seekers from war-torn countries, earning it the well-deserved title of 'City of Sanctuary'. In the year Jamal arrived, there were more than 500 asylum seekers living there. There was also an integration project dedicated to supporting the Afghan interpreters and their families who were arriving under the government scheme. Yet the drab, grey weather and a lack of money meant Jamal spent much of his time missing Lashkar Gah.

Eventually, a local halal supermarket owner gave him a contract for 15 hours a week, and immediately life started to feel better. He liked working on the till and chatting to the customers. He also managed to get himself some translation work at the local refugee centre, which not only put his language skills to good use but also made him feel valued.

By now he had also formed a strong bond with the other Afghans he lived with. The terraced house they lived in was small but comfortable. Each of the tenants had their own bedroom and bathroom – a luxury for Jamal, who was used to sharing both with his many family members. By chance, Abdullah, whom Jamal met at Kabul airport, already knew the other two Afghans from his time in Helmand. But they all made sure to never make Jamal feel left out.

To some extent the Western military bases most of them had worked in back in Afghanistan had prepared them for life in the UK. They were used to seeing women in skimpy gym outfits at Camp Bastion – not to mention the page three pin-ups scattered around every military camp – and already had a taste for the comparatively bland English food. Although meal times in Britain were still a mystery to them. Why did everyone eat separately? And on the sofa? In Afghanistan the whole family would always eat together, no matter how late the father or the brothers arrived home from work. The four men tried to cook for each other, but none of them could cook as well as the women in their families. And even though they were not working for their first few weeks, life in the UK seemed so busy – filling in forms, finding their way around the neighbourhood – that it was hard to find the time. They all longed for their mothers' cooking.

Jamal and Abdullah joined the gym together, and went swimming at the local leisure centre, close to the city's transport museum. They loved swimming so much that some days they went twice. Back in Afghanistan, it was rare to see a public swimming pool. Mostly, they swam in rivers. When he was younger, back in Helmand, Jamal had seen boys swimming in the river and had foolishly decided to jump in, despite the fact he couldn't swim. It was too deep for him to touch the bottom and he nearly drowned. Fortunately for him, a passer-by was able to pull him out. These days he preferred the shallow end. But each time they stayed well over their allocated hour – sometimes as long as three hours – entertaining themselves in the water without, it seemed – to the amusement of the onlooking lifeguards – doing all that much swimming. The pair joked how their skin was turning white like British people because they were spending so much time underwater.

They also explored the local bus routes. The buses were nothing like the ones back in Afghanistan – for a start, they were double-deckers. Also, back home the men would always offer their seats to the women, no matter how old they were, and the driver would also never turn away a paying customer, even if the bus was already completely rammed. But anyway it was much more common for the young men like Jamal and Abdullah to use the local taxis (always Toyota hatchbacks), which seemed to appear whenever you needed a ride. Mind you, they were never particularly comfortable and always seemed to take the longest route to the destination. To pocket the most money from the journey the driver would have two people in the front seat and four crammed into the back. It wasn't unusual to see three or four people in the boot too – which some customers preferred because it was cheaper. By contrast, here in Coventry, the taxis were often too expensive and the buses were rarely full.

They also went to the local mosque, where they mixed with other foreigners, from Pakistan, Bangladesh, parts of Africa. They had never seen such a diverse group of people in one place, and they relished the opportunity to learn about other cultures. However, there were other aspects of life in Coventry that they did not admire. They were shocked at the lack of respect shown to the elderly and women. Back home, it was unacceptable to swear or use 'street language' in front of those over a certain age, or in front of women. Here nobody seemed to care. They got used to hearing spotty teenagers using expletives in every conversation they had. At the weekend the friends even went to nightclubs – something they would never have considered doing in Afghanistan – sometimes taking the train down to London to go to the capital's bars. They didn't drink alcohol, of course, but they had fun all the same. It didn't take long for them to make other friends either. Most of them were Afghans. They had frequent visitors, all intrigued by the newcomers. On an average evening they would have more than six guests knocking on the door for a cup of tea. And when Jamal and Abdullah were together, in particular, they laughed a lot. Jamal would jokingly refer to Abdullah as *khar*, Pashto for 'donkey', because he thought he made stupid decisions, like getting into arguments. He also teased him for writing his name on his food and drink in the fridge. Slowly, slowly, England was starting to feel like it could one day be home.

7

The Ultimate Price: Lashkar Gah, 2019

Taliban infiltration into Lashkar Gah was no longer uncommon. On the day Shaista's eldest son was killed, the family was still reeling from the threatening phone call he had received a month earlier. The unknown voice had referenced his 'son who was an interpreter for the British army' – most likely Jamal. 'You are a slave of the British forces,' the voice had told him in Pashto, warning that the Taliban would not forget the family's treachery.

And then they finally got their revenge.

Rahmatullah, who was married and had a young son, was sitting outside the family house with his friends during Ramadan when Shaista and Razagulla, who were inside at the time, heard the gunfire and the screams in the street. Then there were loud bangs on their door, enough to shake the walls. A group of teenagers shouted their names frantically. 'Your son has been shot! Your son has been shot!' one of them cried. They knew instantly that it was Rahmatullah. Shaista attempted to run outside, but his legs stopped working. He tried to steady himself on the door frame as a wave of nausea swept over his whole body, sending him into a cold sweat. Razagulla ran past him, wearing nothing on her feet and not even a headscarf. 'What's going on?' she screamed to the teenagers, although they didn't need to answer. Behind them she could see a small crowd that had gathered in the aftermath. Seeing her coming, they made way for her, pity etched on their faces. There was her son's mangled body, surrounded by a pool of deep red blood. She flung herself on top of him and, as the world around her fell silent, she wept.

Sometime shortly afterwards – neither of them could remember exactly when – Shaista made it to the scene. But when he got there, his legs gave way completely and he collapsed next to his wife and son. Razagulla's dress was sodden in Rahmatullah's blood, which was slowly oozing out of his body. The next thing Shaista knew he was grabbing hold of his son's face, shaking it violently and shouting for help. Yet he knew it was too late. When the ambulance arrived to take them to the hospital, Rahmatullah was already dead.

Shaista jumped into the back of the ambulance, if only to comfort Rahmatullah's limp body, questions racing through his mind. Who has done this? How can they be so cruel? How will his grandson grow up without his father? He racked his brain to remember the last thing he had said to Rahmatullah, but he couldn't. He suddenly felt panicked. How could he forget? Did Rahmatullah know how much he loved him? He had pain in his heart, and he felt like something heavy was sitting on his chest, weighing it down. When one of the medics asked him a question, he opened his mouth to speak but could only let out a barely audible croak.

Shaista had always said that Rahmatullah – his eldest – was like a best friend to him as well as a son. Strikingly handsome and with a constant smile on his face, sometimes he could make his parents laugh so hard their stomachs ached. As a boy, Rahmatullah had loved school and would scold his parents if they ever made him late, although he was cheeky too – and always getting into fights with the other boys in the street. However, he calmed down as he grew older, becoming a 'gentleman', as Razagulla would say. And now he was a husband and father himself, who had taken his family duties very seriously. How would his wife cope now, and how would his son grow up without a father?

Back at the house, Razagulla was being consoled by anyone and everyone who had heard the news. Within minutes relatives from across the city had been told what had happened and had descended on the house to be by the family's side (it was improper to tell them to go away so they could mourn in peace). Razagulla couldn't remember how she got back to the house, except that she must have been carried. It felt as if her brain was detached from her body and she couldn't move. Her eyes were unblinking as she stared at a mark she had forgotten to scrub on the wall in front of her. There were mutterings in the distance. She thought of her son, lying on the ground. His final moments must have been agony. An hour before he was killed, he had been joking around as usual with his sisters in the kitchen. What did he say to them? What had they been laughing about? She wished she had paid more attention.

Although the family were initially convinced that Rahmatullah had been killed by the Taliban because his father and brother had worked for the British, it turned out there was much more to his story than that. It was a story the family would repeat over and over again to anyone who would listen.

Before Shaista worked at the military base and when Jamal was still at school, he had been employed for the second time by the Afghan police. Despite the dangers involved – and the corruption, which was deeply embedded – he took the job because the family desperately needed the money. Later on, as he made connections and friendships, and after much persistence on Rahmatullah's part, Shaista also managed to get his eldest son a job there. Together they helped man a checkpoint along Highway 601, the main highway connecting Lashkar Gah with the city of Kandahar, in the east. Back then the Taliban controlled the villages along it. Yet it was also a key communications route both for locals going about their everyday lives and for the Afghan forces. And as the Western mission intensified, with more troops and equipment being piled into the region, the route became crucial for the foreign forces too. The checkpoint Shaista and Rahmatullah were stationed at was coming under frequent attack, especially at night, when they were at their most vulnerable. Their job was to stop and search anyone they thought may be acting suspiciously. It was a risky business, although Shaista didn't let on to Razagulla, who would never have allowed them to do it if she had known. Rahmatullah would often tell his father that he would be the first one to be killed if the Taliban got their way. He never explained why. But Shaista would scold him, telling him to stop talking such nonsense. On the rare quiet days when little traffic passed their way, they would talk about the future. Rahmatullah would tell his father how it was his dream to one day leave the police and build a better life somewhere else, in a more stable country. Their countrymen had suffered from too much war for too long. He, like everyone else they knew, was tired of the conflict and just wanted it to end.

When Shaista went to work as a gardener, Rahmatullah kept his position in the police. As activity on the highway intensified, the British forces arrived to set up a patrol base halfway along the road. Rahmatullah watched the soldiers on foot patrol and in armoured vehicles, checking the route regularly for roadside bombs. They had better kit than the Afghans and were keen to keep the highway open. But no matter how hard they searched, buried explosives were common, which made the highway highly dangerous for any civilians who dared drive down it.

Over time, Rahmatullah was given other duties by his superiors, including leaving the checkpoint and going out on patrol scouting around for enemy fighters. The Americans had apparently become frustrated that the Afghan police were not pursuing the Taliban themselves. Although IEDs were being placed near the checkpoints, many of the Afghans were refusing to go out on patrol and/or were requesting air support at the sound of the first shot.[1] If air support was not forthcoming, they told the Americans, they were leaving.

One day Rahmatullah had been out on a foot patrol with another officer in Nahri Saraj, north of the highway, when they spotted a man digging a hole next to the side of the road in the distance. When the man saw them in their uniforms, he started to run away. Rahmatullah assumed he was a member of the Taliban trying to plant a roadside bomb, so they chased him into the nearby village. At some point Rahmatullah lost the other officer and ended up alone, with the suspected Talib in front of him. Breathless and worried that the man was getting away, he fired a shot. He had meant it as a warning shot, to scare the man, he told his family afterwards. But the bullet went into the man's head. The man slumped to the ground. Rahmatullah didn't need to go any closer to know that he had killed him.

His life would never be the same again. The villagers were outraged. They complained that the man was not a member of the Taliban but an innocent civilian. Rahmatullah remained convinced he was an insurgent. Why had he run away if he was just a civilian? Why was he digging the hole? His family also raised all these questions with the community. But they were impossible to prove either way and, despite continuing to plead his innocence, Rahmatullah was put in jail while the investigation continued for more than a year.

For the Guls, that time went painfully slowly. Razagulla aged considerably with the stress, wrinkles forming on her forehead and bags developing under her eyes from lack of sleep. Even her hair appeared to be thinning. She was terrified her son would never be released. But, as any grandmother would, she tried her best to put on a brave face for Rahmatullah's wife and young son, Hamidullah, who were living with them at the time.

Hamidullah, still only a toddler, was the spitting image of his father. He was tall for his age, like Rahmatullah, and yet, unlike his father, he was painfully shy. It made him all the more adorable, in Razagulla's view, though sometimes she worried that he was spending too much time with the women. On the rare moments when she was alone, she prayed for Rahmatullah's release.

In Lashkar Gah, it was not uncommon for corrupt judges to detain people indefinitely – without any decision on their case – until they were handed cash bribes. So it was only when Shaista was able to raise enough money from family and friends to pay a judge that Rahmatullah was released. It seemed the man he shot had indeed been an insurgent. Whatever price they had paid for his freedom, the whole family was overjoyed, giving him a hero's welcome when he at last came through the door. Yet amid the relief, something didn't feel right to Shaista. It played on his mind. Was that really the end of it? He sensed that, as soon as his son had stepped out of the prison walls, the Taliban had started following him. He heard talk. There were rumours that the man he had shot dead had two brothers and one of them was telling people he would never let Rahmatullah live for what he did.

Now no one really knew whether Rahmatullah had been killed in retaliation for the shooting or because Shaista had worked at the military base or because Jamal and Mohmood had been interpreters for the foreigners. They probably never would. Yet Shaista was convinced that the Taliban had targeted him in revenge for the man's death. The local shopkeeper, who knew the Gul family well, would later tell them how two suspicious-looking men, both carrying weapons and with their faces covered, had been sitting casually having a cup of tea at his place a few minutes before the shooting. Nobody seemed to know who they were. According to eyewitnesses, it was they who had shot Rahmatullah. Some locals had tried to run after them and catch them but then, suddenly out of nowhere, some more men had appeared. They too had weapons. The locals, who were unarmed, backed off and the men got away.

When Shaista arrived at the special emergency hospital in the centre of the city, they told him to go home. It was already overwhelmed with casualties arriving from the front line, and they couldn't afford to have visitors clogging up the corridors. There were no beds to spare, and the staff were hollow-eyed with exhaustion. It was no wonder: the hospital was the only free specialist trauma facility in the whole of the province. And at that time there were a lot of trauma wounds. The hospital's doctors were used to dealing with the most horrendous battlefield injuries – babies arriving with bullet wounds in their tiny arms and legs, soldiers half-dead having being blown up by landmines and others with their bodies ripped apart by explosions and air strikes. Not far away was the Médecins Sans Frontières (MSF)-supported Boost hospital, run mainly by foreign volunteer doctors, which would receive war-wounded patients when the trauma hospital was full. Unlike the emergency hospital, much of its focus was on antenatal care and paediatrics, with some 2,000 children suffering from malnutrition coming through its doors every week. But even here there were often more patients than beds for them to sleep in. This year the number of patients admitted was 30 times what it had been a decade previously. Some 3,500 casualties were now arriving every month, compared with 120 back in 2009, when NATO troops began fighting in the region.[2] The sick were arriving from rural areas across the province, sometimes having travelled for hours along dangerous, bomb-ridden roads. Once they got there, many were leaving midway through their treatment, either because they thought it might be the only safe time to leave or because they could no longer afford to keep the taxi they had travelled in waiting for them.

Rahmatullah's body was covered before being transferred to the hospital morgue, where it would remain until his burial. Sometimes as many as ten to twenty bodies were thrown into each refrigerated container because the morgue was so full. And not just the bodies of Afghan soldiers either but some Taliban fighters too. They remained there, piled high, until relatives arrived to take them away for burial. In the short time Shaista was at the hospital he saw a number of maimed bodies arriving and being pushed down the corridor. Although he had seen many war dead, he could not look at them; it was all too much to bear. The floor was sticky and the air thick with the smell of disinfectant.

After decades of war, it was quite common for many Afghans to have seen someone who had been killed – whether a soldier, a civilian or a member of the Taliban. As was customary, Shaista had been to the hospital on several occasions to pay his respects to those who had died. And because of his years spent in the police force before becoming a gardener, he knew a lot of them. As he walked away from the hospital, shaken, Shaista had flashbacks to opening one of the containers and seeing body after body splayed out one on top of another. The stench of flesh swollen in the heat had been enough to make a grown man vomit.

Shaista, who was more wary than most, had often warned his children as they were growing up of the Taliban's tactics, in the hope that it would spook them into taking extra precautions. He told them never to go near the scene of an attack, even if it appeared to be over, because there would sometimes be a secondary bomb laid to kill those who ran to help those who had been injured by the first. He scared them with gruesome stories of seeing the hands and legs of young children lying separated from their bodies on the roadside. He always spoke directly to the family, unafraid of giving them troubled minds – better that than for them to be killed. More recently Shaista had seen a suicide bomber blow himself up. The man, who was wearing an explosive vest, had clambered on top of an ANA tank in the centre of Lashkar Gah, thinking (wrongly) that there were soldiers inside it. In the event, he killed only himself. Shaista couldn't help but think that he must have been inept beyond belief. The impact of the bomb had been so intense that the man's torso was nowhere to be found. His arms and legs had been thrown wildly into the air, much to the horror of those who had witnessed the bombing. It was incredible, really, that no one else had been hurt. Although it was hard to feel sorry for someone who would do such a thing, Shaista had also wondered what had happened in the young man's life to fill him with so much hate. Was he so devoted to the cause? Or was he simply desperate to make money for his family? (Suicide bombers got paid handsomely, by Afghan standards, for their sacrifice.)

Shaista also came close to death himself. It was back when he was in the police and in a convoy providing security to a senior Afghan officer travelling from Kandahar to elsewhere in Helmand. The most dangerous threat to their safety was from roadside bombs. Shaista was in the leading police car when another vehicle suddenly overtook them. It had not been planned. Seconds later it drove over an IED and the vehicle exploded. Bodies flew in their direction – one was missing a head. Plumes of smoke filled the sky, causing Shaista to choke. The charred remains of the vehicle lay scattered across the ground. As it smouldered in front of him, Shaista took pity on its occupants but also thanked God that he was not, as he could so easily have been, among the dead.

At the time of Rahmatullah's death, his wife and son were in Kabul visiting relatives. Shaista and Razagulla didn't want to tell them of his death over the phone so they decided to go ahead with the burial without them. (In Islam, the body should be buried as soon as possible after death.) It was an unusual decision and one that would anger Rahmatullah's wife when she found out later. Jamal, back in Coventry, was also unaware of what had happened. Shaista decided that, as he was so far away and would not make it back in time, now was not the time to tell him. First there was much to sort out. Word had spread quickly among the locals that Rahmatullah had been shot dead. More than 200 of them congregated at the cemetery the following day. Those who could not make it sent representatives in their place. The Gul family's tortured faces were laid bare for all to see. Grief-stricken, Razagulla barely uttered a word, except to politely accept more condolences. After the burial, the family started to receive more visitors at home, including the imam from the mosque who came to recite the Qur'an. This whole process of receiving a constant stream of well-wishers, which could be exhausting in itself, typically took several days.

Three days after his death, Rahmatullah's wife returned home from Kabul to find her whole world changed. The family told her how her husband had died and that he was now buried in the cemetery. Her outpouring of grief was so painful it was hard to watch. Hamidullah, then four, was too young really to understand what had happened, but he knew that his mother was hurting. She was pregnant with their second child, who would never know its father.

As the family mourned, there was talk of peace in the war-torn country – although Shaista was, as ever, sceptical. The US and Taliban were hoping to reach an agreement that would see the complete withdrawal of US and NATO forces in return for a commitment by the Taliban that it would prevent foreign armed groups and fighters from using the country as a launch pad to carry out attacks against the West. Although there were only a few thousand NATO troops left in the country, carrying out training and security missions, like every other Afghan Shaista knew that if the troops pulled out no one could trust the word of the Taliban. How could the Westerners be so naïve?

Indeed, some Afghan leaders believed that the talks had only served to embolden the Taliban. Attacks against interpreters and those connected to the 'spies' appeared to be on the rise across the country. Earlier in March 2019, when the talks had entered their fifth round, an interpreter who was working with the Australian and Dutch forces was gunned down by the Taliban in front of his home in Nangarhar province, east of Kabul. Around the same time, three interpreters who helped the US were reportedly killed in a Taliban ambush and the brother of a former interpreter for the British army was shot by gunmen searching for his sibling. In another attack, an interpreter for the British survived his vehicle being sprayed with bullets by some Taliban fanatics. There was also news of an interpreter, known as Mayar, who had been refused sanctuary in the UK and was working for a charity helping to clear mines when he was ambushed by the Taliban as he was being driven to work.[3] The vehicle was sprayed with 13 bullets, one of which hit the driver in the leg, although Mayar himself survived unscathed. He said afterwards that he believed he was targeted because he had spent three years working for the British troops, and in Taliban eyes he was a traitor. Even before the incident, he had received five death threats. Mayar would be eligible for sanctuary in Britain years later.

At that time more and more interpreters were also being forced into hiding after receiving warnings. Rafi, now living in Birmingham and working as an accountant, was receiving an increasing number of pleas for help from people all over Afghanistan who had worked with the British military and were now trying to leave the country. They knew that at some point he had been in charge of recruitment back in Kabul and had heard he was campaigning for more Afghans to be brought over to the UK. One interpreter called him to say his father had been beaten badly but the UK government did not believe that he and his family were in danger. An Afghan, previously employed by the British military in a different role, said that his brother had been shot dead in front of his family in a revenge attack, but again, when he appealed to the UK for sanctuary his application was refused. Each story seemed more desperate than the last. Yet the solution offered by the UK government was usually to tell these people to change their addresses within Afghanistan. It was a lot to ask and wasn't always practical. It also assumed the Taliban would not have informants elsewhere across the country who would question the sudden arrival of such newcomers. Senior MPs back in London who had started an inquiry into their treatment in 2017 were urging the government to take a more sympathetic approach to their 'intimidation' scheme. Led by Dr Julian Lewis, chair of the defence select committee, they said a major obstacle was the government's 'completely disingenuous' claim that they needed to avoid a supposed 'brain drain' from Afghanistan. Such a policy didn't take into account that those considered to be the brightest members of Afghan society had been forced into hiding.[4] Shaista was grateful that Jamal was already out of the country.

In Lashkar Gah itself, the Taliban had become more brazen in their attacks. It felt like a city on edge, waiting for something dangerous to happen. Bombs, explosions, assassinations had become the new normal. Shaista knew of at least one senior government official who had narrowly missed death when a vehicle exploded near him in an attempted assassination attempt. Car bomb attacks, which seemed to be becoming increasingly frequent, would involve a suicide bomber driving a vehicle packed with explosives into their target. The vehicle could be anything: a car, a lorry, a tanker or a motorbike. It was a common tactic that had been used by suicide fighters belonging to the Islamic State group in Iraq.

Twin explosions inside the city's stadium in March that year resulted in four people dying and more than 30 injured. Two of the four people killed were Jamal's friends – one the deputy of the National Security Department and the other the head of the Directorate of Economy in Helmand, Mohammad Khan Nusrat. The explosions came after a bomb attack in the capital that left a local journalist, Nisar Ahmadi, seriously wounded.[5] According to local police chiefs, a so-called 'sticky bomb' had been attached to his vehicle, which had been detonated shortly after he arrived at the gate of a local TV station. He too was treated at the emergency hospital, where it was reported that he lost his leg. These 'sticky bombs' – small, magnetic devices slapped under vehicles – were having a damaging psychological effect too. Because they were so cheap to make – one could be knocked up in a mechanic's workshop for about $25 – and easy to use, government workers never knew if they would be the next target. Detonated remotely or with a time-delay fuse, and powerful enough to blow up a car, they were also easy to transport and hard to defend against. Sometimes the device was attached when the unwitting victim was stuck in traffic. Sometimes the person responsible for placing it there was a poverty-stricken local too desperate to turn down the cash. With such targeted attacks and now the death of Rahmatullah, it was feeling increasingly like no members of the Gul family were safe.

8

Behind Bars: Lashkar Gah, August 2021

The third knock was so loud that Razagulla instinctively jumped up from their hiding place. Whoever was there was not going to go away. She looked at her husband, terror in her eyes. Shaista blinked and nodded at the same time – their sign – and Razagulla knew what she had to do.

'Where's the interpreter?' the Taliban fighter asked as she opened the door. He was dressed all in black and was holding an AK-47. Behind him stood another man, dressed almost identically. 'He left years ago. We aren't in touch,' she said, struggling to speak as she stood frozen on the spot, trembling with fear.

'Where is the gardener?' the Talib probed.

'There is no gardener here,' she said.

He didn't believe her. Shaista, who could hear the conversation clearly from the underground room in which he and the rest of the family were hiding, prayed that his quails, of which there were now nearly 30, would stay quiet.

'We are going to burn this house down if you don't get Shaista Gul for us,' the Talib added, dark and menacing. Then, holding her in his stare, he turned away slowly and walked down the path with his companion.

They knew Shaista by name.

Razagulla closed the door behind her, her heart still racing as she watched them through the window. They walked back across the street to the house where the family of Jamal's wife Spozhmai had lived before the Taliban had broken in and forced them out. They appeared to have converted it into a makeshift office that was being used as a base for the patrols they were sending out regularly to taunt the locals. It was a clever, cruel strategy. By doing so, they were keeping the people in a permanent state of fear and anxiety, thereby exerting their control over the population.

'He's gone,' Razagulla whispered down to Shaista. They had created the underground room in which he was hiding years earlier to protect them from any rocket fire or shelling. Razagulla joined him, quaking yet again at the sound of gunfire in the street. They stayed there in silence, contemplating the ramifications of the visit: the Taliban were looking for Shaista himself. It wasn't the first time they had knocked at the door in recent days, and every time it happened Shaista became more and more convinced that they were coming for him. Now he knew it.

Back in April the US had announced that NATO was withdrawing all of its remaining troops from Afghanistan by 11 September – 20 years on from the deadly attacks on the Twin Towers. But there had been no conditions attached to the pull-out, much to the horror of the Afghan government, effectively meaning that the Taliban could do whatever they liked. Unlike many Afghans, Shaista did not feel angered by the withdrawal because he believed the British and Americans had made huge sacrifices for his country, and his people were ungrateful. After two decades of war, NATO had done everything it could. To him, there seemed no point in them staying, given that nothing was getting any better. However, many others believed that the Americans had betrayed their Afghan allies by pulling out their few thousand remaining troops. For several years the NATO forces had managed to hold a fragile peace, even though they were no longer fighting on the front line, not only by providing training but simply through their presence. As the deadline loomed and the US started withdrawing its troops and equipment at the beginning of May, the Taliban were taking village after village, edging ever closer to the provincial capitals.

Luckily for Jamal, Spozhmai had managed to get out of Lashkar Gah the previous year and join him in Coventry. By that point she had waited almost five years for the British government to grant her a visa. Neither she nor Jamal had had any idea that it would take so long when he had originally moved to the UK. Like many in their position, they did not know that the British had a policy of only allowing Afghans to bring their wives to the UK if they originally arrived with their husbands. It was only after the UK government came under pressure from campaigners that this policy was changed in March 2019 so that loved ones could join their partners later without having to apply under normal immigration rules. The Afghans had found a sympathetic ear in Sajid Javid, Home Secretary from April 2018 to July 2019, who told journalists 'we owe these unsung heroes a huge debt of gratitude for their service' as he overhauled the policy.[1] This announcement came after he waived visa fees for those Afghans who were struggling to afford £2,400 to apply for indefinite leave to remain. Dropping the large fees had been one of his first acts in the job.[2] Although dropping the fees would benefit interpreters like Jamal, the policy change on bringing over wives added further complication for Jamal, who had only married Spozhmai after he had moved to England – in 2016, during a brief visit to his homeland. (It was the grand wedding that Spozhmai had dreamed of, with the couple inviting 1,800 people from across the district. Leaving his security fears aside, Jamal forked out $29,000 to pay for it all and wore a fancy suit that he had brought from Britain.) The timing of their marriage mattered because the policy stated that they had to have been together at the time of the initial relocation. Jamal had to go through an arduous process to prove that he and Spozhmai were in fact engaged to be married when he flew to Britain years earlier. Luckily for him, he had told senior officers at Camp Bastion about his relationship when he first started the process so there was paperwork that would eventually prove it. From Kandahar (around three hours by car from Lashkar Gah) Razagulla and Spozhmai's mother had flown with her to Kabul, where she had to go to provide her biometric information, such as fingerprints, for her British visa. 'I'm ready to fly from the house,' she cried to Jamal over the phone when he received the email saying she had been accepted. She didn't believe it until he sent over a screenshot. She arrived in Britain on 22 June 2020, a date Jamal would never forget. He was allowed to meet her at the terminal at Birmingham airport on condition that he would go into quarantine with her for ten days to comply with coronavirus restrictions. There was no way he was letting her go through that on her own. When they saw each other, they didn't hold back – Britain wasn't like Afghanistan. Jamal grabbed her and kissed her and Spozhmai kissed him back before bursting into a fit of excited giggles.

Jamal and Spozhmai weren't the only ones to spend many years apart as a result of the government policy. Abdul Suboor, another interpreter who served three years on the front line in Helmand with British troops, had arrived in Britain in

December 2015, not long after Jamal. He came with his eldest son, Shakeel, believing the rest of the family would join them later. Yet after arriving he was told that his wife, who gave birth to their third son, Muzzammel, the day Abdul left Afghanistan, no longer qualified because he had not brought her with him on the same flight. He spent years bringing up Shakeel alone in Manchester as he juggled ten-hour night shifts working for an online retailer. Abdul, a generous man who used to take sweets for the local children when out on patrol with British troops, had to take Shakeel to see a psychologist because he was so miserable in Britain. 'He told one of his classmates that he was going to harm himself because he's missing his mum,' he told journalists at the time. The family finally joined them in July 2021. It took so long because Abdul was told by the local council that the Home Office needed to be sure his accommodation was suitable for the whole family and the council didn't have any spare houses.

Any piece of good news for the Gul family always seemed to be dampened by something bad. Almost a year to the day after Spozhmai arrived in Britain, in June 2021, Shaista's grandson Shir had been kidnapped from one of the villages on the outskirts of Lashkar Gah. He was only 16. Salma, Shaista's eldest daughter and Shir's mother, had been inconsolable ever since. He had gone to school at 7 a.m. one day, never to return. That evening his teacher told Salma and her husband, Said, that the Taliban had come for him. Apparently they had told Shir that his mother's brother had been an interpreter for the British army and that he was sending money back to the family. Her son, who rarely showed signs of weakness, cried as they bundled him into a car. What would happen to him? Salma was sick with worry.

Not long after the kidnapping Salma's house was hit by rockets, forcing the family to move in with Shaista and the others. The

Taliban were getting ever closer to Lashkar Gah. Jamal, who was trying to do his best for his family remotely, knew that he needed to get his parents and siblings out of there before it was too late. Shaista had already applied for sanctuary in the UK, but his case had been rejected because he had not served on the front line. By then, the Defence Secretary, Ben Wallace, a former Scots Guard who understood the value of interpreters, had been so taken by the stories of those who had been left behind that he, along with Priti Patel, the Home Secretary, changed the policy again. Now interpreters could come to the UK if they had served 18 months on the front line at any point during the conflict. Also, it no longer mattered if they had then resigned – before that they had to have been made redundant to be eligible. This change of policy was designed to help dozens more interpreters and their families seek sanctuary in Britain, but it did nothing for people like Shaista, who had never served on the front line. Shaista's cousin Sayed, who had also been a gardener at the base in Lashkar Gah, had been employed by a contractor – not by the British military directly – and so his chances of escaping were even more remote.

Later ministers announced a new scheme, the Afghan Relocations and Assistance Policy, known as ARAP. Coming into force in April 2021, to reflect the increasing turmoil in Afghanistan, this scheme was indeed open to Afghans such as Shaista who had worked directly for the British in roles other than as patrol interpreters. However, they did not get their visas automatically: they had to show that they were facing imminent risk, such as intimidation or threat to life. But it provided the Guls with hope that if they could prove Shaista was at risk and put enough pressure on the government to act urgently, then he would be allowed into the UK. Sayed, on the other hand, still didn't meet the criteria.

Jamal swung into action and, using his many connections with former soldiers and journalists, arranged for Shaista to do a television interview appealing for help, to be broadcast in the UK on ITV.[3] They decided that revealing Shaista's identity on television was a risk worth taking if it meant that the British government would grant the family a visa. Ed Aitken, a former captain with the British army who was co-founder of a group called the Sulha Alliance which campaigned for the government to relax its rules on former Afghan employees, explained to journalists how the Taliban couldn't care less if the person they were after was a front-line interpreter whose employment had been terminated or a pot-washer in the kitchen. They would kill any and all of them without hesitation.[4] Jamal started to build up the case that his father really was in danger.

But after the TV interview the situation on the ground became rapidly more hopeless. Everything was moving so fast. The family were all together at home at the end of July when they heard that the conflict had reached the outskirts of Lashkar Gah. The city had become a refuge for people fleeing the fighting in the rest of the province. The fighting became so intense that the ANA told all remaining civilians to leave. Not knowing what else to do or where to go, Shaista and the family stayed put.

The Taliban were moving ever closer to their home. Now they had surrounded the police headquarters and the provincial government office. Shaista had a secret vantage point, on the roof of his house, where he could see what was happening in the streets without being seen himself. His worst nightmare was unfolding before his eyes. The Talibs were running around firing weapons and fighting in hand-to-hand combat with the Afghan forces. Bullets and rockets were landing on the street outside, some of them leaving pockmarks on the walls. His recurrent gasps were drowned out by the cacophony of battle. He knew the family needed to get out, but every time they thought about opening the door and running for it there was another attack. There were so many knocks on the door by now too that they just bolted it shut and didn't answer it to anyone. The Taliban were shooting at the troops before running into civilian homes in order to hide themselves. Bombs were being dropped from the sky to destroy their hideouts, killing men, women and children in the process. Shaista had heard that some of their neighbours had been killed accidentally by an ANA helicopter circling above. He didn't see how they would get out of there alive.

'Leave Mum and the boys, run out of the house and go somewhere else,' Jamal urged his father. He believed that if Shaista was found he would be killed as a traitor, though the rest of the family might be spared. But Shaista didn't want to leave without them. And where would he go anyway? He urged Jamal to carry on trying to find a way for them all to escape together.

And that was when the Taliban came knocking for him. By now the family were getting very hungry and knew that it was only a matter of time before one of them would have to go outside and get some food. Razagulla had been churning out batches of naan bread, as all they had left was flour and water, but even the flour was now in short supply and there was no electricity and no fuel. Would they die there?

When government and senior military officials flew by helicopter out of Lashkar Gah under the cover of darkness a few days later, on 12 August, the Guls knew that it was all over. Some 200 members of the Afghan security forces who had remained in the governor's compound surrendered to the

Taliban.[5] If they had given up, what hope was there for the rest of them?

In the UK, Major James Bolter, a reservist in the British army, received an alarming message from Jamal. Two members of the Taliban had been to his family house asking for Shaista by name. He needed help to get his family out. It was only by chance that James knew Shaista from 2011, when he had served in Helmand. He was desperate to do something, having spent years fighting for his own interpreter, Hashmat Nawabi, known as Hash, to be allowed sanctuary in Britain – and eventually succeeding. He now referred to Hash as '007' after he once escaped from Afghanistan in the boot of a car to dodge a Taliban road block. James, a generous man, always thinking of others, reached out to journalists he knew and senior officials in the MoD to tell them of Shaista's plight.

He had fond memories of Shaista and his garden, which took him back to his childhood and memories of his grandmother planting roses in her garden. When they met in 2011, James had been a captain working as an operations officer within the Labour Support Unit, in charge of locally employed staff. Although he was based at Camp Bastion, he visited the MOB frequently. The first time he went, a senior interpreter insisted he visited the garden. He was not disappointed. There, in that tranquil refuge, James and Shaista bonded over flowers. James didn't know any Pashto, and Shaista spoke barely any English, but James pointed animatedly at the roses. Instantly they understood each other. James couldn't believe how well kept the garden was or the hours that Shaista must have put into tending to it. The next time James visited, Shaista recognized him immediately. 'Ah, Mr Rose.'

James understood immediately how vulnerable all the Afghans who had been employed by the British were. After arriving in Helmand he had been told that the Taliban had put a $10,000 bounty on the head of a patrol interpreter, and slightly less for Afghans working in the more menial roles. These were huge amounts of money for anyone in Helmand province, where the ANA was paying its recruits a healthy salary of $240 a month in 2009.[6]

He also made it his mission to make sure that the interpreters wore their body armour so they didn't stand out too much from the rest of the troops. By this point most of them had been issued with the same kit as the regular soldiers, but some were choosing not to wear it, believing they were invincible. James knew about this *laissez-faire* attitude of 'If I get shot, I get shot' and he was keen to put an end to it.

And yet there was only so much he could do. All too often, interpreters and other locally employed staff were going home on leave and not coming back. Family members and their friends were telling the soldiers they had been killed. He found it all too easy to believe.

On an earlier tour, James was told that as many as seven Afghans had been lost to the Taliban. When it came to returning the bodies to their families, there were so many that the soldiers almost got two of the bodies mixed up. From then on the British instituted a formal identification process.

The first Afghan James lost was a pot-washer in the kitchen at one of the remote sites. He had wandered outside the base to a small stream and had been shot by a Taliban sniper. His body had been recovered and repatriated back to Lashkar Gah. His family, who lived nearby, came to collect it in a pick-up truck. James took them to the refrigerated room where the body was stored and unzipped the body bag for them to identify him. They collapsed in grief.

During his first six to seven weeks in Helmand there had been another two deaths. Both of them were patrol interpreters. One had strayed away from an area cleared of IEDs, had his leg blown off and then bled to death; the other went swimming in a canal, got caught up in some debris and was dragged underwater. Initially, no one knew what had happened to the second interpreter, so, fearing that the Taliban would find him and parade him with his head chopped off in order to put off any would-be interpreters from signing up, the British troops poured resources into a manhunt. Even with special forces and drones, it took more than three days for them to find his body. He had drowned.

Towards the end of James's tour a further two interpreters were shot by the Taliban. One was sitting under a tree during a patrol when a bullet pierced through his ankle and up his leg. Three weeks after he was discharged he was back at work, having told his British bosses that he was 'bored'. The other was caught in an IED blast but again returned to his job a few weeks later, presumably because the money was so good. James also overheard phone calls from the Taliban to a number of his interpreters. The threats were all quite similar: leave your job or one of our brothers will collect a handsome reward for your head. In addition, there were the night letters. Afghans returning to the base from leave would show James what their families had been sent while they were away. The letter was usually addressed to the head of the family, ordering him to force his son to stop working for the British. There was also the implied threat that, if he didn't, the whole family would be at risk.

As the Guls waited for any information from Britain, they heard on the radio that Kabul itself had fallen, a feat that surprised even the Taliban. News of their victory spread across the country as a sense of fear and panic gripped the capital.

Witnesses said it was like something out of an apocalypse. Those who had lived under Taliban rule before remembered their brutality. Women ran out of the university, terrified of history repeating itself. Police took off their uniforms in the streets. Make-up artists abandoned their beauty salons. Women and girls who had been wearing jeans and trainers in the morning were in black burqas by the afternoon, petrified of being lashed for showing too much flesh. At the heavily guarded British embassy, Foreign Office workers scrambled to get on the next flight out, leaving documents with the contact details of Afghans working for them, as well as the CVs of locals applying for jobs, scattered on the ground.

Already in hiding was one young woman, Arifa, who had been trained by British troops at the 'Sandhurst in the Sand' academy in 2016–2017. She had gone on to become a first lieutenant in the female tactical platoon of Afghan special forces. Hours earlier, she had been at a military camp in Kabul carrying out exercises and 'preparing for war and possible enemy attack' when she was suddenly sent home. The 26-year-old said the President had ordered forces to "retreat" and had fled Afghanistan.[7] She would later make it to America, although the journey would not be easy.

A human catastrophe was unfolding as thousands of Afghans fled to Kabul international airport, desperate to get an evacuation flight out of the country. These flights were being carried out by the military forces of participating Nato countries to evacuate stranded foreign nationals and Afghans eligible for visas, many of whom had worked with foreign troops during the fighting. Britain's military operation to fly people to safety was code-named Operation Pitting. In the chaos, hundreds of people managed to make it onto the tarmac and ran alongside a US military aircraft as it taxied along the runway. Some clung to the side of the plane, and at least two apparently fell to their deaths from the undercarriage immediately after take-off. Video footage purported to show the bodies of three people – two men and a woman – lying on the ground amid the chaos.[8] The cause of their death was unclear. Other accounts put the figure of those killed, either by gunshot wounds, in a stampede or after clinging to aircraft, higher. As the Americans regained control of the airport, the crowds outside its perimeter grew bigger and bigger as Afghans flocked there from across the country. Even as they were being beaten by the Taliban, desperate mothers threw their babies at the British soldiers standing guard above them. Some of the babies fell on the barbed wire, bringing even hardened paratroopers to tears.

Jamal told Shaista that other Afghans whose British visa applications had been rejected, either because they had been dismissed for various misdemeanours or because they had not served on the front line, had started making their way to the capital. It seemed they were hoping that, once they were actually standing in front of them, the British and American troops would take pity and allow them on to the evacuation flights. It wasn't clear to Jamal whether their efforts were proving successful or not. What was apparent, however, was that the number of evacuation flights was being ramped up, with some RAF aircraft being diverted from other operations to support the mission. But they would not last for ever.[9]

Jamal called one of his friends in Lashkar Gah, begging him to go and pick up Shaista from the house and get him out of there. He knew that by the time they heard anything back from the UK government it could be too late. But when the friend got to their street, some militants fired at his car and he was forced to pull back.

Shaista was getting desperate, believing it was only a matter of time before the Taliban would find him and the family. And yet he was also wary of making the journey to Kabul through Taliban checkpoints when there was no guarantee they would be allowed to board a flight.

Then, as if the situation couldn't get any worse, one of his teenage sons, Esmatullah, was taken. As their food supplies dwindled, it had been agreed that Esmatullah would go and get some more items. But he barely reached the street and was on his phone when he heard the screech of tyres. A car pulled up, inside which was a group of men, all wearing turbans and carrying AK-47s and pistols. 'Is that you, Esmatullah?' said one of the men, feigning surprise. He had a familiar face. 'Yes,' he replied. Two of them got out of the vehicle and grabbed him. They put him in handcuffs and shoved him in the boot. The boy had never been so frightened. Where were they taking him? What did they want from him?

Then he let out a silent scream. He realized who the man with the familiar face was. It was the son of the imam at the mosque. Esmatullah had prayed alongside him many times. He was a Talib. How had he not realized before? Esmatullah felt like he was suffocating. It was so hot trapped in the boot that he was dripping in sweat. He shouted for the Talibs to let him out but it was no use. Then he thought about Jamal, about all the times his brother had returned home and prayed at that mosque. Perhaps it was the imam's son who had fired at Jamal's car that day?

He needed to warn the rest of the family what had happened to him but he could not get out of the vehicle. He tried banging with his feet but it was dark and he couldn't see what he was doing. There was a lot of noise outside; they must be taking him into the heart of the city, he thought. In the few minutes he had been locked away in the boot of that car he had decided he would be brave, no matter what. He wouldn't tell the Talibs anything about this family or where Jamal was now. If they knew he was in Britain, then that was effectively confirmation that he had worked for the British and the whole family could be implicated in his perceived crimes.

Then suddenly there was daylight. The boot was opened and Esmatullah was dragged out by his hands. He gasped for air, welcoming the chance to breathe properly again. The hot afternoon sun was beating down on his head. And then he realized where he had been taken. It was the police station which the Afghan government had controlled only a few days before. It seemed so surreal that it was now in the hands of the Taliban. Esmatullah was taken in by the back door, although he didn't understand why the Talibs seemed so keen to avoid taking him through the main gate at the front. When he got inside, another man attached cuffs around his ankles, took away his phone and threw him into a tiny, windowless room. He waited for what felt like hours, wondering what they would do with him. Did he have the strength to fight back? What would they do if he refused to tell them anything? He had heard so many stories about the cold-blooded brutality of the Taliban. The strangulations, the beatings with sticks, the public floggings. In one province they had sliced a man's arm muscles off. Last month they had killed a well-known comedian, Nazar Mohammad, better known as Khasha Zwan. As fighting had raged on the outskirts of Kandahar, Nazar, who had previously served in the police, had been dragged from his home and then slapped and abused while being held down by two men in a car. Footage of them taunting him had gone viral on the internet. Later photographs emerged of him backed up against a tree and then of him lying on the ground with his throat cut.[10] Militants were said to be going from house to house searching for government workers. And now it seemed that the hunt for traitors had reached Lashkar Gah, where people were being detained at random.

Nothing had prepared Esmatullah for being tortured.

The door opened. One of the Talibs sauntered in holding Esmatullah's phone and smiling menacingly. 'Where is your brother Jamal?' he asked him. Esmatullah was prepared for this question. 'He is in Iran.' The man with the long beard knew he was lying. He held out the phone and went on to his WhatsApp conversation with Jamal. Then he played one of Jamal's voice messages. There was no mistaking it was him. 'This phone number is British,' the man said. Esmatullah protested. 'No, he is not in the UK.' Then came the whack over his head. The pain seared through him as the man used the butt of his AK-47 to strike him repeatedly. His hands, still handcuffed together, offered him little protection. He felt the blood trickling down his face and on to his *shalwar*. He collapsed into a crumpled heap.

As soon as the family realized Esmatullah had been taken by the Talibs Razagulla went to the village elders begging for help. He was only a boy – it wasn't right, she said. They agreed, and the elders went with her to the police station asking for Esmatullah's release, but to no effect. There was no way her son was being let out that easily, she was told. There needed to be a full investigation. Into what exactly, Razagulla had no idea. She waited all day outside the police station, under a punishing sun, before returning home alone to Shaista, her face blotchy from crying.

There was still no electricity in the city at that time. At the police station Esmatullah sat in his dark, airless cell, wishing there was an open window. There was no bed and because of the way his hands and legs were tied he couldn't even lie down on the floor properly. Every few hours one of the guards would come in to check on him and hit him with his rifle, just for the fun of it, as he left. Esmatullah lost count of the times he had been hit. But he was on alert the whole night through, not wanting to fall asleep in case they caught him by surprise.

The following morning he was taken out of the cell and made to sit down outside. Here he came face to face with one of the senior commanders. The Talib hurled questions in his direction. 'What is your tribe?' he wanted to know. 'Barakzai,' Esmatullah replied feebly, not sure where the conversation was headed. He was hit again over the head. The commander didn't explain why. Perhaps they were from a different tribe? There were a lot in Afghanistan. 'Where's your father? What is he doing?' he asked next. 'Nothing,' replied Esmatullah. The commander was asking the questions at lightning speed, trying to catch him out. 'You were working in the Afghan forces,' he said next. Esmatullah replied a little too quickly. 'No, I was not,' he said. Another Talib chipped in. 'Yes, I know you. You were there working with me,' said a man he had never seen before. Had the Talibs allowed former Afghan soldiers into their ranks? 'No, I was not there,' he persisted.

As it happened, back in Coventry, Jamal had received a phone call a few days earlier from one of his friends in Lashkar Gah. He had warned him that he had spotted Esmatullah sitting with some ANA soldiers, holding a rifle and in a uniform, at the military headquarters in the city. The friend believed Esmatullah had been trying to join the fight. Concerned for his safety, Jamal's friend went up to him. 'Esmatullah, you are very young. You can see Lashkar Gah has been surrounded. Go home,' he told him. Jamal was told his little brother had refused. He got on to Shaista straight away. 'Dad, go and get him from the military headquarters. He is going to get himself killed. He is young. He's never even been trained!' When Shaista arrived at the headquarters he couldn't find him, and when Esmatullah came home later he denied ever having been there. The exact truth remained unclear, but the Taliban were clearly toying with him now.

The commander moved on to the topic of Jamal. 'Where is he? Is he in the UK?' he barked. Esmatullah repeated his previous answer, that Jamal was in Iran. 'If he's not in the UK, then how come you are not working? Why is your father not working? Where are you getting your money from? How are you paying for your food?' the man probed. Esmatullah stumbled on some of his answers, not sure how to explain how they were managing to survive. 'I have no communication with my brother,' he told them. But then the commander said something that really worried him. 'We have heard that you, your mother, father and brothers are trying to run away to the UK. You're going to join your brother,' he said, as one of the Talibs slapped and kicked him. 'No, that's a lie. Whoever told you that is lying, it is not true,' came Esmatullah's response. He didn't know how much longer he could keep up the denials. The interrogation was exhausting. But they were getting nowhere with him.

The commander nodded and one of the Talibs grabbed him by the arm and took him back to the tiny cell. 'It's too hot in there, please put me somewhere else,' Esmatullah pleaded in the politest voice he could muster. The stench of sweat coupled with the summer heat was suffocating. Much to his surprise, the man took pity on him. He led him back outside and put him with a group of other prisoners who were herded up behind some wire mesh. The makeshift holding pen looked rudimentary but there still didn't seem to be any way out. Another Talib had been watching what was happening and intervened. 'He's too young,' he told him. Esmatullah, who was about 16, wasn't clear why his age suddenly had any bearing on where he was held. They moved him to a nearby tree, uncuffed his hands and feet and tied him to the tree with a chain like a dog. He was left there overnight, although he was grateful for the fresh air. Anywhere but that tiny, foetid cell.

Having managed to drift off to sleep, Esmatullah was woken up just before sunrise with a grunt and tug on his shoulder. It was time to pray, he was told. One of his captors removed the chain from around his legs. They allowed him to wash his face and his legs, and then he got down on his hands and knees and prayed towards Mecca.

It was now just about light and Esmatullah was taken inside to a room holding 17 other prisoners. Three of them were the family's neighbours. It was a small comfort, but he was relieved to see some people he knew. Then he remembered that they had all been working for the Afghan government and he took pity on them. That must be why they were here – and everybody knew what the Taliban did with such people. He had never met the rest of the men, but was told they were ANA soldiers. They all looked as frightened as he felt. One by one they were dragged outside for an 'investigation'. Grown men returned crying because they had been beaten so badly, their clothes torn and their faces blue with the bruising. Esmatullah tried hard not to look, wondering what the Talibs had in store for him.

His turn came the following morning. There were electric cables laid on the ground outside. Upon seeing them he could feel his body convulse involuntarily. 'Why do you not dress in Afghan clothes? Where is your cap?' one of the Talibs asked him. They said that his clothes were too short and too loose. They also told him that he should have his head covered. Esmatullah was confused. He was dressed like most boys of his age he knew in the city, in traditional Afghan clothing but not as long and baggy as the Talibs. He didn't reply, not sure what answer they were expecting from him. With that two men grabbed his bare feet, holding one each. Another put his foot on Esmatullah's throat so that he was crushed against the ground and couldn't move. Lashes rained down on Esmatullah's feet. He had never felt pain like it before. After what seemed like forever the fourth man – his torturer – spoke. 'Hold out your hands,' he demanded. Esmatullah blanked out.

As it got dark, he was taken back to the tree. He longed for something cool to soothe his bleeding hands and feet. Another boy about his age was tied to the tree next to him. Esmatullah had no idea who he was or what he had done to be there, but he realized what he himself must look like as the other boy looked at him appalled. By the following morning the Taliban had decided they had punished Esmatullah enough and roused him from his exhausted slumber. 'Do you have someone who can be your guarantor?' 'Yes, if you go to my house someone will come,' he told them. He hoped that his father would still be in hiding.

Salma and her husband, Said, were in the house when there was a loud bang at the door. Said answered. After a brief conversation he rushed out to speak to the tribal elders and they agreed to go back to the station with him. The Taliban were satisfied that if they demanded to see Esmatullah again, then the elders would ensure that he was brought swiftly to their presence. 'You must pray five times a day, Esmatullah. And make sure you change your clothes,' one of the Talibs shouted as they released him. Then it was as if he had read his mind. The man reached out to grab his arm. 'And make sure you do not run away from your country,' he spat.

Esmatullah returned home, broken. He had bruises on his head from where he had been beaten and gashes on his hand and feet from the lashings. But at least he was alive.

9

Journey to Kabul: Lashkar Gah, Monday, 23–Tuesday, 24 August 2021

Shaista's phone rang shortly after sunset. He answered immediately. It was Jamal. 'You've been accepted, Dad. You're coming to Britain.'

Shaista dropped to his knees, as if about to start praying, unable to believe what his son was saying. He had spent so long locked in the house by that point that even the wind rattling the doors outside was making him jump.

'But I don't know if Mohmood can come. He might be too old,' Jamal added, tentatively, afraid of Shaista's response.

'We aren't leaving without Mohmood,' Shaista told Jamal.

'You have to, Dad. This might be your only chance. When you get to England, we will make sure they let him come,' Jamal pleaded. There was no point debating this any further now. Jamal had been given no detail on which family members were allowed to join Shaista in the UK. He told his father to wait for more information from the MoD about who was on the list before making any rash decisions.

Hours earlier, in the MoD main building in Whitehall, Defence Secretary Ben Wallace had been handed a list of

Afghans with special circumstances who had not yet been given permission to come to the UK. On the list was Shaista. His case had been raised by Wallace's special adviser, Peter Quentin, who had served in Afghanistan and who had been to Shaista's garden himself. Eleven years on, he hadn't forgotten it. The minister, who had broken down in tears earlier in the month in a radio interview when he admitted that they might not be able to get everyone out, had promised to review any contentious claims personally. He was keen to do away with the 'Computer says no' mentality and to take a more human approach. With the stroke of a pen, he decided Shaista would be allowed in.

After the decision was made, everything moved quickly. That afternoon the British team at the MoD sent an email to Shaista, which Jamal received on his behalf while at a protest in London. The email asked for the names and ages of all his children. Jamal replied for his father, who like many Afghans of his age had no access to email, and included Mohmood on the list. Jamal was uncertain as to whether he would be accepted. Even though he struggled to walk following the Taliban attack on him back in 2015 and his parents had to help him to shower, he was over 18 and so was not considered a dependant. Jamal had not applied for his sisters to come to the UK because they were all married, and so were considered the responsibilities of their husbands' families. Mohmood was married too, but under the new Taliban regime his wife could no longer go out of the house unless escorted by a male relative. She would struggle to take care of him without his family's support.

Just 20 minutes after Jamal had sent the list of his five brothers to the MoD, an official emailed back to tell him Shaista was being evacuated to the UK and to head to the airport immediately. It didn't mention anything about the rest of the family. Reading the email chain again, Jamal realized to his horror that he had put down Mohmood's age as 22, rather than 20. Would it make a difference? It probably didn't matter anyway. He still counted as an adult.

After the call with Jamal, Shaista agonized over what to do, as any father would. It was entirely possible Mohmood would not be on the list. And he was torn between a better life for his wife and the four of their sons (including the traumatized Esmatullah) who had been offered sanctuary in the UK and staying in Afghanistan but with all the family, except Jamal, together. It was the sort of dilemma that was facing many Afghan families, especially those with older parents who would normally be cared for at home until the day they died. Leaving them, and their war-ravaged country, might have seemed like an obvious choice given the new regime, but it didn't make it an easy one.

Shaista made his decision. If it came to it, they would leave Mohmood behind. But they didn't have much time. It was only a matter of days – maybe even hours – before the British forces would leave the country for ever. He shouted to Razagulla, who came running with the younger boys. They jumped up and down excitedly. 'Shh,' Shaista whispered to them sharply, terrified the Taliban would hear their cries. They all started running around the house packing anything they could get their hands on.

'Can I come?' asked Mohmood, who had appeared in the corner of the room. 'Yes, can he come?' Razagulla repeated to Shaista. She had never got over the death of Rahmatullah and didn't know if she could bear losing another son to the Taliban. 'I'm not sure, Mohmood, we are waiting to hear from them,' he replied, referring to the British. Mohmood looked into his father's eyes and knew deep down it was hopeless. Even if they could get him out, he also had his wife, Gulali, to think about. They hadn't even mentioned her in any of the applications, so getting her on a flight would be an added complication. But should they go to the airport and try their luck anyway?

There were many other Afghans who had gone to Kabul that night in the hope that the British soldiers would take pity on them and wave them through. One such was Mohibullah, the younger brother of an interpreter friend of Jamal's who had been killed in June 2010, and who had reached out to Jamal for help. He had rushed to the airport hours after the Taliban seized Kabul and had been one of the people who had watched in horror as two desperate men fell from one of the planes. Mohibullah's brother Naveedullah, a local boxing champion, had been killed while out on patrol in the Sangin district of Helmand province, then considered the deadliest area in the whole of Afghanistan. Straddling the sun-scorched desert and a lush river valley, Sangin, which the Taliban had not stopped fighting to control, had rarely known peace. Mohibullah, who shared his brother's bravery but was more cautious, was just 15 when his father received the letter from Naveedullah's commanding officer saying that he had been killed performing an 'invaluable service'. There were no other details of his death, although the town of Sangin had become notorious for the huge numbers of roadside bombs that were being planted there by the militants. 'This is terrible news and such a waste of a truly good life,' the letter went on. When the family went to collect Naveedullah's body two days after his death, his injuries were hard to stomach: his face was unscathed but the rest of his body had been torn apart by a bomb blast. Mohibullah would never forget what he saw.

The family weren't angry. In fact, Mohibullah's father had been so proud of Naveedullah's service with the British army that he believed his death had not been in vain, but had been for the greater good of the stability and freedom of Afghanistan. Yet he was unprepared for the impact on his family. After his son's death the news spread in the village that Naveedullah had worked for the British army and the family were branded 'slaves of the infidels'. Letters were pinned to their front door, one of them even accusing them of not being Muslim. Mohibullah was singled out in particular because he was studying English at the time and was accused of receiving money from Britain. The family stopped going outside and in the end were forced to move to Kabul in the hope that no one would recognize them. Now Mohibullah, who had kept Naveedullah's army bag tag on him, applied for the British government's relocation scheme, even though he knew his chances were slim.

Desperate to leave the country, he had taken his brother's papers with him to Kabul airport. As he wrestled through the crowd, his arms cut on the wires, his clothes torn, 'My life is not good. The Taliban keep threatening me,' he told an American soldier who had a brief look at his documents. 'Go to Abbey Gate – that's where the British are,' he was told. Mohibullah shoved the papers into his underwear, afraid that the Taliban would see them and arrest him. Having spent several hours wading through raw sewage and the clamour of his desperate countrymen, he made it to the right gate. 'Where is your email?' asked the British soldier at the gate, referring to an email sent by the MoD to eligible Afghans confirming they had a place on a flight. Mohibullah had no email. Shots were fired from a distance. It was the American soldiers and the Taliban trying to control the crowds, although all it seemed to do was create panic. Like thousands of others, he was turned away.

A few hours later, in the middle of the night, just as the Gul family were packing to leave, Shaista received a call from an unknown number. It was an interpreter working for the British government.

'Shaista?'

'Yes.'

'Make sure you get yourselves to Kabul as soon as possible.'

'Yes, we are coming in the next few hours.'

'But Mohmood cannot come as he is over 18,' the interpreter said, confirming Shaista's worst fears.

'But Mohmood is disabled, he has been shot multiple times. How can I leave him here?' Shaista pleaded with the interpreter, who was only doing his job. It was worth a try.

'I'm sorry, there's nothing we can do.'

The call ended. The interpreter had many more calls to make that night.

Mohmood had been in the room listening, hanging on to his father's every word. 'Mohmood can't come, he's too old,' Shaista confirmed to the whole family, before looking at his son with sadness in his eyes. They all stood still, Razagulla's eyes darting between her husband and her son. They all knew that it was coming, but how would he take the news? Mohmood said that he understood, but he was holding back tears. Shaista promised him that they would try their best to get him and his wife out afterwards.

Shortly after the phone call, Mohmood took himself to bed, without Gulali. He didn't want any company. It was too painful to witness all the excited commotion in the rest of the house when he knew that he would be left behind in Afghanistan, fearing for his life. The Taliban would surely be angry once they found out that the rest of the family had fled. What would happen to him when they were gone? It didn't bear thinking about. He cried himself to sleep.

As the family were leaving, Shaista went to Mohmood's door and opened it quietly. He could see him sleeping and thought for a moment about waking him up. But he knew that if he did so it would be much harder to leave. He took one last look at his son and slowly closed the door again, creeping away silently.

Razagulla breathed slowly and deeply, trying not to cry – or panic. Her hands were shaking as she checked her handbag one last time to make sure she had everything. She always thought she'd spend the rest of her life in Lashkar Gah, with her children and her grandchildren around her. Now the family was being ripped apart and she might never see Mohmood or her daughters again. Salma, who had appeared in the doorway, smiled reassuringly to her mother, as if she knew what she was thinking. Despite her lack of education, she was a wise woman and knew that, because she and her four sisters had husbands, and therefore technically were cared for, they had no hope of coming to England.

'Only one suitcase between us all,' Shaista whispered loudly, concerned at the number of items that seemed to be piling up. Jamal had told him that the British would only allow a small amount of luggage on the flight. Two or three sets of clothes each; everything else to be left behind. Shaista shoved packets of medication into his pockets – he had a cunning plan to use the medication as a way out. He would pretend to be sick. He then phoned a taxi driver, a man he had never met, who arrived shortly after 5 a.m. He took one last look at his beloved quails, the pomegranate tree in the garden bulging with fruit, the house he had worked all his life to make a home. He knew he might never return.

Now he opened the front door, checked that nobody was around outside, and under the cover of darkness darted for the taxi.

No driver would take the family all the way to Kabul, so they would take the taxi to the central bus station in Lashkar Gah before getting another one to Kandahar, the Taliban's ethnic Pashtun heartland, which the insurgents now controlled. In Kandahar, Jamal had told them, they would meet with one of his friends who would give them some money for the rest of the journey. They were lucky he had so many connections.

Less than 20 minutes into the journey from the bus station, their second taxi approached the first Taliban checkpoint. Shaista was in the front passenger seat, with Razagulla and the four boys squeezed into the back. They had all agreed on the same cover story. They were going to Kandahar for treatment for Shaista because he couldn't get the right medication in Lashkar Gah. It was risky, especially as it made no sense for them all to be crammed into a taxi heading more than 80 miles east during such a chaotic period, but they had to try. Everyone was well aware that one wrong word could lead to execution on the spot.

Shaista wore a black *lungee* (turban) draped across part of his face so he would not be easily recognized. 'Where are you going?' the Taliban fighter asked him, peering through the taxi window. 'We are going to Kandahar to see the doctor,' Shaista told him, perhaps rather too confidently. 'I need more medication, there are not the doctors in Lashkar Gah,' he added, spluttering. He got out the packs of medication from his pockets and held them up for the Talib to see. Some of the packets spilled onto the floor. Most of the pills were not even his. He could feel himself trembling uncontrollably. Razagulla, who had covered her face with a black niqab, held her head in her hands, pretending to be unwell too. The boys sat silently in the back, having put on traditional Afghan caps in order to make themselves look more pious. In a lighter moment, they might have all laughed. Instead they stared down at the ground, not wanting to catch the eyes of the Taliban. They were waved through.

Once in Kandahar, Afghanistan's second biggest city, they met with Jamal's friend, who gave Shaista 15,000 afghani (about £140), and they caught yet another taxi bound for Kabul. To get to Kabul, they had to drive down Highway 1. Once a great symbol of America's reconstruction effort in the country, heralded by President Hamid Karzai as bringing Afghanistan back to the civilized world, it had become a death run for ordinary Afghans hoping to make it to the capital.[1] There were hidden bombs everywhere and the Taliban lurked in trees and houses along the route, ready to fire on any passers-by. Shootings, kidnappings and ambushes were almost routine.

But now the 300-mile stretch of battered roadway, which was supposed to reduce the journey time from Kandahar to Kabul from two days to six hours, was fully in the hands of the Taliban. The very people who were once blowing it apart were now its guardians. Shaista wondered if that was a good thing or a bad thing. At least they knew where the IEDs were hidden, he thought wryly.

They passed checkpoint after checkpoint, each as daunting as the last. Most of the time they were waved through, although sometimes they were stopped and asked questions. Shaista used the same rehearsed routine, although this time he told the fighters that they were headed to Kabul for medical treatment. The militants checked their identity cards, referred to as the Tazkira, and asked them which province they were from. Each time they were stopped Shaista wondered if anyone would recognize him from the television interview he had done for Jamal. It was a constant source of worry for him, even though the chances seemed remote.

They slowed down at one of the checkpoints, where they saw the insurgents pulling people out of their cars and searching them from head to toe. Shaista took a deep breath and readied himself for what might come next. His documents, which proved that he had worked with the British, were stashed away in the boot. The driver opened his window as they got closer to the checkpoint. One of the Talibs looked at Shaista, pointed, and shouted 'Get out!' His legs were shaking. The militant patted him down, more rigorously than seemed necessary, and then paused. Shaista wondered what would come next. His heart was pounding so fast he thought he might be having a heart attack. What if they put handcuffs on him and led him away? What would happen to the family if he never came back? But no, he had passed their invisible test.

Next it was the boys' turn. Shaista gave a look of reassurance to Esmatullah, who was also shaking. The poor boy had already been through so much. One by one they were told to get out of the car while the Talib searched them. Razagulla, who feigned a coughing fit, was spared the ordeal. Satisfied with their cover story and, crucially, their lack of luggage, which suggested they weren't going too far, the militants waved them through.

By now it was early afternoon and the highway had become much busier. Vehicle after vehicle raced past, crammed full of people and their belongings trying to flee to the capital. Some had solemn faces; others looked excited with anticipation. Shaista assumed that many were people like them, attempting to get on flights to the West.

Over the next few hours they passed by decaying American-built security posts lining the route, a couple of which were now flying the white banner of the Taliban. As the road snaked through towns and villages, the deep ruts made by overturned lorries and the blast holes from roadside bombs became worse. Some stretches were barely passable. Shaista admired the driver, who was having to slam on the brakes repeatedly to avoid an accident. Some cars had pulled up along the side of the road for a pit stop, although there wasn't much open. The Guls continued; they didn't want to waste any time.

Just as Shaista and the family were getting closer to Kabul, the US president, Joe Biden, was having a virtual emergency meeting of G7 leaders. Boris Johnson, the British Prime Minister, and others were trying to persuade him to extend the humanitarian airlift out of Kabul beyond his self-imposed deadline of 31 August. The day before, the Taliban had already firmly ruled out an extension to the withdrawal date, threatening dire consequences if the Western troops didn't leave on time. Yet there were concerns among UK ministers and officials that thousands of people who were eligible to come to Britain would not make it on to the flights. They would be left behind to face the Taliban, whom they had spent the best part of two decades helping the West to oust. How could they abandon them after all the promises that had been made? But the leaders failed to persuade Biden to delay the deadline. He believed that each day the American troops were there the risk to their lives increased.

There was intelligence to suggest that a branch of the Islamic State group in Afghanistan was seeking to target the airport. And they were ruthless. The group, known as Islamic State–Khorasan province (Isis–K), which attracted defectors from the Taliban who felt that they were not purist enough, was the most extreme and violent organization in the whole of Afghanistan. As far as they were concerned, the more foreign troops they could kill, the better. And, as unseemly as it was, the West was dependent upon the Taliban's co-operation to prevent that happening, because it was they who controlled access to the airport. Too many American and British soldiers had already lost their lives in the country. If any of them died at this late stage, after Biden had made such a point of carrying out an orderly drawdown which would prioritize the safety of US troops, it would be nothing short of a humiliation. With that in mind, there were reports that US troops had started to pull out of Kabul already. In Whitehall, some MPs suggested that US–UK relations were about to enter their lowest point since the Suez Crisis in 1956.

If anything, the episode highlighted how reliant the British were on the Americans.

After the virtual meeting, rumours were rife that the British government would have to stop its evacuation flights in the next 24 to 36 hours to give them time to pack up before the end of August. To make matters more complicated, the British troops were wholly dependent on the 6,000-strong US force for security and the smooth running of the airfield. Once they left, everyone else's time was up. Yet it was difficult for the MoD back in London to know exactly when that would be.

Such headlines did little to calm Jamal's nerves, who was waiting anxiously back in Coventry. There were potentially hundreds, if not thousands, of Afghans waiting outside the airport who, like the Guls, had been told they were eligible to get on one of the RAF evacuation flights. Jamal wondered how his family would manage to break through the crowds in time.

One former interpreter, who had worked in the British embassy in Kabul for 17 years and had been shot at by gunmen, had just made it to Manchester after waiting 14 hours overnight outside the airport.[2] As they pushed through the crowds, his daughter had fallen unconscious. He only knew she was still alive when he poured water over her head and her hand moved. The family then witnessed a woman in her forties and a boy aged five or six die in the crush. Would Razagulla have the strength to push through the crowds like them? And what about Jamal's brothers? They were so young and timid. Jamal prayed they were prepared for what was to come.

Standing under the beating sun that afternoon was also an interpreter named Qais, who had with him his wife, their three small children and two of his teenage brothers. They had been waiting outside the airport for three punishing days. Like Jamal, Qais had served in Nad Ali, but a year later, in 2011. He was baby-faced, with one neat curl of hair pressed against his forehead. Qais had been in the thick of it for around nine months before he went home on leave. When he returned to Helmand, he was told they didn't need an interpreter any more, so he was offered a job at one of the patrol bases, which had been set up in a shop. He considered it for a day but then heard others dismissing the job as beneath them, so decided to quit and return to his family. That decision became the biggest regret of his life, because had he stayed in the role for several months – until December 2012 – he would have been eligible for a British visa as early as 2014. Now, nine years later, he was making a last desperate attempt to get out of the country.

When Kabul had fallen a few days earlier, Qais told friends the scenes in front of him were like a horror movie. He never thought he would see such things in real life. He had watched from the roof of his house as the Taliban had freed dangerous inmates from Pul-e Charkhi prison, a notorious high-security facility on the outskirts of the capital. Once used by the Americans to hold thousands of Taliban fighters, it had now fallen into the hands of the militants. He saw plumes of smoke rising from the sprawling complex as the prisoners ran amok outside and helicopters roared ahead – presumably American ones observing the chaos. The prospect of hundreds of dangerous men roaming the streets of the capital haunted Qais for days.

Then, at last, he received the phone call saying that he and his family were eligible for an RAF flight out of the country. What was more, following months of indecision, his teenage brothers were allowed to come too. But all that meant confronting his worst nightmare of standing face to face with the Taliban, whom he would need to get past to catch the flight.

Now he and his family watched appalled as the Taliban thugs hit people in the crowd with sticks and rifle butts. The blows were indiscriminate; not even children were spared. The sound of them crying was only occasionally drowned out by the thunderous noise of the aircraft taking off above. When the people surged forward, the Taliban fired into the air or by their feet as a warning not to get any closer. Qais couldn't see where the bullets were landing, but he wouldn't have been surprised if someone in the crowd had already been killed by one of them.

They fired again. And that was when he lost his three-year-old daughter, Hadia. Qais's wife, Fahima, who looked like a doll, with plump, rosy cheeks and pink lips, had put her down for a second, but at that very moment the crowd had broken out violently in all directions in response to the volley of gunfire. Suddenly Hadia was gone. They screamed and shouted her name, but there were so many people that they could neither see nor hear her above the clamour. But they were lucky. Qais's cousin, who was there too, found her after what felt like an eternity, crying for her mother. They persevered.

Other Afghans had tried to get to where Qais was but had given up trying. Ahmad, the interpreter who had been considering paying people smugglers back in 2015 and decided to do so, had called up his brother-in-law from France, where he was now living, having claimed asylum there in 2016. His wife and family were still in Afghanistan, and now he was urging his brother-in-law to take them to the airport.

A few weeks previously, before the fall of Kabul even looked likely, he had received an email from the MoD out of the blue saying he was eligible for relocation in the UK. Not only that, but his wife, Janah, and their three children – the youngest of whom had been born when he was travelling through Iran to France – would be able to join him too. Ahmad had paid $3,000 to get them passports, a feat that would be impossible now that the Taliban controlled the government and therefore effectively the money supply. But the British visa appointment, given to his family, was scheduled for about a week's time in Kabul. Ahmad could not wait until then.

'Leave everything behind and get to the airport,' he told Janah when it looked like there was no other way out. She did what he asked and left their house in Khost with nothing but the family's passports and identity cards. When they arrived at the airport, the children were petrified, clinging on to their mother as they were pushed back and forward by the surging crowds. The Taliban fighters – the angry men the children knew not to trust – were still firing sporadically into the air, and families were getting separated from each other in the crush. They gave up: there was no chance Janah and the children would get through. They returned to Khost, where, over a year later, they remained as they waited for further instruction from the British government.

Back with the Guls, it was early evening by the time they arrived in the centre of Kabul. The journey had taken far longer than the six hours they had been told it would, but the driver had managed to navigate the highway without incident. It was now more than a week since the Taliban had seized the capital.

The sound of planes taking off cut through the hum of the subdued city, now dotted with Taliban checkpoints manned by bearded men wielding Kalashnikovs. Chinooks and Black Hawk helicopters were buzzing nearby. There was a rumour that the militants were searching people's phones for any signs of communications in English. They were also going to the homes and offices of Afghans they believed to have been in contact with Westerners. All the banks were closed, and food prices had rocketed. The cash machines had long been emptied and money transfer firms had pulled out, so the flow of transfers from abroad had dried up. One fast-food restaurant popular for its kebabs and ice cream had been selling 40,000 afghani (about £370) worth of food and drink a day before the Taliban arrived. Now it was taking as little as 5,000 afghani.[3] Some people had resorted to selling their household belongings on the street in order to raise just a little bit of money before trying to flee to safety. Staff in clothes shops who had been wearing jeans and T-shirts only ten days ago were now wearing traditional Afghan dress, fearful that otherwise they would be beaten to a pulp.

By now, as the sun started to fade on the anxious, adrenalized city, the Taliban were declaring that the route to Kabul airport was only open to foreigners. It was unclear if that was a ruse to clear the airport's gates of the thousands of Afghans who had arrived without the correct papers or a move by the insurgents to exert control over the fleeing masses.

The Guls pressed on regardless. As they got closer to their drop-off point near the airport they couldn't believe the sheer number of people in the streets in front of them. It seemed as if half of Afghanistan's population was trying to leave the country. It was clear to them all that their window of escape was rapidly closing.

10

Hell on Earth: Kabul, Tuesday, 24–Thursday, 26 August 2021

'Shame on you for abandoning your country!' roared the Taliban fighter as he lashed out at Shaista with his stick. The air was thick, the heat was punishing. Shaista had spread his arms as wide as he could, trying to protect Razagulla and the boys from being trampled on. The crowd had gone crazy; people had lost their minds. Then Shaista made the horrible mistake of looking down at the ground, only to see a dead girl lying there bleeding from the mouth. She must have been crushed to death. The stench was unbearable but he had no time to dwell on the horror of it.

Now Razagulla was pushed to the ground, as the crowd surged forward when one of the gates into the airport opened much further ahead of them. Men, women and children were stepping all over her and she was crying out in pain. Shaista held on to her shoulders so no one could stand on top of her. He then used all his strength to pull his wife up towards him. The Taliban, many of them armed with sticks and cables, fired their AK-47s into the air to stop people pushing forward. Shaista heard screams as the bullets fell back to the ground.

Children were being dragged under foot, too weak to stand up unaided. The closer the Guls got to the gate to the airport, the louder the shouts from men, women and teenagers holding up signs with names on, trying desperately to catch the eyes of the soldiers. Kicked-up dust clung to the hairs of Shaista's nostrils. Rubbish lay strewn on the ground, leaving a rancid smell in the air. A message arrived on Shaista's phone, which he struggled to retrieve from his pocket because his arms were so tightly squeezed in by the people around him.

'Take a picture showing where you are,' the text read, from an unknown number. By this point he had received so many messages from so many different people that he was not sure who this was.

He handed the phone to Esmatullah, who took a photograph of what they could see – in the hope that it would then be passed on to the British troops inside the airport, who would recognize where they were and come and rescue them. It was dark and the photograph was blurry. No way would anyone be able to work out their position. Esmatullah turned on the flash and tried again. This time he saw a huge sign taped on to the gate a few metres in front of them and took a shot of it. It read 'BRITISH PASSPORT HOLDERS', in capital letters. They were so close, but so far away.

A Taliban guard spotted the flash and waded forward, hitting Esmatullah with a stick. Then he slapped Shaista across the face, cursing him and shouting, 'You are a spy!'

Feeling utterly humiliated and exhausted, Shaista thought about leaving there and then. But he couldn't; for the sake of the family he couldn't. By this time the Taliban were firing warning shots to disperse everybody. Those who were waiting at the gate would be shoved backwards a few metres, then the Taliban would move on to another part of the gate, and do the same thing again and the crowd would surge forward again. If you could make some ground in those few seconds then you were doing well. It was a pattern that had been going on for days.

The family knew that Jamal was doing all he could back in the UK to reach out to a group of British army veterans who were liaising with soldiers on the ground to try and get eligible Afghans inside the airport. But the whole process was chaotic – and many people were still waiting for responses to applications they had submitted to the MoD months before, under the ARAP scheme. Others were waiting for their biometrics to be carried out, a prerequisite for getting on a flight. And then there were those who had received an email telling them to go to the airport but who did not have any papers and had no idea what they were supposed to do or where they were going. The veterans swung into action. Some of them teamed together and, using their army training, they created their own sort of informal task force, with everyone assigned different roles. They created a database of all the people they knew about who might be eligible to leave but were still in the country – which was probably the most up-to-date and accurate list of Afghan interpreters and other former staff held by anyone. At one point during the evacuation they had some 50 people on their list – and that was just the ones who had been told to come to the airport. There were many more who had still not received the email. Once an eligible Afghan had made it through the gates of the airport, they got in touch with him to collect vital information, such as what documents he still needed and which routes he had taken to get there. They then passed these details on to the soldiers on the ground.

Major-General (ret.) Charlie Herbert, a former commander in Afghanistan, Ed Aitken, the former captain who co-founded the Sulha Alliance, and Major Andrew Fox, a paratrooper who had served three gruelling tours of the country, did much organizing, managing to get many Afghans through the gates, sending them maps of the ground and pinpointing to them where the Taliban were positioned. Many others were involved too. These included Pam French, a former intelligence officer who had initially come to the rescue of her former interpreter who had mistakenly been denied entry to the airport, but then stayed on to help others, and Sara de Jong, a political scientist who had co-founded the Sulha Alliance campaign group with Ed Aitken and who had spent years supporting the interpreters who had been left behind. The veterans all knew of Shaista through Jamal, who had kick-started a Herculean effort spanning the globe to get his father to Britain. From their stations in Somalia, Dubai and the UK, veterans were passing on any information Jamal had from his father – who couldn't communicate with them directly because of his poor English – to serving soldiers they knew inside the base. These included many in the 2nd Battalion, the Parachute Regiment (2 PARA), who were part of a 600-strong British contingent from 16 Air Assault Brigade, a brigade always held at high readiness for emergencies like these, who had been urgently deployed to the capital to help manage the evacuation. It was harrowing work. Some broke down, having been forced to turn away desperate Afghans because they did not have the right papers. For all the government and army work that was going on in terms of processing people, these were the people who were having to make the split-second decisions that could determine whether someone might live or be killed by the Taliban the following day. One senior soldier who had completed tours in Afghanistan, Iraq and Northern Ireland, believed that Operation Pitting was the hardest thing he had ever done.

Behind the scenes, there was friction between the MoD and the Foreign Office, which had pulled all its officials out from Kabul, with the exception of Sir Laurie Bristow, the ambassador. This had left the staff at the MoD processing huge numbers of complex cases without the help of any consular staff. A team of four MoD civil servants ended up volunteering to come to Afghanistan to help process some of the applications after the officials fled. Three days after the diplomatic staff left, the Foreign Office sent a replacement team. But even then it consisted of only around ten people, including Border Force officials from the Home Office. That was nothing like enough people to handle the hundreds of fresh applications that were flooding in daily. One minister believed that the Foreign Office's decision to withdraw its diplomatic staff cost the evacuation effort several days, with between 800 and 1,000 fewer people being evacuated as a result.[1]

The lack of staff and planning and a vast underestimation of the numbers of people who would need to be evacuated also meant that mistakes were being made. Some Afghan nationals believed they had been cleared for evacuation only to be turned away at the airport. Others were being allowed through the gates even though they were not eligible. One source in the MoD admitted it was possible errors were being made because 'people are writing on pieces of paper who is getting on the plane'.[2] There was also a disconnect between the MoD and the Home Office, with the MoD telling some Afghans that they were eligible for visas, only for the Home Office to reject them following security checks. Hanif Ahmadzai, one of Charlie Herbert's former interpreters, had woken up in the middle of the night in June to find an email from the British government saying he was eligible to travel to Britain.[3] Now in his late thirties, he had worked with UK forces for less than a year in Kandahar before working with the Americans. During his time with the British troops, in 2007, he had interpreted for Charlie, and Charlie, who had been a senior NATO adviser to the Afghan police until 2018, knew that he had faced 'chilling' death threats and that there was no doubt of the Taliban's intention to kill him.

Despite the pressure he was under, Charlie thought Hanif hysterical (in a good way): he was hilarious, light-hearted and loved by all the British officers. When Hanif was on leave, he would buy Charlie and the others local clothing. He once dressed up as a Talib for some group photos. Hanif, an avid reader and intellectual who was well respected by Ashraf Ghani Ahmadzai, the Afghan president, with whom he worked for years previously, had few true friends, but regarded Charlie as one of them. He was so happy when he got the email from the MoD that he went out and bought new dresses and shoes for his three daughters and one son, all of whom had striking green eyes. He even started teaching them English.

After completing his biometric tests a month later he was given a date of the end of July for their flights. But the day he was due to collect his visa he was told by the British embassy they had not received it yet and that he would have to wait for a later flight. And then, on 11 August, he was told he had been refused the visa because he did not meet the requirements of the immigration rules. There was no other explanation. Senior MPs who learned about his plight were horrified by the decision but were being told that there was a genuine reason for the refusal. One source in the MoD said it was something to do with suspected involvement in terrorist activity. Hanif was so baffled by the decision that he asked Charlie whether the government had got him confused with a man of the same name who had been the spokesman for the Taliban in 2006 – and had been subsequently killed.

When Kabul fell, Hanif moved his family to another house, fearing the Taliban would come looking for him. He was told they had twice knocked on his door asking for his whereabouts. Now, not willing to tell his children that they would no longer be going to Britain, he decided to take the family to the airport to try and see if they could get through the gate with the papers they already had. But when he saw the shots being fired and, he thought, tear gas being used, he decided to take them away. Of everything that he had witnessed he was most alarmed by what he believed to be the Taliban following and then taking photographs of interpreters arriving at the gates in order to identify them later on. When he returned home, rumours were rife that the Taliban were going from house to house in his neighbourhood, arresting people they suspected of working for the West. He was told that, while he was at the airport, his neighbour's house had been searched and that he had been taken away, reported as missing. Those who knew him went to the local police station to ask for his release, but were told he was not there. And then, a few days later, Hanif was given the good news that the Americans were prepared to put him on a flight out of Kabul. His daughters would finally get to wear their pretty new pink and white dresses. However, his case raised serious concerns about the UK government vetting process.

Despite the endeavours of the veterans and the soldiers on the ground, there had been dozens of failed attempts to get people to safety almost every day. And there were still hundreds of people like the Guls who had been told to make their way to the airport but who could neither get through the checkpoints nor get past the final gate. Now, more than a week since the Taliban had taken over Kabul, everyone was becoming increasingly frustrated.

Jamal received a message from Charlie, which he passed on to Shaista. 'You need to stay there all night if necessary,' he told him. Both Shaista and Jamal knew that doing so would require patience and perseverance, both of which Shaista was now lacking. He clutched his 11-year-old son Najeebullah's hand tightly and, even though he did not feel like it himself, he told him to be brave and stay put. Although he was only young, Najeebullah was a clever, observant boy and knew exactly what was going on. There was no way he wanted to go back home. He had spent years telling Jamal, to whom he was extremely close and whom he adored, to get him to the UK. This was his chance.

Rumours were circulating that the Americans could leave within hours. And if the Americans, who were responsible for securing the airport, went, then there would be no more flights. But the desperate crowd showed no signs of giving up. Shaista watched in horror as young men tried to clamber over the razor wire to get inside the airport. If he hadn't had Razagulla and the children with him, he might have tried himself.

It was impossible to sit down comfortably or safely, so they used each other to lean on. Every ten to 20 minutes it seemed the British troops further up ahead were opening the gate and shouting people by name. No one called out for Shaista or the rest of the family. The Taliban lashed out some more, and the butt of an AK-47 caught Shaista's head. This time he had had enough. He messaged Jamal. 'I don't care about the UK, I don't want to go there. They are beating us, swearing at us,

I can't accept this any more.' Then: 'I'm tired, Jamal, leave us, leave us to die here.' Jamal knew that his father was exhausted and not thinking straight. He pleaded with him to stay put, which he eventually accepted.

And then Shaista received another phone call. Later that night or in the early hours of the morning, when it was darker and quieter, the gate would be opened and the British troops would grab members of an elite group of Afghan troops known as Afghan Task Force (ATF) 444, who had been trained and mentored by the British military's Special Forces Support Group and integrated into Afghan police special units. They had been working with members of the Parachute Regiment throughout Helmand and were deemed to be at considerable risk, and so were being pulled immediately. Shaista and the family would be allowed in at the same time, so they had to make sure they stayed close to the soldiers. It would be relatively easy to pick them out of the crowd because some of the British forces already knew the Afghan troops and what they looked like.

But as dawn approached, the family had made very little progress. And then Shaista received another call from yet another unknown number. They must make their way to the Ministry of Interior Affairs, across the road, where they would be picked up and taken right inside the airport. The voice told Shaista that the British had found that they were unable to open the gate to the airport because every time they tried to do so, too many people pushed forward and were trying to jump over the walls. If Shaista and the family could arrive in a vehicle, the Taliban might, in theory, let them in a less congested entrance. They decided to give it a try.

It was believed at that time that some British special forces soldiers had been dispatched outside the airport on secret missions to try and pick up stranded British citizens and others who were considered high priority. Perhaps they were coming for them? But by the time the family got to the Ministry, it seemed that it was too late and the contact number Shaista had been given no longer worked. He was so tired and emotionally drained that his legs had almost stopped working and his arms were aching from trying to protect Razagulla and the boys in the crowd. All he wanted to do was sleep. But by now the whole family was beginning to panic.

It was now Wednesday – two days since they had been told to go to the airport to catch their flight – and the evacuation effort was reaching its final stages. Although the RAF had already flown out more than 11,000 people, over 10,000 were still thought to be waiting at the airport. Among them were as many as 2,000 Afghan interpreters and others who had worked for the British government.

The Foreign Office updated its travel advice for Afghanistan, warning of an 'ongoing and high threat of terrorist attack' and urging people not to go to the airport. Those who were already there were told to go to a safe location and await further advice. It appeared that the mood back in the UK had changed. Ben Wallace came out and said that any Afghans wanting to flee the country would be better off heading for a border and trying to make their way to a third country rather than travel to the airport. Did they know something they weren't letting on?

Yet people were still getting through. In his makeshift office in Mogadishu, Charlie Herbert received news that Qais and his family had finally made it inside the airport. Excited messages were exchanged among the veterans, all of whom had been rooting for them. It seemed to make all their efforts worthwhile. A triumphant Qais shared a photograph of himself wading knee-deep through sewage water in a duct that ran parallel to a 500m stretch of road to the Baron Hotel, where the British were processing evacuees. He had passed through it twice – once by himself to get close enough to a British soldier to give his papers and then once more to carry his family through, although even then it was not straightforward: they had to clamber through a hole in a chain-link fence. Next they had to join the queue for biometric tests, which seemed to go on for ever. Fahima, Qais's wife, was at this point so sleep-deprived that she was no longer making sense. 'We are going to die now,' she told her husband. She made him nervous, even though they were safely inside the airport with the British army. Were they really going to make the flight out of there?

As the situation had become more desperate, and the British raced to evacuate as many people as possible, the soldiers on the ground, some of whom had seen their comrades murdered by the Taliban, found themselves having to work with the Taliban in order to try and bring forward those who were eligible but were stuck in the crowds.

The job of the Taliban, who had arrived suddenly one day and positioned themselves in front of the paratroopers with riot shields who were guarding the perimeter fence, was to provide public order alongside the US and British troops at two of the entrances: the North Gate and the one near the Baron Hotel. A fortified complex for Western contractors to the south of the airport, this had once been one of the most prestigious hotels in Afghanistan, boasting a gym, a swimming pool, shops, a café, two restaurants, a beauty salon and a spa. Now it had been turned into a processing point. But even then, the plan wasn't always working. Many of the Afghans on the ground didn't trust the Taliban and didn't want to show them their papers. Why would these people, who had spent years trying to track them down and kill them, suddenly wave them through to safety? A British soldier who was on the ground believed the Taliban co-operated because they knew that once the evacuees were out the Western forces would also leave. It was essentially a matter of expediency on both sides.

There was also the money, because there was allegedly another way of getting into the airport without going through the crowds – one that wasn't really talked about. It was believed that the South Gate was being used for the exclusive use of those considered higher priority by the West. According to a soldier on the ground, the Taliban were accepting payments to shuttle through VIPs for both the Brits and the Americans. There was a huge US presence at the gate, as well as a smaller British contingent of Pathfinders (rapid reaction troops skilled in covert operations, often deep behind enemy lines).

The veteran volunteers could never work out what was going on behind the scenes. None of the Afghans they were helping – several dozen, at least – had managed to get in any of the cars or buses destined for the South Gate, yet others who did not appear to qualify for sanctuary under the British scheme seemed to have made it through easily.

At 8 p.m. that evening a bus finally arrived to collect the Guls and a large number of others – they had no idea who they were. At least three buses reached the airport gate, including the one the Guls were on. Although incredibly weary, they were also excited, believing this was now it and that soon they would be on a flight to Britain.

'They just got to the bus,' Jamal messaged Charlie, who had been using all the connections he had garnered during 25 years of service in the British army to get Shaista into the airport.

'We've just got to pray that the Taliban let them through,' he replied on WhatsApp, which had become a lifeline for fleeing Afghans who were able to use the free social messaging service to communicate with their contacts in the West.

'*Inshallah* [God willing],' replied Jamal.

'I'm a nervous wreck, I can't begin to think how you feel,' added Charlie.

However, the Taliban refused to let the bus through. The driver told his passengers that the Taliban had had an argument with the British soldiers that was yet to be resolved. As a result, they had closed the gate to all vehicles and were not allowing anyone inside. 'Just sit here and hopefully in the next few hours you will be allowed inside,' the driver announced hesitantly. He didn't inspire confidence.

A couple of hours later Charlie messaged Jamal to tell him that there was a rumour going around that the Americans were trying to help. By this point the family had not eaten properly for more than 24 hours and they were feeling both hungry and desperate. Yet they could do nothing but wait.

It was getting late, and Jamal worried that they were wasting time sitting on a stationary bus when they could at least be making some progress by pushing through the crowds. He messaged Charlie again, asking him what they should do.

'We're all desperately hoping that they will let them through, but at the moment it's not looking great. We are right out of options at the moment,' Charlie replied, swiftly. He was doing all this from a shipping container with a single bed in it in a UN compound in Mogadishu, where he was meant to be working as an international adviser to the Somali Ministry of Internal Security. However, when the withdrawal happened, he felt a moral compulsion to help the people who had done so much for him and his men during his time in

Afghanistan and had asked for a couple of weeks off. Now he was on his phone all hours of the day and night doing everything he could to get these people out of Kabul.

'So should I tell them to stay in the bus?' Jamal asked.

Charlie hesitated, not wanting to give a firm answer should it turn out to be the wrong one. 'I just don't know, Jamal. My head says yes. I'm not hearing of anyone getting into the Baron Hotel on foot. I think this is the only option.'

Jamal told his family to stay on the bus. He was feeling emotional. He messaged Charlie: 'I will never forget your help, I have too many military officers I have worked with shoulder to shoulder but today they didn't care about me. You are the only one having all the stress and I have no word how I'm going to say thank you.'

Charlie was touched by the message. 'Jamal, I want your father evacuated. Simple as that. A lot of my interpreters haven't got out, but getting your family out would make it all worthwhile. Keep your phone on tonight. And your father. It may or may not happen but this could be our last chance.'

The Guls stayed on the bus until the afternoon of the following day, Thursday, when the driver went off and came back. 'That's it, everyone should leave the bus. The Taliban are not allowing us to go inside the airport,' he shouted down the aisle. Everyone on that bus was tired, hungry, desperate and angry. They hurled questions at him. What should they do next? How would they get inside? He had no answers.

Shortly afterwards Jamal received a phone call back in Coventry.

'Tell your father to go to the front door,' said a man's voice, which Jamal understood to be that of a British soldier. An officer in the Joint Task Force Headquarters helping to oversee the operation had been given a list of those Afghans who were both eligible to go to the UK and waiting outside the airport, but who were unable to get past through the series of checkpoints. Miraculously he had managed to get a message through to the Taliban fighters guarding the final checkpoint into the airport and they had agreed to allow Shaista safe passage.

But the message came through too late. The Guls had got off the bus. Overwhelmed with exhaustion, they had given up and were walking away when Jamal got on the phone to Shaista. 'Dad, you have to go back, they are going to help you!' For Shaista the thought of having to push back through the crowds where lifeless bodies lay strewn on the ground was almost too much to bear. But it was their last chance.

British soldiers on the ground dispatched a Taliban escort to walk Shaista and the family to the front gate of the Baron Hotel. It was a highly irregular move and one fraught with risk. The Taliban had proved time and again that they were not to be trusted and, although they were being cooperative at that moment – on the understanding that it would speed up NATO's departure – there was no telling what they would do afterwards.

Now Shaista and the family made their way to the gate nearest them. They saw the door to the hotel. But what they did not realize was that it was the back door, not the front door. Jamal messaged his British army contact to tell him where they were. The man rang back immediately. 'Where is your dad?' he asked, panic-stricken. 'He's there,' Jamal replied. 'Tell them not to go to the back gate because there is an attack about to happen. They need to leave now,' the man urged.

What Jamal hadn't appreciated was that, the previous day, a government minister back in the UK had warned of a potentially lethal terror attack at Kabul airport within hours. James Heappey, the Under-Secretary of State for the Armed Forces and a former army officer himself, who had spent hours helping Afghans who were trying to escape, said the information was based on very credible reports of what he described as a 'severe' threat. It was clear that intelligence reports had indicated that some terrorists were planning to carry out an imminent attack. The crowds and the troops at the airport made them an obvious target for the sort of mass-casualty attack that Islamic State had become known for. Even the British soldiers manning the gate had retreated further inside the airport for their own safety. They would have remembered the attack at Manchester Arena in May 2017, when a suicide bomber blew himself up as thousands of fans left an Ariana Grande concert. The bomb killed 22 people, including many children, in the deadliest attack in the UK since the London bombings in July 2005. Yet many of the Afghans on the ground either didn't hear the warning or didn't take it seriously enough – or maybe they were simply so desperate that they thought it was worth the risk.

Jamal called his father immediately. 'Leave, leave, leave!' he shouted.

They ran for it.

Four minutes later there was an explosion. The intelligence was correct. A suicide bomber who had rigged himself up with roughly 20 lb of military-grade explosives had walked into the throng of families waiting outside the gate and blown himself up.[4] A deadly concoction of ball bearings and shrapnel flew through the air, ripping into anybody within the vicinity. Many Afghans who had been trying to get closer to the Western troops to show them their records were killed instantly. Some were flung by the blast into the sewage ditch.

Shaista Gul in the garden at the Main Operating Base (MOB),
Lashkar Gah, 2012

Jamal in Marjah district, 2011

Jamal working at the Provincial Police Headquarters in Lashkar Gah, 2013

Jamal and Captain Richard "Rich", 2013

Main Operating Base Lashkar Gah in Helmand Province, March 2014
© photgraphed by Joe Giddens, PA Images / Alamy Stock Photo

Shaista, Razagulla and children waiting for the bus to get into the airport in
Kabul, August 2021

Outside the Baron Hotel, Kabul, waiting to be let inside for an evacuation
flight, August 2021 © Esmatulla

The Gul family outside Chimney House Hotel, October 2021. From Left to Right - Razagulla, Shaista, Najeebullah, Mohammed Sahil, Jamal (in foreground in white), Edrees, Esmatullah © Larisa Brown

Mohmood in Baramcha, near the border with Pakistan, November 2021
© Abdul Wali

Abdul Wali, Shaista's brother, on his way to Pakistan, November 2021
© Mohmood Khan

The water turned red. Standing only a few hundred metres away, Shaista and Razagulla looked on in horror as they saw people running towards them covered in blood, some without shoes, some holding injured children, others missing limbs. One woman, her dress soaked in a deep red, was holding her dead child while screaming up at the sky. Another woman had a gash on her head, with blood pouring from it. Esmatullah couldn't keep his eyes off a man trying to get away with his leg torn off. In the distance, Shaista spotted the bodies of two American soldiers lying on the ground. They looked so young and innocent.

Then the medics started arriving. A Taliban fighter started hitting the crowd, including Shaista, with a stick. 'Look at that, we killed the infidels. Get out now or we will kill you as well!' he cried. In fact there was no reason to suspect the Taliban were behind the attack (which Islamic State later claimed credit for) – they too had their fighters out there and were reeling from the explosion. But if they hadn't already scarpered, the warning was enough to frighten more of the crowd away.

The Guls went further back and waited to hear from Jamal, who was frantically messaging the British soldier. 'There's been an explosion. Tell your dad to wait,' came the reply.

Inside the airport another British soldier tried to get through to the Guls' Taliban escort to ask him to go back for the second time to help Shaista. But for that he needed an interpreter, and he had been sent off to help with the fallout of the explosion. The Taliban refused to consider any further movement towards the gate.

Ten minutes later Jamal's contact messaged again. 'Tell your father I'm waiting at the gate, tell him to come now, this is the right time.' But although the way forward was clear of the crowds, the Taliban were not letting anyone through. Razagulla, overcome with emotion, went up to one of the militants, begging him to allow them through. 'We have the right documents,' she implored. But it was no use. Jamal then told her to try and hand the phone to the Taliban so that he could speak to him, pretending to be an interpreter on the ground. She went back. 'Go straight to the interpreter, he's on the ground and is telling us to come,' she told the Talib. 'No, our leaders will not allow anybody through,' he replied dismissively. Becoming more and more frantic, Jamal messaged his contact yet again. 'I'm out of the gate with one of the interpreters waiting for him. I'm waving my hand, just tell him to come!' came the reply. Jamal was relaying his messages as fast as he could to Shaista, but 'I can see him but I can't go any further. They won't let me,' Shaista told Jamal. The whole family was becoming exhausted. They had come so far, they had been through so much, but now they knew that it was time to give up.

'We've been left behind. We will never get to see Jamal,' Esmatullah said weakly to his father. They walked away, their clothes torn and dirty and their dreams shattered.

Escape from Afghanistan: Kabul to Pakistan, Saturday, 28 August– Wednesday, 13 October 2021

By the time the last RAF flight left Kabul airport the following day, Shaista and the family were hiding in one of Spozhmai's father's empty apartments in Shahrak-e-Aria, a relatively plush gated residential complex near the airport. It had been a relief to simply wash and change out of the clothes they had been wearing for four days straight. Esmatullah, who was in total despair, was sent out of the apartment with his brothers to get the family some food from a run-down but popular restaurant a few hundred metres away. Shaista stood nervously at the gate waiting for them to come back, worried sick that he might be spotted by the Taliban, who were manning every checkpoint across the city. His body jolted at the sound of a distant car door closing. He could see some remaining families nearby packing up their belongings, still intent on leaving the country. But everything had changed. Rather than the constant sound of car horns and ice cream vendors as you would get on a typical day in Kabul just days before, now there was only the periodic noise of aircraft or helicopters flying overhead. And, apart from that, quiet.

The boys returned with bags of okra, fresh bread and thick slabs of meat – enough to make your mouth water. As they ate dinner that evening, silently, deep in their own thoughts, Shaista reflected on the chaos at the airport. He had no idea how anyone had actually managed to make it through the crowd; it had seemed totally impossible. He was also very concerned for the boys, who had been so excited when they first arrived in Kabul, truly believing they would be living in the UK by now. Yet at least they were all still alive thanks to the British military, unlike the dozens of people who had perished in the crowds and in the blast at the Baron Hotel. And the apartment they were staying in was comfortable enough. It was fully furnished, with three spacious bedrooms, enough for them to spread out. But most importantly, it felt safe.

Meanwhile Jamal was fuming. He had been listening to the news of how Paul ('Pen') Farthing, a former Royal Marine who was the founder of an animal charity, had managed to get inside the airport in the final hours and take a private jet out, along with numerous rescue pets. To Jamal, it seemed like animals were being prioritized over people like his father, who had so loyally served the British for years. 'I think it's totally unacceptable. How come animals are somewhere safe but human beings are left behind in hell?' he asked a British journalist. The case of Pen Farthing and his animals had split public opinion in Britain, with Ben Wallace causing outrage by saying he would prioritize 'people over pets' during the evacuation. Farthing countered by saying that he had fundraised enough money to charter a private aircraft into Kabul airport with a capacity for 250 passengers – enough room for his 140 dogs and 60 cats – but that he was awaiting crucial documents from the MoD.[1] The two sides briefed against each other. At one point Pen Farthing sent an audio message to Peter Quentin, the government adviser who had raised Shaista's case originally, threatening to 'fucking destroy' him if he did not arrange for the animals to be evacuated.[2] Yet the Prime Minister, Boris Johnson, whose wife, Carrie, was a vociferous animal-rights campaigner and in touch with Dominic Dyer, a friend of Farthing's, appeared to take a different perspective from his Defence Secretary. In a high-level meeting earlier in the week, Johnson was said to have issued an instruction to call forward Farthing's team for evacuation.[3] Apparently, soldiers had been told to get ready to receive him at the South Gate – the one typically reserved for VIPs – as early as the Thursday, but then the explosion happened.

What Jamal, and most others, didn't know was the full extent of the discussions taking place over Farthing and his animals. A soldier who was at the airport at the time said he was told by the Pathfinders that the UK had paid tens of thousands of dollars to the Taliban – in cash – to allow them through the South Gate. The figure circulating among serving personnel was up to $50,000. There was said to be 'an air of consternation' among the troops about this. Yet an MoD insider said that although there was a cash float to pay the Taliban to extract people if necessary, none of it was used, raising questions as to why those on the ground thought otherwise.

Shaista had been told earlier that day by someone still inside the airport – presumably a soldier – that the last Afghan eligible under the ARAP scheme had been allowed in and 'No more'. That last Afghan was Sayed Wafa, a former interpreter from Kandahar who had been blown up while on the front line in 2011. Coincidentally, he was the one who had briefly trained Jamal in 2010 before they deployed together to Nad Ali. Jamal had not spoken to him in a long time but remembered him to be a quiet man. He had received permission to go to Britain months previously. However, his wife had given birth a few weeks before the flight, so officials had asked him to submit more details about his family, which had delayed the process. As Kabul fell to the Taliban, the family's passports were stuck at the British embassy. By the night of Friday, 27 August, Sayed, along with his wife, tiny daughter and three-year-old son, had spent more than 100 hours trying to get inside the airport, to no avail. But British ministers were so taken by his case that they stepped in at the eleventh hour. And in the early hours of Saturday morning Sayed, who by this point had lost all hope of ever going to the UK, received a phone call from an interpreter working for the British government telling him to come to a gate used by the Americans by 2 a.m. When the family got close, the interpreter guided them by phone, giving them step-by-step directions to the gate. But the crowds were still so great that Sayed and the family could not get past them. So then the interpreter came up with another solution. 'Leave that area and come to the other side,' he said, telling them to follow the laser light. Sayed, who had jet-black curly hair and a reddish tinge to his skin from the hours spent under the glaze of the sun, spotted the light and led his family towards it. When they got to the wall below it, they saw a British soldier who pulled his children up and over the barbed wire. His wife was next and then, finally, Sayed entered the airport, safe at last.

Over the next ten days or so Shaista and the family stayed in Kabul, hoping against hope that there might be another way out or that the RAF would restart the evacuation flights. But as each day passed those hopes faded. Jamal didn't give up, though, staying in touch with all his army contacts to make sure that, if there was a flight, then his family would be on it. He was anxious that, despite assurances to the contrary to the watching world, the Taliban were stepping up their search for people who had worked with the NATO forces or for the previous Afghan government. He knew that militants were going from door to door, hunting down targets and threatening family members. What if they found his father?

'If we can organize a flight from Mazar-e Sharif, can your family get there?' asked a man on an unknown number who contacted him a few days later. Jamal assumed he was from the British military. Mazar-e Sharif, a traditional anti-Taliban bastion in north-west Afghanistan, had been captured by the militants just before the fall of Kabul. It would be a long journey – possibly more than nine hours by bus – and there was no clue as to how the unknown caller planned to get Shaista and the family out of there. But they were desperate. Jamal asked his father, whose immediate answer was 'Yes'. 'Yes, I can send my parents there,' Jamal replied a few minutes later.

Then, only a few hours later, Jamal was told that it wouldn't happen. Yet another disappointment. The family was in limbo. There was no way they could get out of the country by air, but they couldn't go back to Lashkar Gah either, as by now everyone knew they had fled to Kabul in order to escape. The Taliban had already knocked on the door of their home, asking Salma and Faiz about Jamal and Shaista, as if they didn't know perfectly well.

Shaista was among some 260 Afghans who had worked for the British and had been approved for an RAF flight but who hadn't made it into the airport in time. Some of them had by now received an email from the British government telling them it was 'sorry' they had been unable to get to the Baron Hotel before it closed, but that if they were able to make it to another country, they should do so as soon as possible and that their application to the UK would continue to be supported. 'Our priority is your safety. Please go wherever you feel safest – either at home or another country if you are able to make the journey,' it ended.

With no one else to turn to, those left behind ended up messaging the veterans asking what they should do next. Former officers like Charlie, skilled in military planning and strategy, started shifting their attention to trying to help people move towards the border. With the Taliban manning checkpoints across the country, it would not be easy. Many people, like the Guls, were still stuck in Kabul. The city was unfamiliar to them, and there were road blocks around the capital. They were also justifiably afraid that they would be beaten if they tried to leave.

Charlie assessed the options. He knew of five crossing points between Afghanistan and Pakistan, in between which was a 1,600-mile metal fence snaking through snow-covered mountains and treacherous ravines. There were the two most obvious ways. The first, and possibly the one that made the most sense, was to go to the dusty town of Spin Boldak in the southern province of Kandahar, accessible via a long desert route. Charlie, who had spent time there with the Afghan border police in 2007 and knew the region fairly well, quickly learned that to get across the border fleeing Afghans would need to buy fake identity cards making out that they came from Kandahar (the only Afghans officially allowed over the border). Or, if that wasn't possible, they could try and get a medical visa and pretend that they were going to see a specialist doctor. Those could cost the equivalent of around US$50 – a small fortune for some of those trying to escape. There was also an abundance of people smugglers making a handsome profit from the chaos, so paying those men to help bribe their way across the border might also work.

The other main option was the Torkham border crossing, an old smugglers' route nestled into a mountain valley. Not far from Jalalabad, it offered the most immediate route from Kabul. But it was now manned on the Afghan side by armed Taliban militia, and there was confusion about whether the pedestrian part of the crossing was open at all. There were also other old narcotics routes through porous areas in southern Helmand, one of which went through a town known as a hub for the heroin trade. But Taliban fighters were flowing freely in and out of it and some people were understandably incredibly nervous about heading down such a dangerous path.

Charlie was also in touch with people considering heading west to Herat, the historical city that had sat on the Silk Road between the Middle East, Central and South Asia since ancient times. One of the first major places to fall to the Taliban, there had been horror stories coming out of it about the Taliban's brutality – for instance, cutting off the hands of thieves. But from there it was theoretically possible to cross the border directly into Iran, although Taliban checkpoints made the route dangerous and expensive. And, crucially, it was not clear how welcoming the Iranian government would be to people who had worked for the British, given the sour relations between Iran and Britain. That option made more sense for those Afghans who weren't eligible for visas but thought that they would try to make it to the UK illegally – although even then it was seen as possibly less dangerous to try and reach Iran along a mountainous route through Pakistan. Then there were the other bordering countries of Uzbekistan and Tajikistan, although the routes seemed complicated and again it wasn't certain how much help the fleeing Afghans would get at the other end. A few people had come up with their own ideas about how to get out: one individual, who must have had plenty of money, had managed to get himself on to one of the first commercial flights out of Kabul to Islamabad, although he apparently hadn't worked out what to do after that.

Initially, the veterans started sending Afghans who were sure they wanted to leave the country to Spin Boldak. At that time many of them were desperate for money, having spent all they had on getting to Kabul. Julian Perreira, a former Grenadier Guard who completed three tours of Afghanistan but who was by now working for NATO from his new home in Cornwall, saw a gap and started to help. Earlier in the summer he had heard about Ahmad, an interpreter struggling to afford the $600 for the documents he needed to get to Britain, so he had set up a fundraising page. Donations flooded in from both veterans and ordinary members of the public who were watching the crisis unfold on the news and wanted to help. One woman who donated was the mother of a soldier who had been killed in Afghanistan. She told Julian that her son had spoken to her of the work the interpreters were doing for them and so she felt it was important to help them in some way. It became obvious that, through such generosity, Julian would be able to assist many more to get out of the country. What had started with one interpreter soon became an operation to help more than 30 people, all in need of financial help. He raised almost £30,000 in the end.

To begin with, Julian urged any Afghans heading for Pakistan to make sure his name was saved on their phone as an Afghani name. He had heard reports of the Taliban widely stopping people and checking the messages on their phones for anything linking them to the West. He also sent them instructions on how to wipe their phones clear of certain information so that, again, they wouldn't raise suspicion at a checkpoint. Once they had received money from Julian – via Western Union, the worldwide money transfer company – they were to hand that and their phones to their wives in the hope that the Taliban would respect the Afghan culture of not searching women. In the end, the money covered all sorts. Food, hotels, border crossings – there was a lot to pay for. Sometimes Julian would book hotels for them so they had somewhere safe to stay. One Afghan interpreter had found a taxi driver who could get his family across the border but he needed the money to pay for it. Others just needed money for something to eat. On the days when Julian struggled to make payments via Western Union, which appeared to be decreasing the daily limits for how much money could be taken out in Afghanistan, Jamal, who knew someone in a money exchange shop, stepped in.

When both Jamal and Shaista were certain that there was no way the family would be leaving the country on a flight out of Kabul, Shaista went to the bus station to buy tickets back to Kandahar. From there the plan was to hide in another house belonging to Spozhmai's father, where one of her brothers was living. All Shaista really wanted to do at that point was to go back home to Lashkar Gah and be with the rest of the family, but he understood that it was just too risky. Once they got to Kandahar, they would decide where to go next.

The dusty bus park in the west of the city was bedlam. Families clutching bags were pushing their way through the crowds, shouting to drivers to let them on to packed buses. There were no orderly queues, only jostling for the next available seat. Every now and again a car would pull up with suitcases hanging out of the boot. Children were crying, scrabbling for a place in the tiny strip of shade under the unrelenting afternoon sun. Everyone wanted a way out, whether it was to Iran, Pakistan or elsewhere in Afghanistan. A small office selling tickets, hardly visible among the market stalls that filled the street, was unable to help Shaista. Finding six spaces on a bus out of the city was not going to be easy. He ran to every bus he could see, begging the driver for help. Prices had rocketed. In the end, only the most expensive option, on one of the more luxurious buses, was still available. He handed over 2,000 afghani (some £20) from the money Jamal's friend had given him in Kandahar. At least it was cheaper than a taxi.

The highway back to Kandahar seemed much further than before. The passengers' faces were gloomy and despondent, no longer caught in the buzz of excitement. The bus was stopped at Taliban checkpoints multiple times. Each time it slowed down, the Guls held their breath, terrified of what would come next. When the Talibs got on as they stopped at one of them, the Guls averted their eyes, hoping to avoid their attention. 'You, come out! You, come out!' one of the militants said, pointing to two men who happened to be travelling alone. And then to another two. The man nearest to them turned as pale as a corpse. It appeared that the Taliban had descriptions of the people and faces they were looking for. Shaista prayed that the men would come to no harm. They waited at the side of the road as they were searched by the Talibs. But after a few minutes it became clear that they were going to be held for a while, so the driver just left without them. Shaista had no idea who they were or what happened to them next.

It was still daylight as they finally drove into Kandahar, the birthplace and spiritual home of the Taliban. What Shaista saw did not inspire him with hope. He witnessed the Taliban beating two men with an AK-47 before putting handcuffs on them and shoving them into the back of a car. Others were having their pockets searched for mobile phones. Everyone else just stood by or ignored them. It was as if it was almost normal. Those fighters who were not on foot were cruising around in the back of captured police pick-ups. There was an unmistakable air of suspicion in the air – more so than in Kabul – and it frightened him.

As soon as they arrived at their new hideout, Shaista stashed some of his certificates from his gardening days in a cupboard with Razagulla's clothes: no Talib would dare search there. Jamal called, telling them they must stay there for a while as he worked out how to get them to safety. 'Do not go back to Lashkar Gah, it's too dangerous. But if you stay where you are, I can follow the news and everything the UK government is saying. The British have a plan to evacuate everyone from a third country, I just need you to stay there until everything is clear.' No matter how miserable he felt, Shaista understood that his son was right.

As they stayed inside the house, news spread of a former ANA sniper who had been gunned down by the Taliban in front of his family in Kabul. Only 28, and with five children, Noor, as he was called, had been in the elite Afghan unit, Counter-Narcotics Force (CF)333, known as Triple 3, which had been mentored by British special forces and integrated into Afghan police special units, like ATF 444. When they were younger, his older brother, Shakar Chi, who was also a sniper, had trained him in how to use the weapon. Shakar, who was well known for his specialist skills in using a night vision rifle with heat sensors to track the enemy, had been warned two months before Kabul fell that everyone in his family would be killed, 'even the chickens'.

The brothers had always had a strong bond. They had been there for each other since they were little boys. When Noor signed up to CF333, he quickly became the fittest man in the unit. Shakar always admired how his little brother could go from making him laugh one minute to killing the enemy in the other. When he was in the heat of the battle, Shakar knew he showed no mercy. Such was his strength that Noor once carried a fallen comrade nearly two miles across the hilly district of Achin in Jalalabad, where temperatures sometimes rose to as high as 40 °C.

During the withdrawal, Noor had been among 25 to 30 Afghans who had been picked out of the crowds to go to the Baron Hotel because of his service in 'Triple 3'. But in the final hours of the evacuation he had been told, according to his brother, that the only seats remaining were for UK passport holders. As a result, he was forced to return to the Taliban-controlled streets and into hiding, without his wife and children. Shakar, who had got on an earlier flight and had been promised his brother would soon follow, said that by pulling Noor and the others out of the crowds, the British had unintentionally allowed the Taliban to identify them, thereby putting them in further danger.

On the morning of his death, 13 September, Noor had messaged Shakar saying, 'We will stay safe. We promise.' Later that day he had left his hiding place to go next door to the family shop to pick up a phone charger when some Taliban pulled up in a green Ford Ranger pick-up previously used by the Afghan police. This was followed by a man on a motorbike. Noor was told to put his hands up, which he did, before being shot five times through the chest and twice through his arm. He never got a chance to meet his newborn daughter. Witnesses reported that his death was celebrated by the local Taliban in Logar province, near where the family was from and where Noor had been based with the military.

It was stories like this that made Shaista realize, if he hadn't already, that it was time to move on. The British government was still advising anybody who hadn't made the flights out of Kabul to make their way to a 'third country', where they could be processed and flown to the UK. He and Jamal decided that the family should make their way to Pakistan via Spin Boldak.

Much of the taxi journey to the Spin Boldak border crossing was by highway. Desert wind blew through the open window, leaving a gritty taste in their mouths. The family changed their cover story. If anyone asked them, they were from Pakistan, had been visiting relatives in Afghanistan and were now on their way home. It seemed plausible, given that the family had lived in Pakistan several years before and knew the country well. And, being from southern Afghanistan themselves, they could pass for Pakistani.

As they came closer to the crossing, they saw thousands of little dots in the distance: all Afghans trying to cross the border. The taxi driver, whose clothes had a whiff of stale cigarettes, could not take them any further, so they got out and walked the rest of the way. As they approached the border, they saw guards wielding sticks and rubber pipes trying to control the frenzied crowds. Men wearing traditional flat pakol hats, sweating under the weight of their luggage, crammed themselves and their families into a narrow corridor fenced off with barbed wire that led to the checkpoint. People – some white-bearded and ancient, and others barely out of the womb – were being pushed back violently. Shaista, Razagulla and the boys attempted to make their way through, but, as feared, the Pakistani authorities said they were only accepting the Tazkira of people from Kandahar province, where the crossing point was, not from Helmand province. The rules were confusing and often subject to bribes; however, in

August 2019, the Pakistani government had limited border crossings to those from Kandahar province and the Spin Boldak district only – despite the fact that people from other parts of Afghanistan also went over the border regularly, in many cases for work.

There was no way they would get across, so Jamal rang up one of Spozhmai's brothers, who knew the area well, to ask if he could get hold of someone at the border who could get them fake IDs, claiming they were from Kandahar.

'Give me three hours and I'll find someone,' he replied. There was no time for chit-chat. Not long after, he called back. 'I've found someone. He wants 20,000 Pakistani rupees [about £60].' There was an excited tone to his voice. This was cheap: some smugglers were asking for 30,000 rupees. For Jamal it was a huge chunk of money, never mind for Shaista and the family. But it was their only hope.

'No problem, I'm going to transfer you the money, please do it,' he replied. But the brother told him to wait before sending the money because it would be virtually impossible for him to collect it from anywhere.

'Once everything is sorted you can give me the money back,' he told him.

The deal was that the smuggler would get the family fake ID cards and would take them across the border. He would receive the money only once they had all crossed safely. When Shaista, Razagulla and the boys met him they were pleased that he could speak both Pashto and Urdu, considered essential if you are to bribe anyone in Pakistan. A tall man with a beard as black as coal, he lived on the border as a dual-national, and so knew his way across easily. His first job was to take everyone's photographs and then stick them on cards with their name, father's name, age, face colour and eye colour. All of these would be accurate. Then in the part where it said province and district, he would put Kandahar and Maiwand district, in the south of the province. These were the lies. The smuggler went away and returned with the cards. They looked good but he did not point out the extra detail of the district – a crucial mistake.

Shaista, Razagulla and the two youngest boys, 9-year-old Edrees and 11-year-old Najeebullah, crossed first, but, in the chaos they became separated from the other two. They had been simply waved across, but Esmatullah, 16, and Mohammed Sahil, 14, were stopped by one of the guards. They were asked what district of Kandahar they were from and became confused as to what to say. As they looked at each other through the corners of their eyes, clearly in a state of panic, the border guards knew that they were lying and turned them away.

The smuggler had stayed with Shaista, who became very distressed when he realized that two of his children were not with them. How could they have left them behind? And why hadn't the smuggler pointed out the district on the ID cards? It was getting dark and soon they would stop letting people cross. Thankfully, the boys had a phone so they could contact them.

'Stay there tonight and tomorrow, I'll come back for you. I'll try my best so you can join your family,' the smuggler told Esmatullah, who was unsure whether to believe him. In good faith, Shaista handed over the 20,000 Pakistani rupees. There was nowhere for the two boys to sleep at the crossing, except on the ground where buses and cars were pulling up. Exhaust fumes filled the air. The two boys huddled together, more for comfort than for warmth. The sound of revving engines and car doors slamming made it impossible to sleep.

Meanwhile, the rest of the family were safe at last. It was an hour's journey on foot from the Pakistan side of the border to a passable road that cars could drive down. They had managed to get a message through to Razagulla's uncle, who lived in Quetta, close to the border, who had come to pick them up and take them to his house. He was a relatively wealthy businessman who was born in Afghanistan but had grown up on the other side of the border. He always had plenty of spare rooms for guests.

After a sleepless night, Esmatullah and Mohammed Sahil made it across. This time they stayed extremely close to the smuggler, who appeared to be paying bribes to several officers as they went along. And then the uncle came back to pick them up too and take them to his house.

Everyone was at last out of immediate danger, and it may have felt like the final hurdle was behind them, but there was still a long way to go. Still working from Somalia, Charlie was using his connections with the Foreign Office to reach out to staff in the British High Commission in Islamabad, the capital of Pakistan. He had put an efficient system in place whereby he would wait until he knew that the family he was in touch with had crossed the border successfully and then would pass on their details to the consulate. In doing so, he was providing a vital link between the fleeing Afghans and the British government. It had its frustrations, though. Sometimes the British team in Pakistan would reach out to the Afghans quickly and sort them out with somewhere to stay. More often than not, though, it was taking much longer and the Afghans would need some money simply to keep them off the streets. Charlie made sure that anyone who made it across the border would then speak to the family who was coming up behind them to share any tips.

Shaista didn't have to wait long before a case worker from the High Commission, a man he knew only as Tom, reached out to him. He promised to try and organize some transport to get the family to Islamabad, some 550 miles to the north-east. They were told not to try and make the journey themselves because they would probably be stopped without a proper visa. Yet after nearly a week of waiting, and feeling frustrated at how little progress his family had made, Jamal told them to make their own way to the capital. 'They're on their way,' he told Tom, who sent them the address of a hotel to stay at, the Islamabad Hotel: easy enough to remember. 'Tell them to go there, mention their name at reception, and they'll have a room,' replied Tom.

When they arrived at last, it all suddenly felt somewhat overwhelming and unreal. The Islamabad was a four-star hotel – much more comfortable than they were used to – sitting in the footsteps to the Margalla Hills, a mountain range known for its monkeys and cheetahs. Although it was a little run-down, there were omelettes for breakfast, barbecue for dinner, a kettle in the room and free slippers. At least one paying guest would later complain about 'refugee children running round the hotel and corridors, with little or no supervision'. But for the Guls there were still more hurdles to overcome. Within days, Shaista was taken to the airport for questioning by Pakistan's intelligence agency, the ISI, which had long supported the Taliban. At first he was extremely hesitant, wondering why he had been singled out and what they wanted from him, but when he arrived at the holding centre where they were conducting the interviews and he saw all the other people queuing there too, he realized it must just be routine. He was interrogated for about an hour about his work for the British army and his journey to Pakistan. The officials also wanted to know how much money he had and who he knew in the UK. He felt that he had no choice but to give them truthful answers, but he could not help but wonder what they would do with all that information.

By now the entire family had been living out of one suitcase for well over a month and were getting fed up with wearing the same old tired clothes. Sure that they would be heading to Britain any day now, Shaista took the boys shopping for Western clothes. Each of them was allowed to choose a pair of trousers and a T-shirt. They were delighted. Going outside the hotel and being able to breathe fresh air again felt like a big adventure. Unlike dusty, chaotic Kabul, Islamabad was leafy and green, with wide streets which seemed to go on for ever. And for the first time in months the boys could wander around, browsing the shops and the marketplace, without having to look over their shoulders all the time. Jamal transferred them some spending money. With its tech stores, designer boutiques and Western fast food outlets, there was something of fascination for everybody in Islamabad. They returned to the hotel with three suitcases bursting with clothes and gifts for Jamal and Spozhmai. Over dinner that evening the boys chattered excitedly.

There were other families staying at the hotel who, like the Guls, had been through a lot. Razagulla met a woman whose husband had been blown up in the suicide bombing near the Baron Hotel, which had killed at least 170 Afghans and 13 US service members. She was left trying to escape with her only child, a boy of about two, whom she lost in the chaos. They were eventually reunited and were now coming to Britain on their own, with no idea of what to expect or where to go. Razagulla realized how lucky she had been.

Then, with only a few hours' notice, on 13 October, and amid concerns that terrorists could try to take down the plane or attack its passengers, the family were put on an RAF flight from Pakistan to Cyprus, and then hopefully to the UK.

Left Behind: Lashkar Gah, October 2021

'What's your name?' asked the militant outside the house. 'Mohmood,' replied the man, who was sitting there, next to his father's plants, early one evening. There were another 11 Talibs standing behind the man. Mohmood felt unbelievably nervous answering him, knowing that he was at risk of reprisals from the Taliban both because of his own work as an interpreter and because of who his family was. He was acutely aware that his parents and brothers were about to take off on their flight to Cyprus, and for a split second he wondered if that had anything to do with the sudden interrogation. 'Where's your father?' came the next question, as if they were reading his mind.

The man had piercing dark eyes, which were staring at him with such an intensity it made it hard to concentrate. 'My father is in Pakistan because he is not feeling well,' he lied. 'No, he isn't, tell me the truth,' the man demanded. 'That is the reality, they are in Pakistan. They went for treatment,' he replied, trying not to fidget. They would never believe him. He looked at their weapons and their massive beards. They had arrived on foot, as if they were out on some sort of patrol, although they were probably just trying to cause mischief.

'Where is Esmatullah? We want him. Go and get him,' another commanded, holding up a grainy photograph of his younger brother. Although he thought it peculiar, he didn't have time to make out any of the details or give it too much thought. 'He's gone with my dad to Pakistan.' That seemed to make them angry. Mohmood recalled anxiously the warning Esmatullah had been given weeks earlier not to leave Lashkar Gah. Then one of the Talibs took out a second photograph. This one would send shivers down his spine. Totally unmistakable. It was himself, many years ago. He was in the former police headquarters in Lashkar Gah where he had worked as an interpreter, wearing a yellow helmet and jacket. How did they get that? Who took it? Were the people he worked with back then secretly working for the Taliban? All these thoughts were racing through his mind.

He needed to give them an explanation for what he was doing there. Anything that didn't corroborate that he was working for foreigners. As he stumbled for words, it seemed that it was already too late.

'Go!' instructed the Talib, pointing towards the street.

'I can't walk because of my leg,' he told them, pointing down at his foot.

But it appeared they already knew. That was the whole point.

'You have to walk,' replied the Talib, forcefully.

He had no choice but to begin limping down the road, wincing as he went and hoping that they would take pity on him. But of course they didn't.

After he had been shot at in 2015, Mohmood had been diagnosed by the Red Cross as having drop foot, a condition usually caused by damage to a nerve as a result of trauma. Little was known about it in Lashkar Gah, but it meant that

Mohmood was unable to lift the front part of his right foot properly. As he walked, his toes effectively dragged along the ground, making it easy to trip up and extremely difficult to move at any pace. But not just that; he had issues with his left leg too. He would find out later that there were still seven pieces of shrapnel in it from when he had been shot.

The Taliban were deliberately making him walk, knowing that it was causing him agony. Every time Mohmood tried to rest, one of the militants would pinch or punch him hard. He cried out in pain. But that just made it worse. His tormentors made fun of him, calling him names and then laughing with each other as they took it in turns to force him to continue to walk. 'I can't walk any more,' he said, pleading with them to let him stop. His voice trembled. Then one of them kicked him in the backside while holding his hair.

It felt like this torture was going on for ever, but even after they had finished beating him they didn't let him go. Instead, they took him to the same former police station that Esmatullah had been taken to several weeks earlier. Barely able to stand, he was led to a tiny cell with nothing but cold concrete on the floor. It may even have been the same one that Esmatullah had been held captive in, although it was impossible to tell. It was incredibly uncomfortable, but Mohmood was so overcome with exhaustion that he closed his eyes and fell into a deep sleep.

Back at the house, Salma, who had taken on a more mothering role to Mohmood since the rest of the family had left, was getting more and more distressed. She paced up and down the kitchen, picking up her phone every couple of minutes to check if she had a missed call. He hadn't arrived home for dinner and nobody had heard from him for several hours. It was unlike Mohmood to just not turn up without calling her, as he knew the family would be waiting for him to appear before eating. And now Lashkar Gah was under control of the Taliban, he knew she would worry. She called a few of his friends, but they didn't know where he was either, which was unusual. Then she sent out a search party. Her husband and sons started knocking door to door, trying the neighbours first and then heading to the local shops, which were luckily still open despite the time of night. Finally, someone said that they had seen something. Mohmood had been taken by the Taliban.

Meanwhile at the police station, at around 2 a.m. – it was hard to know exactly when – Mohmood was dragged out of his cell by the Talibs and had cold water poured over his head. He winced. 'Where is your father?' demanded one of them. Then they got out a razor. What were they going to do with it? he thought. Would they cut his wrists until he bled to death? No, they had another, more subtle punishment. Once his head had dried, they shaved off his hair. That might not have seemed like much but, without shaving foam or warm soapy water, it was so dry that it hurt – a lot. But they just laughed when he yelled in pain. For them it was like one big joke. Bits of his scalp were bleeding and red raw from the blades.

Mohmood was sent back to his cell and fell into a deep, exhausted sleep. A few hours later he woke up and looked down at his feet, which were badly swollen from the walking. If he had been at home, his wife would have soaked them in some water. But he was in a cold, hard cell wearing damp clothing with guards outside just waiting for the next opportunity to torment him.

Then there was further questioning. His two interrogators were obsessed with his family's whereabouts.

'Where is Esmatullah?' he was asked again.

Feeling braver than the previous day, having decided that they wouldn't kill him, he gave them an explanation. 'When you took Esmatullah and detained him, you beat him really badly. He suffered from mental health problems after that. That's why my dad took him to Pakistan for treatment, because of what you did to him,' he replied, matter-of-factly.

When Esmatullah was taken by the Taliban they had repeatedly asked him if he wanted to go to the UK. Now it dawned on Mohmood that they clearly already knew the family's intentions to head to Britain to join Jamal.

'Where is Jamal?' came the next question.

'Kabul,' he replied. It was pointless.

'What are you doing for work?' they asked next.

'I'm not working,' he told them.

Mohmood's disability obviously limited what he could do, but now many able-bodied men in Lashkar Gah were also struggling to find work. Foreign aid had dried up, as had many other projects that had previously provided people with an income. A lack of proper governance also meant that many of the official roles that had existed previously now ceased to exist.

The Talibs had prepared their next question already. 'Well, how are you living in such a beautiful house, and where did you get the money from?'

He responded with a vague answer about other men in the family who had jobs.

'Where is your father?'

He had already told them he was in Pakistan with Esmatullah – they were trying to catch him out. After that, they stopped asking the questions. This was about control, not about extracting any worthwhile intelligence.

'Where you gone?' Salma texted Jamal frantically the next day. A day after Mohmood had gone missing, she had finally managed to put some credit on her phone (which was becoming more and more expensive and many people couldn't afford at all). Normally he was so quick to respond but now, when she needed him most, he wasn't picking up. She started pacing up and down the room, her husband, Faiz, telling her to slow down and be patient. She had no idea that Jamal was working at the supermarket so didn't have time to answer. She tried messaging him again – this time more to the point. 'I don't want to stress you, Jamal, but the Taliban came yesterday afternoon. They took our brother,' she wrote. Jamal saw the message flash on his screen, stopped what he was doing and called her back.

Salma told him that Mohmood had been sitting outside the house when the Taliban came for him. 'They had a picture of Esmatullah,' she added.

'What? How? Where did they get it from?' Jamal responded.

Salma had no idea. She told Jamal that Faiz had gone to the local Taliban station, where they were detaining people, to ask why they had taken a disabled man. Jamal knew it had been a risky move for him, because there was no telling how the Taliban would react. Yet Faiz was a brave, principled man who would do anything to protect his family. Salma explained how Faiz had been told that the Taliban had received a report that Mohmood's parents and his brother Esmatullah had fled to the UK. Jamal wondered how on earth they had found that out. Did they have spies everywhere?

'They are in Pakistan. My wife's father is sick, so his son has taken him to Pakistan for treatment, not to the UK,' Faiz had assured them.

But his interrogator had not been so easily fooled, Salma told Jamal. 'We know he is in the UK, one of your relatives reported it to us,' the Talib had replied.

Was he telling the truth or was he just trying to create paranoia within the family? Who might have betrayed them, and why? Jamal thought to himself. It was hard to know who to trust and where people's allegiances really lay. Some men had joined the Taliban as a means of survival, because they had no other source of income. Others disliked the idea of Westerners meddling in their country's affairs. Even Spozhmai's departure to Britain to join her husband had raised eyebrows among some of her own family members, with one uncle accusing his sister (Spozhmai's mother) of giving her daughter away to a 'man who is a slave to the Western country'.

His shift at the supermarket now finished, Jamal went back to the flat in the Tile Hill suburb of Coventry where he lived with Spozhmai in a perfunctory four-storey block of flats, all of which were in need of renovation. It was not beautiful, but the young couple felt that they had little to complain about: the building was surrounded by trees and grass, there was a woodland and nature reserve nearby and they had a small balcony to sit on. Jamal was paying £650 a month rent, which he could just about afford with help from the government. Any money left over and he would take Spozhmai out for dinner, sometimes for Turkish food, or sometimes to her favourite local Indian restaurant because she loved its spicy dishes. Spozhmai, who by this point was 22, was also starting to make friends within the Afghan community. But she wanted to go to college and learn English, and it was her ultimate dream to train as a nurse. When Jamal told her about Mohmood, she too was appalled by the news. Such lawless behaviour was a world away from England, where people might complain about late buses or the price of bread but there seemed to be rules and regulations for everything.

They sat and waited for news of his parents' flight to Cyprus. They must be on it now.

For Shaista, Razagulla and the boys, it was their first time ever on an aeroplane. And, wow, were they excited! This aircraft seemed extra special because it was a military one – an RAF Voyager A330. Shaista wondered at first whether it might be like one of the Chinook helicopters he used to see land in Lashkar Gah. But no, it was a proper plane, much bigger than a Chinook and even more impressive. Inside, it was similar to a civilian passenger jet, with rows of seats and a toilet at each end, only this one had other functions too. It had carried out missions over Iraq and Syria, serving as an air-to-air refuelling aircraft, ensuring that the fighter jets dropping bombs and missiles could stay in the air for longer. It had even been used for royal engagements.

The Guls couldn't believe their luck. When they got on board, they were astonished at how clean and comfortable its shiny blue seats were and how it had proper seat belts in case of turbulence. Back in Afghanistan, it was highly unusual to see such safety measures. 'Look at this table!' Shaista remarked to Razagulla excitedly as he realized that they each had their own individual table that they could open up and eat on. For lunch, they were served chicken and rice – even better. Every now and again he glanced over at the boys, who looked so smart in their new Western-style clothing. He was so proud of them for making it this far. Each of them was beaming – even Esmatullah.

The Guls were, at the time, among some 60 Afghans eligible for visas who had made it to neighbouring countries out of the more than 300 who had failed to get inside the airport. Also among the 60 was Sharif, another former interpreter who had served three years with the British, who knew Jamal and who also happened to be from Lashkar Gah. Having found it impossible to enter the airport, he was kidnapped by the Taliban just days later. In a story similar to Mohmood's, he had been taken by a group of about 25 Talibs to a detention centre where he had been beaten and held for four days in a tiny cell where he could barely breathe. He was only released after his local elders intervened and his relatives managed to pull together a staggering $21,000 in payment. Sharif had told friends back in August that the Taliban were searching for him.

During Sharif's time with the military he had been a supervisor for 120 interpreters, yet he was originally rejected for relocation to the UK because, despite his insistence to the contrary, official records showed that his employment had been terminated. And then, at 10 p.m. on the night before the Taliban took Kabul, he was told that he was eligible for relocation but that he still had to submit his passport information and carry out biometrics. This could take months, and there was no way he could wait. Sharif fled Lashkar Gah with his wife and four children and headed for Kabul. They were told that they could board a flight two nights after Shaista got the same email. But their chances of making it inside the airport seemed next to none. They left having tried to get through for six hours, after the Taliban threatened to fire into the crowd unless everyone went home. However, they did make it to Pakistan.

Even as Sharif and his family were waiting in a hotel in Islamabad to find out whether they could get to Britain, the Guls were taking off for Cyprus – some of the first Afghans to have made it from a third country to Europe. Their departure from Pakistan, along with dozens of other Afghans on their flight, would mark the beginning of a new phase of a continuing effort by the UK government to bring people to whom it had promised sanctuary to safety. But, not wanting to do anything to jeopardize their safety – or its plan – it was taking every precaution to make sure all details of the evacuation flights were kept secret. Although it seemed obvious to most that the flights were coming from Pakistan, the MoD would only confirm that they were from a 'neighbouring third country'.

Officials appeared especially nervous after a major blunder a few weeks earlier in which an email sent to more than 250 Afghans, all of whom were eligible for the ARAP scheme, asking for updated information was copied to all applicants rather than being blind copied. This meant that any Afghan in the email chain now had the details for all the others who had worked with the British troops. Some of them even had their photographs attached to their email addresses and many were in hiding across Afghanistan. Had anyone in the chain been a Taliban informant, the implications would have been catastrophic. It was classed as a significant data breach. Jamal, who was receiving emails on his father's behalf, was on the list. He had then received a second email shortly afterwards as the MoD tried to recall the first one, warning him that his email address 'may have been compromised' and that he should change it. He was understandably annoyed and told a journalist that, rather than trying to save Afghan lives, the MoD was putting yet more people at risk – which was true, as the Taliban were checking the phones of people they had arrested – although he felt slightly reassured that at least now they were taking security seriously.

The other families on the flight were just as excited as the Guls. Some kept going to the bathroom or walking around the aircraft just to take a look. Most were former interpreters, like Jamal, but all had worked with the British in one way or another. They were also from all over Afghanistan: Kabul, Jalalabad and even Lashkar Gah. One of these was Shaista's long-time friend Hanif, whom he had first met back home some 30 years ago. Although he had been on an aeroplane before – to Germany, several years earlier – he was as excited as the rest of them. Many, though, were keeping quiet about their pasts, perhaps because they were still worried they could be in danger.

At about the same time as their flight, a second RAF aeroplane took off heading to Europe. On board were 31 Afghans, including their wives and children, along with members of the British media. One Afghan on that flight told reporters that he had tried to go to Kabul airport every day of the evacuation but found it impossible to get through the crowds. A family heading into the airport on a shuttle bus when the suicide bomb went off had no choice but to turn back. One couple's son had been executed as a punishment because his father had worked for the British.[1] Every family had its own tale of unimaginable suffering to tell.

As the Guls' plane descended to land at RAF Akrotiri, in Cyprus, Shaista stared out of the window, mesmerized. The clear blue waters and sandy beaches of the Mediterranean were like nothing he had ever seen before. And yet it was also hard not to feel an element of sadness. This was it. They had given up hope on their own country and, like tens of thousands of others, they were running away, probably never to return.

Any feelings of regret, however, quickly evaporated when they got off the aircraft and were greeted by a small group of smiling British troops. 'Welcome to Cyprus,' said a British officer via an interpreter to all the gathered Afghans. It was a lovely balmy evening with a slight breeze, and something about the weather seemed to put everyone at their ease. The Afghans were quiet, eager to know what the British had in store for them next. 'You're going to be staying here before your next flight. You'll have accommodation and food and anything else you need. Then you'll fly to Britain,' the officer told them. To Shaista even the fresh air here tasted like freedom. And he suddenly realized that for the first time in a long while he had been made to feel like a human being.

After the briefing they were given some tea, made the British way, in a cup with an offering of milk, rather than black in a little glass. Shaista thought that the British must love drinking tea as much as the Afghans, although he wouldn't say as much to Razagulla, who was certain to disagree. They were also shown where they would sleep for the night – in a huge accommodation block that was typically used by soldiers, with women in one section and men in the other. What particularly intrigued them all, though, were the bunk beds, which many of the Afghans had never seen before. Then they were taken to dinner. Just like Jamal all those years ago, when he had arrived at Camp Bastion on Christmas Day, they were somewhat overwhelmed not only by the quantities but also by the choice. At the counter there was tray upon tray of different dishes – chicken, steak, anything you could think of – as well as an array of sides that they joked were enough to keep them full for a week. And then at another counter there were desserts – fresh fruit, cake and more – followed by more tea and coffee and juice. As they all sat together, chatting animatedly about their first few hours in Europe, it was easy to forget all their worries back in Lashkar Gah.

It was only once Shaista and Razagulla were back in the military accommodation and they were shown how to connect to the wifi that Shaista saw Jamal's missed calls. The blood drained from his face. He called his son immediately, only to be told about Mohmood's capture. It was his worst nightmare realized – what if they killed him? – and he began to question whether leaving him behind had been the right thing to do. Racked with guilt, he relayed the conversation to Razagulla. She called to the boys, who hurried in to listen to the conversation. The happiness they had felt only moments earlier quickly turned to hopelessness.

With Jamal on speakerphone, the family reeled off the names of family members, wondering who could have told the Taliban that they had fled to England. They also couldn't understand how the Taliban had got hold of a picture of Esmatullah, although the discussion about which relative was to blame was a welcome distraction from thinking about Mohmood being tortured in a prison cell merely because his family had fled to safety. A small part of Jamal did wonder whether this had all stemmed from Esmatullah, who he was sure had been telling the children in the neighbourhood about the family's hopes to leave for England. But Esmatullah was only a teenager, so how could he be blamed? The call ended with mixed emotions for everyone. The family were weary from travelling, anxious about Mohmood but exuberant to think that in less than 48 hours they would be reunited with Jamal in England. As Jamal was about to hang up, he heard Shaista call his name one more time.

'Jamal, when I get to Britain we need to do everything we can to get Mohmood out. I will never enjoy my life if the Taliban takes my son because of me.'

13

The Hotel: Crewe, October 2021

'We love you Afghanistan,' read a children's drawing in English pinned up on the wall of the Chimney House Hotel, a three-star hotel half a mile off the M6 motorway near Crewe. Another poster displayed the translation from Pashto to English of 'Don't fight'. Spozhmai and Razagulla sat next to each other in the conservatory watching a cricket match between Pakistan and Afghanistan on a mobile phone. Spozhmai, her hair dyed with flashes of blonde, was wearing a velvet purple dress, with brightly coloured pom-poms and diamante open-toe shoes. That morning she and Jamal had driven from Coventry, which was normally just over an hour away, although it had taken much longer because of climate change protesters on the motorway. Razagulla had also dressed up for the occasion, wearing a long fuchsia-pink scarf with different shades of blue tassels wrapped over her multicoloured *firaq partug*, her wedding ring with its mint-green stone glistening in the autumnal light.

Other Afghans staying at the hotel were watching the cricket too, but on a projector screen inside the lobby, which now resembled an enormous family living room, full of children craning to get a better look. There was juice and nibbles on the side, and everyone cheered whenever Afghanistan scored a run.

Some of the families had spent several months living at the hotel, which had closed its doors to normal guests and padlocked the front gate. It was also manned by a security guard, although this was probably to stop the children running out on to the main road more than anything else. Set in 8 acres of private grounds, it was a safe place for the children to play. A couple of tiny ones with grubby faces were racing around on scooters, each trying to go faster than the other. Their parents were happy to leave them unattended, knowing that they would come to no harm. The older children had been taken to the local schools on buses, as the families waited to be given permanent accommodation. There were thousands of Afghan refugees like these people, and the Home Office didn't have anything like enough houses to accommodate everyone.

Near Razagulla, in the dappled autumn sunlight, sat a little boy clutching a plastic Barbie doll and surrounded by crisp crumbs, clearly intrigued by the newcomers. Donations of clothing had flooded in from across Britain for the families, and the Guls had been quick to choose the most fashionable styles. Esmatullah, Mohammed Sahil, Najeebullah and Edrees were wearing smart trousers and trendy warm jackets.

It had been an emotional few days. The best news they'd received was that Mohmood had been released from his cell – with a warning: 'If we find you are talking to your mother and father and they have gone to Britain, we will bring you back again.' He had spent a further two nights in that cell, during which time he had been hit several times with cables. Some of the Talibs who were hitting him were boys as young as 15 or 16. They opened the door at random hours just to tease him. One would hold his leg and the other would whack him with all the strength he could muster. But, in the same way that they had intervened with Esmatullah, the village elders had come to his rescue and acted as his guarantors. He would have to check in at the station every 12 days, but otherwise he was free to go – for a payment. 'You've been here three nights and the rent is 3,000 afghani [about £30],' one of the Talibs told him, grinning. Mohmood didn't dare argue. Yet perhaps what shocked Jamal and Shaista most was that, when he went to the local mosque afterwards to pray, Mohmood was approached by the imam, whose son Esmatullah had discovered was a member of the Taliban. 'You never knew my son and I were working for the Taliban,' he smiled, like it was some sort of joke. Maybe it had been him behind the beatings after all.

A couple of days after Mohmood's release Jamal received an email from the British government saying that he had been accepted to enter the UK. Jamal replied immediately, asking whether they would also allow in Mohmood's wife, Gulali. Until then, the British government knew nothing of her existence. It was almost too much to hope that Mohmood would be able to start his own journey to Pakistan.

The family had recently left quarantine in a hotel in Coventry, where they had been held for ten days because of arbitrary coronavirus restrictions placed on all arrivals from Afghanistan, although they were among the lucky ones – many families had been forced to stay much longer than ten days because the Home Office had been unable to find them alternative accommodation elsewhere. Some felt they were being imprisoned because they were not allowed to go outside even after completing their quarantine. This had happened to a group of Afghans in a hotel on the outskirts of London. At most, they were allowed outside for a 20-minute walk around a car park next to Heathrow Airport. Even then, they were escorted by a security guard. It seemed the same rules were being applied across all the quarantine hotels, affecting potentially hundreds of people. But they had to stay there until they were provided with alternative accommodation – either social housing or at one of the 'bridging hotels' designed for longer-term stays.

Some of those who had moved into social housing already were disappointed. One former interpreter, Ahmad, found himself living in one room with his pregnant wife and baby and sharing a bathroom without a shower and a kitchen with three other families. He didn't even have enough space to lay down his prayer mat. He explained to the Home Office how his wife was crying the whole night long because she was so depressed. There also seemed to be a postcode lottery in place: what they were given in the way of supplies depended on which council area they ended up in, with some Afghans arriving to fridges stocked full of food while others were provided with the bare minimum. Ahmad was one of the unlucky ones, having been sent a loaf of white bread, six tomatoes and just a few other staples. In the five weeks he and his family had been in their accommodation they had been given £310 to live on and were struggling to afford to eat.

Ahmad had been an interpreter for nearly three years from 2011, serving in some of the most dangerous locations across the province, including in Nad Ali, Babaji and Gereshk. But he made the difficult decision of resigning from his job in 2013 after receiving many threats back in his home village in the Deh Sabz district, north of Kabul. This was well known as a particularly unsafe place for people like him because of its strong Taliban ties. Everybody in the village seemed to know he was working with the UK troops, and it became impossible to pretend otherwise. His father seemed to bear the brunt of the threats, receiving them on a regular basis either while out walking or when he went to pray at the mosque. One man came up to him and told him that one day the Taliban would be in power and that they would take revenge on him unless his son quit his job.

Ahmad took such threats seriously and decided to quit. But even then he felt exposed. When ministers changed the rules on who could come to the UK to include those who had resigned, he became eligible for sanctuary. But it still took him many months to get the right papers. In the end he and his family flew to the UK on 1 August, and after a brief period in hotels, they had been in the shared house ever since. When he arrived in Britain, he was offered a scholarship to do an online International Relations Masters course, but had been forced to postpone it as there was nowhere for him to study in the cramped single room he now shared with his young family.

The Guls would have a better experience. When they had first arrived at the quarantine hotel a few hours after touching down from Cyprus, they had no idea where they were. Shaista had messaged Jamal to say 'London'. It didn't help that none of them could understand English. It was only when Jamal asked for a photograph and they sent them one of the hotel with its name on it – Ramada – and he recognized the building that he realized they were just a few miles away from him and Spozhmai in Coventry. 'That's close to my house!' he messaged back to his father. They couldn't believe their luck. Although slightly unsightly from the outside, the hotel's towering views over the city and four-star bedrooms were a world away from what most of its temporary visitors had ever experienced.

There was no time to waste. Jamal got in his car immediately and drove to see them, as excitable as a little boy at Eid. What if they were hungry? He knew he couldn't turn up without food. So he stopped at a takeaway and bought them burgers and chips, enough for more than one each. When he arrived, Jamal, who could normally charm his way into most situations, was slightly taken aback when the receptionist told him he wasn't allowed inside the quarantine hotel. Rules were rules. But he had food! In the end she relented and agreed that he could call one of his brothers and they could come downstairs and collect the food from him. It seemed like a fair enough compromise, although the people he really wanted to see were his parents.

All four of the boys turned up, eyes sparkling and grinning so widely that they could probably fit a whole burger into each of their mouths. The receptionist didn't have the heart to reprimand them, so left them to it. They all stood there hugging each other in the foyer for several minutes. Nobody needed to say much: the boys knew that Jamal understood what they had been through to get here. Then a security guard came up to Jamal. 'You can go now,' he told him. Jamal knew that he had bent the rules too far, but it had been worth it, if only for these few minutes.

Those first few days in the quarantine hotel were hard, with Shaista complaining often about how rigid the rules were in Britain. They had barely considered coronavirus as an issue back in Afghanistan, where they had been squashed together in crowds of thousands, nobody wearing masks. Now, in the UK, it seemed like there was an obsessive paranoia about the disease. They were not allowed into each other's rooms;

they were banned from chatting to other people face to face; and their food was left for them outside their doors. Shaista had never seen anything like it. 'It's like a prison,' he told Jamal, although Jamal reminded him that they hadn't been vaccinated, so perhaps it was a good thing for all their sakes.

Now, having moved to Crewe, they were for the first time able to spend some proper time together. Shaista, Razagulla and the boys would be staying here while more permanent accommodation was found for them elsewhere.

It was a day Jamal and his father had given up believing would ever happen. As they gathered around a table in the conservatory to drink some black coffee, Jamal's eyes darted to and from his brothers, and back to his father. He couldn't stop smiling. For perhaps the first time in months, Razagulla also felt at ease, delicately placing her feet on top of her precious silver shoes; Shaista was keeping warm in his new black padded coat worn over his dark grey *kamez* and polished brown shoes.

There were long pauses as the conversation dropped and Shaista and Razagulla thought about all that the family had been through. Some things were still too difficult to talk about. Any mention of her daughters who were still in Afghanistan made Razagulla go very quiet.

Then came sudden outbursts of laughter as the couple thought back to their escape from the Taliban. Shaista's black *lungee*, Razagulla's niqab covering her whole face and the boy's caps – their 'disguises', as they referred to them – had all been discarded as soon as they got to Pakistan.

But when Shaista really came alive was when he and Razagulla started talking about the flowers in the garden back in Lashkar Gah. Razagulla tried to help her husband remember some of their names, and Jamal attempted to come up with their English equivalents. But then there was a brief moment of silence as it dawned on Shaista that the flowers might soon be destroyed by the Taliban.

'When I was growing up, I knew I needed to be a gardener,' he said to Jamal quietly, before diverting his attention to his wife. 'She loved the flowers more than me. She loved the flowers too much,' he added, laughing, wondering how different their lives would have been if the British troops had not entered their city. He thought of Mohmood and the perilous journey ahead of him. What would he do if his wife was not accepted into the UK? Would he still come? Shaista also feared for his brothers, who had been left behind with no hope of escape. Having also worked for the British, they were as much targets for the Taliban as he had been. And what would life be like for his young sons in the UK? Would they be able to learn English? What if they didn't like school? Where would they all live? He had heard of one family being sent to the Isle of Skye, 500 miles away in Scotland, far from all the other Afghans. Most of all he thought of his daughters – his eldest, Salma, especially – and the life that they would now have under Taliban rule. He stared, wide-eyed, over Jamal's shoulder and through the window dirtied with watermarks as memories of the previous Taliban regime's treatment of women came flooding back to him. Anyone looking closely would have noticed him shudder.

The sun was almost set and Shaista excused himself from the conversation to retrieve his prayer mat, one of the few precious items he had brought with him all the way from Afghanistan. He would take his time. That evening, more so than any other, he had a lot to pray for.

Although the Guls had little to compare it to, the Chimney House Hotel was much better than some of the other 'bridging' hotels because it only housed Afghan refugees, with no paying guests. There they could relax. One of the hotels in London had tried to accommodate both, with one side having paying guests and the other about a thousand Afghan refugees from all walks of life – former soldiers, diplomats, judges, female activists and even lorry drivers. It was much more chaotic. There were even Chevening scholars, who had previously studied in the UK, and a female MP. One young woman, Monwara, had been halfway through her degree in economics and banking in Kabul when the Taliban took over. As her mother worked for the government and her father was in the military, she was eligible for a flight. Her dream was to become a doctor. With her chestnut-brown hair and wide smile, she exuded confidence and had already taken to helping the hotel managers and charity workers with distributing clothing among the other Afghans. Yet, although most of the Afghans at the hotel were like her and wanted to study or find work, it was becoming apparent that it would not be easy. Many of the arrivals had been given temporary six-month visas, which council workers believed meant they struggled to find long-term or well-paid jobs, or indeed any jobs at all. They were still waiting to be given what is called 'indefinite leave to remain'. Some had job offers based on the condition they would be given the more basic Biometric Residence Permit. One pilot had been refused entry to an aviation college because of his visa status.

There was also an issue with their identity documents. Banks were refusing to let them set up accounts because many didn't have passports, as it had been impossible to get them done in the days after the Taliban took over. Schools were often already over-subscribed, leaving Afghans stuck in hotel rooms relying on charities to teach them English. With the central London hotel, in particular, there were only 200 primary school places for some 500 children. There was less space here than at the Chimney House Hotel, with families crowding around the few benches outside and screaming children running around. Charity workers were handing out bags of warm clothing because many people had arrived with nothing but the clothes they were wearing. Some had arrived in just sandals. One woman had given birth upstairs because the ambulance had been unable to get to the hotel in time. A charity worker who happened to be a part-time nurse had stepped in and delivered the baby. It was something she had never done before.

Yet at every hotel there was a huge backlog of cases. In Crewe the days turned into weeks as the government struggled to find suitable housing for the newly arrived Afghans and their often quite extensive families. Meanwhile, the Guls settled into life at the hotel with its hundreds of other long-term occupants. In a way it was starting to feel like one big family. They had two rooms between them: one for Shaista, Razagulla and Najeebullah, and another for Edrees, Mohammed Sahil and Esmatullah. 'Not too big and not too small,' was how Shaista had described it to Jamal. He was fascinated by the radiator and delighted to have a kettle in his room again to make tea (although there was free tea and coffee down at reception any time of the day). They had set mealtimes around banquet-style tables and the chefs at the hotel had made quite an effort to prepare Afghan food, which was usually flavoursome.

Their time there was also vastly improved by the government-launched 'Operation Warm Welcome', which was aimed at making Afghans who had recently arrived in the country feel more at home. Councils were able to request

£28 per person per day to help support the Afghans in the hotels, plus extra money for English classes. As well as being taught basic English, Shaista, Razagulla and the boys had regular fitness classes and a separate course on British culture. They found the fitness classes hilarious – they had never done anything like that before. Razagulla had joined the one for women and Shaista a separate one for men. They now knew what a squat was, much to Jamal's amusement.

Shaista thought the culture classes were more interesting. They looked at the law and various other rules, some of which were notably different from the customs in Afghanistan. Things like the law prohibiting people from beating women or slapping their children, the latter being particularly surprising to many Afghans, who were not used to being told how to raise their own children. But the day trips were their favourite. Every week a list of activities was scribbled on a board in the foyer. Typically a bus came to pick up a group of them and they would be taken somewhere new, equipped with a packed lunch. The visit Shaista enjoyed most was to a museum with an old aircraft on display and uniforms of pilots of different ranks from the Second World War. In particular he marvelled at how old everything was, telling Razagulla how some of the artefacts were more than a hundred years old. Other days the staff at the hotel would drop them off in nearby towns or cities such as Crewe and Manchester to go and explore. There were trips to the local swimming pool – which the boys, like Jamal, loved – although Shaista avoided going because he was too embarrassed to be seen in just some swimming trunks by women he had never met before. Every Afghan over a certain age felt the same. Sometimes the family would just wander around the streets and remark on how different the houses were from those in Lashkar Gah. Many looked exactly the same as each other – especially if they were on the same street – only with different-coloured doors and windows. There were also signs everywhere so you always knew where you were, and there were street lights that worked and bins that would actually be collected.

In the evenings Shaista would play cards with the other men of a similar age. Often they chose to play Teka, a whist-based game with four players that is one of the most popular games in Afghanistan. One of those he played with was Hanif, his friend from Lashkar Gah, who had also ended up in the same hotel. Hanif was happy to admit that Shaista was much better at the game than him, although he joked with others that he once managed to scrape a win.

Back in Lashkar Gah, although they had both worked at the military base, Hanif had actually been employed by the British Foreign Office in the provincial reconstruction team (PRT), of which there were dozens across the country, providing security for humanitarian missions and helping with reconstruction in the local area. Hanif would always grasp any opportunity to chat to Shaista in his garden because he too loved flowers. Shaista enjoyed the company and trusted him with just about anything. Hanif's role was as a management assistant and supervisor to Afghan civilian workers, also employed by the PRT. He, like Shaista, had been lucky to be accepted to go to the UK, given that he had not been working in a front-line role. Many of his colleagues had not, though, and he was still in touch with some of them, forced into hiding in fear for their lives.

By sheer fluke, Hanif, who was nearly 50, had taken the same route from Lashkar Gah to the Chimney House as Shaista, at almost exactly the same time. Two days before Kabul fell he had had an appointment at the British High

Commission to discuss his application. After that, he was told to make his way to the airport. For three days and three nights Hanif, his wife, Hanifa, his elderly mother and two of his children, a son aged 11 and a daughter aged seven, had tried to make their way through the crowds to the airport. His mother, who had been granted eligibility because Hanif's father had passed away and there was no one else to take care of her, found it especially difficult as she got tired more easily. 'It's not possible to get inside, Hanif,' she told her son many times. But Hanif told her they must try. However, having failed to get through, they had made their way to Spin Boldak via Kandahar, with Hanif growing his beard as long as possible in the short time available to him and buying a black turban in order to look more like a Taliban. Without it, he was told, crossing the border would be impossible.

Like many others who had worked for the British, he was incredibly anxious that the family would be stopped by the militants. Ever since he had been made redundant by the Foreign Office in 2014 he had been looking over his shoulder. Also like many others, he had received phone calls from anonymous numbers and had had letters pinned to the door. 'You worked with the foreigners, you should be dead,' one of the letters said. On one occasion he was on a day trip with a friend who had also worked for the British to Qala-e-Bost, a fortress built three thousand years ago, some 30 minutes south of Lashkar Gah, when their car was shot at. Two bullets hit the back of the vehicle, although they remained unharmed. They never found out who it was that had been shooting at them, but they assumed it must be the Taliban.

When Hanif and his family arrived at Spin Boldak, they tried a different technique from the Guls to get over the border. Rather than using a people smuggler, they simply

paid money – 5,000 Pakistani rupees (about £14.60) each
– to the border guards to let them cross. It worked. Then,
after a long, arduous journey from Quetta to Islamabad, they
reached the Islamabad Hotel, where, much to their mutual
surprise, Hanif bumped into his good friend Shaista. And,
as the days went on, they realized they would be on the same
flight, would be staying in the same quarantine hotel and
would end up at the Chimney House Hotel together. It was
an enormous comfort to both families. Now, like Shaista,
Hanif enjoyed the classes on British culture and way of life.
He also listened hard about how to find a job, determined to
use his English skills to start working as soon as possible.

As the two friends played cards, Razagulla and Hanif's wife,
Hanifa, would sit together in the conservatory drinking cups
of tea and chatting – mostly about what was happening back
in Afghanistan. They also met many other women like them,
people they would hope to keep in touch with in the future.
And the boys made friends too. In fact, they were having so
much fun that Shaista would have to tell them off when it
was their bedtime. If he didn't, they would stay downstairs
until all hours playing games with the other teenagers and
watching television. Edrees, who was normally a shy boy who
never started a conversation with anyone he didn't know, even
joined in with the others. All in all there was very little for the
family to grumble about at the Chimney House Hotel. But
they could not stay there for ever.

14

The Smugglers' Route: Lashkar Gah to Pakistan, November–December 2021

The bleating of the goats at the doorway, together with the piercing sound of high-pitched wails coming from the street, jarred on Salma's ears as she hurried to put on her burqa. A group of armed Talibs were ushering the residents out of their homes – politely at first, although Salma knew what would happen if they didn't listen.

A few moments later they were outside: Salma, Faiz – a farmer by trade, and a good man with a kind heart – and their three remaining children, Haji, Azat and Wali. All of them were paralysed by the scene in front of them. Salma tried to shield her children, who had never witnessed an execution before. In truth, she wasn't sure if she could handle it herself.

A group of Talibs brought forward their prisoner, throwing him to the ground as if he was a sack of grain. Salma was close enough to make out his faint, resigned cries. Indeed, for a moment she caught a whiff of his body odour and for once she was grateful for the burqa covering her face. 'This infidel is guilty of murder,' shouted one of the Talibs in Pashto on a cheap megaphone. He was wearing the standard Talib garb of a black *shalwar* and black sandals, and he looked like he could crush a man's skull with his bare hands.

'It's the soldier,' Faiz whispered in her ear. He knew how little Salma could see through the masked mesh across her eyes. She gasped. She knew exactly who he meant. Their neighbour's son; he was only 19. Most people in the neighbourhood knew he had been a soldier for the previous Afghan government – his family had been so proud at the time. Like thousands of others, he had wanted to escape the country when the Taliban took over but hadn't managed to. His mother was nearby, a crumpled heap on the ground, with her other son and daughter next to her.

His death happened quickly. Two of the Talibs wrapped a shabby rope around his neck and hoisted him up for all the crowd to see. Salma covered 12-year-old Haji's eyes. The teenager's body writhed spasmodically before finally going limp. Blood trickled from his mouth.

They found out afterwards that he was suspected of killing a member of the Taliban. As usual, there was no evidence of his alleged crime.

This wasn't the first time the Taliban had so publicly displayed such gratuitous brutality. Only last month they had driven a parade of trucks carrying the bodies of hanged men through the city.[1] Jamal, who had been following events in Helmand closely, had watched a video of the ghastly scene, which showed the dead men swinging at the end of a crane, followed by a flurry of motorbikes. He believed the savagery of what he referred to as the 'desert court' in Helmand was part of a calculated attempt to spread fear among the people.

Life in Lashkar Gah had become like a prison for Salma, who could now only leave the house if escorted by a man. Even then, she had to wear a burqa which covered her head to toe except for a small mesh across her eyes which made it impossible to see sideways. Sometimes there was so little air for her to breathe inside that burqa that she felt like vomiting.

Mohmood and his wife, Gulali, had left for Pakistan the previous month in the hope that they would make it to Britain. Although they did not yet know the result of Gulali's application, Jamal had told Mohmood to get out of Lashkar Gah as soon as his had been accepted, fearing that the Taliban would come and arrest him again. Abdul, Shaista's brother, who had worked as a chef at the military base, had gone with them even though he, like Gulali, had had not yet been accepted for sanctuary in Britain either. However, they were willing to try their luck, believing that once they got to a third country the British government would feel sorry for them and let them in. The night before they left they feasted on curry, rice and Afghani naan at Abdul's home, where he lived with his wife and many of his ten children. Mohmood had also been staying there ever since he got his acceptance email, afraid the Taliban would come looking for him back at Shaista's house. Salma, Faiz and Salma's four sisters were also there to say their last goodbyes.

Mohmood's departure was a significant moment for the women, who until now had always had a brother there to protect them. The sisters spent most of the evening crying, showering him with hugs and kisses. Salma had told Jamal that life without any of her brothers would feel like no life at all. Somehow losing the last one, Mohmood, made her suddenly feel more vulnerable, even though she had her husband there with her – and she knew the others felt that way too. But another part of her was happy for him: he had been so miserable since the others had left and she knew that he couldn't stay in Afghanistan any more. He would be safe in England. And at least he and Gulali would have Abdul to look after them on the journey. They would surely need him, given how much Mohmood struggled even to walk.

Abdul had long been adored by Shaista's children, who visited him often. He was the youngest of Shaista's brothers and perhaps only in his late thirties, although, as ever, no one was keeping count. He always carried a pen in his chest pocket, and although he rarely used it, it made him look like a professor from the city. He had been made redundant from his job at the military base in 2013 and had struggled for money ever since. Now he had barely enough to feed his family. Abdul believed that if he could get to Europe and find a job he would be able to send money back home.

Jamal had sent the three of them 60,000 Pakistani rupees (about £175), which he had been told was enough for them all to pay the drivers and then the smugglers who would take them into Pakistan. The fee for the smugglers alone was 30,000 rupees. The price was higher now than when his parents and the boys had gone over, as the smugglers were seeking to cash in on the huge influx of refugees trying to leave the country. Also, this time it wouldn't be possible to go to Spin Boldak, Jamal had been told by some of his interpreter friends who had tried the crossing and been turned away. Apparently it was closed, with the Pakistani authorities refusing to take any more bribes. However, another of Jamal's friends, Shahwali Habibi, had taken the Baramcha route – considered one of the most dangerous – and had made it across successfully with his wife and six children. Mohmood, Gulali and Abdul would try and do the same.

The Baramcha crossing point was in a remote part of Helmand province nearly 200 miles south of Lashkar Gah. There they would meet a smuggler who would take them through the mountains to Pakistan. 'The smuggler wants money but he will organize everything,' Shahwali had told Jamal on the phone, and he could apparently be trusted. To get there, Mohmood, Gulali and Abdul would stop off at Garmsir, the capital of an impoverished district comprised mainly of hot desert. In the heart of Taliban country, Garmsir had long been a thorn in NATO's side, and the Americans had poured hundreds of troops and millions of dollars into securing it, but now it was back under Taliban control. Shahwali had passed through there a few weeks earlier, just to pray and eat, before heading on to the border town of Baramcha, famous for its drug bazaars and heroin-processing facilities. NATO had also once known it for being where weapons and ammunition were stored, and for housing bomb factories and foreign fighter training facilities.[2] It was not somewhere Mohmood and the others would want to stay for long.

Shahwali, a relatively short man whose glasses gave him an intellectual air, had explained to Jamal that in Garmsir they must not tell anyone they were heading to Pakistan, in case they were stopped by the Taliban. When quizzed by a Talib himself, he had claimed he wanted to go to Baramcha to visit relatives – which they seemed to have accepted. Mohmood would try the same cover story, made more believable by the fact that he, Gulali and Abdul were carrying barely any belongings. Shahwali had other tips too. Like Shaista's friend Hanif, he had grown his beard, but had also left all of his papers from his British army days back home in Lashkar Gah, along with anything else that might arouse suspicion, such as his degree certificate. As an extra security precaution, he had also switched off his mobile phone and given it to his wife so she could hide it under her clothes.

So much had changed for Shahwali in such a few short weeks. Before the Taliban had taken over in August and he had been forced out of his job, he had not wanted to leave his country. He had been employed by the British military for five years, working mainly in the 'crimestoppers' unit in the police headquarters, like Jamal. He was known there for his laugh, which was so loud it carried through the walls. His job had been to work both as an IT mechanic, fixing the computers and also answering and translating calls coming into the 110 helpline from across the region. Members of the public would ring in to report, say, an IED being planted or that they knew of an impending attack, and Shahwali would pass it on to the relevant department. It was a clever system – a British idea which to some extent mirrored the 999 system back in the UK – which had never previously been tried in Afghanistan. However, even then Shahwali had been more cautious than many and, fearing Taliban reprisals, had insisted that the British always referred to him as Jan.

When the British troops left in 2014, Shahwali stayed on to do a similar job for the Afghan government. Over time he was given more senior tasks, such as connecting President Ashraf Ghani with the local governor, and he was making good money. But everything had changed earlier in the year when the Taliban had marched across the region. There was no telling what would happen to him if he stayed in Lashkar Gah. He applied for the ARAP scheme and took his family to Kabul, awaiting the outcome of his application. But on the day he went to the post office to collect his passport, he saw people running around the streets shouting that the Taliban had arrived. After that, he realized that he had no hope of getting hold of his documents. And so, like so many other people, he joined the crowds outside the airport. But with six children in tow, including a baby, he realized that he had little hope of getting through the gate. However, he waited until October before finally making the decision to leave Afghanistan on foot, by which time the Spin Boldak crossing was closed.

When Shahwali and his family arrived in Baramcha, they could find nowhere suitable to stay, so he decided to move on quickly and immediately started making inquiries about how they could get across into Pakistan. 'No, no, no, you can't do it on your own,' one of the locals had told him. He was eventually introduced to a smuggler who gave him two options. The first was to take the mountain route, which was longer, more physically demanding but avoided any checkpoints – for which he would charge 25,000 Pakistani rupees. But how would the children manage? Shahwali decided that his eldest son, who was 12, would be fine, but the others were too young to walk far. That's when the smuggler mentioned the second option. If he paid him an extra 10,000 rupees he could get them identity cards that claimed they were refugees living in Pakistan and he would drive them straight across the border in a car. The deal was done.

The journey by car was incredibly nerve-wracking, with Shahwali, his wife and the oldest son spending the entire time rehearsing what was written on their fake identity cards. They had new first names, new family names and a new address elsewhere in Helmand. When they arrived at the checkpoint, Shahwali's baby daughter was crying, desperate for milk, and writhing uncomfortably in the sweltering heat, which added to the anxiety. Nervously, he told the guard that they had travelled far and that his children were sick. But, when it came to it, the guards showed little interest in checking their documents – presumably because they were being given a cut of the smuggler's money – and allowed them straight through. Other Afghans, those without children, were being pointed towards a much longer queue, where they were being far more rigorously checked.

At last they were in Pakistan. The smuggler took them to his family home and, despite having been unnerved by his Taliban-style appearance when they first met, Shahwali decided that he was indeed a good person. Fluent in three languages, he was against the Taliban because he believed that they were destroying Afghanistan. His home was a very modest mud house in Girdi Jangal, some 30 miles from the border with Afghanistan, which had grown from a small village before the Russian invasion of Afghanistan in 1979 into a town of some 60,000 inhabitants, most of whom were Afghan refugees. But as it had grown in size, it had turned into a hub of criminal activity.[3] And it was clear from Shahwali's journey, and the experience that Mohmood would later have, that criminal activity had not gone away.

In an attempt to make them feel a bit more at home, the smuggler's wife baked the family some bread and offered them some black or green tea. While Shahwali was given a room in the guest house a short distance away, his wife and children stayed in the smuggler's house. Then, having at last been able to rest properly after their stressful journey, they were picked up and taken to Quetta. Only then did Shahwali begin to feel safe. Not long after, he had a call from Jamal, asking for advice about the best way into Pakistan for Mohmood, Gulali and Ahmed.

Shahwali told him that, because they were all adults, it was probably better for them to take the mountain pass, where they were less likely to be stopped by border guards. None the wiser, they were happy to take any advice they could get. Jamal got in touch with the same smuggler that Shahwali had met in Baramcha, and the plan was hatched. The three of them set off for the mountains. After a brief, uneventful stop in Garmsir, the trio continued to Baramcha by taxi. Gulali was unusually quiet on the journey, probably thinking about her parents, whom she was leaving behind. They were reasonably wealthy because they had plentiful land handed down through the generations, so for them, unlike many Afghans, money was not an issue. They also had their sons, Gulali's brothers, nearby to take care of them. But that did not stop her worrying about them and about what the future might bring both for them and for her. For most of her life she had lived on their farm in the Nawa district, upstream from Lashkar Gah on the River Helmand. She had never been to school (there were none where she lived) and had spent her childhood playing and then working among the apple orchards and the fields full of fruits and vegetables of the area. She had never been so far from home before, and she had no idea whether she would ever go back. Now she was going to be smuggled into a foreign land with no promise of ever even being able to get out of there. She was terrified.

They stayed in Baramcha for one night. The following morning a smuggler with a Taliban-like beard appeared on a motorbike. He told Mohmood that he could only take Gulali and that he and Abdul would have to wait. She would stay in his family home overnight without them. His words were met with silence. Mohmood didn't like that plan at all. How could he leave his wife with a man he had never met before? What if she got lost in the mountains? What if they were caught by the police? Gulali, who found the smuggler scary, also seemed horrified by the idea. The couple caught each other's eyes, knowingly. Mohmood called Jamal. 'This guy is saying he will take Gulali first. How can I trust him?' he asked, trying to keep his voice down so the smuggler wouldn't hear him. Jamal, who had learned to trust no one, was immediately suspicious. He called up Shahwali. 'Don't worry, he will take her safely to his house. There's nothing to worry about,' he told Jamal, assuring him that the smuggler was trustworthy and that he himself had been to the man's house with his family. 'He has a wife and children there,' he added. That settled things. Jamal was reassured and told his brother to go ahead with the plan. Gulali set off with the smuggler on the motorbike.

A few hours later two more smugglers turned up to where Mohmood and Abdul were waiting. Mohmood could see that they had bags packed full of heroin covered by blankets. He and Abdul looked at each other. There was no way they wanted to be anywhere near the drugs. It was far too dangerous, and if they were caught with them that could jeopardize their chances of ever getting to Britain.

'We don't want to go like this. It's far too risky for us,' Mohmood told the men.

'If you don't want to go this way, then we can't take you,' one of them replied, his voice unwavering.

Mohmood thought the men were from the ancient Baloch tribe, historically a nomadic group whose lands straddle the borders between Afghanistan, Iran and Pakistan. They are generally to be found living in mud-brick homes in rugged mountains, parched river valleys and dry desert regions. But their adoption of a moderate form of Islam has exposed them to brutal repression from fundamentalists, with the Taliban once issuing a fatwa (an Islamic edict) in Nimroz, near the Afghan–Iranian border, calling for their ethnic cleansing.[4] Mohmood didn't know too much about them other than what he'd heard: that they were generally speaking uneducated but very rich (largely from the drugs trade). And trustworthy? That he doubted. But he and Abdul didn't really have a choice. They couldn't possibly navigate their way through the mountains on their own, and Gulali had already gone ahead. How else would they link up with her? Had Jamal known of their dilemma, he would never have let them go. But he hadn't and, despite their misgivings, they agreed to go with the smugglers, praying to God that the Pakistani authorities would not catch them.

For the first part of the journey they would all have to walk before being met in the mountains by another two smugglers on motorbikes who would take them to the bearded man's house. Mohmood explained that he was disabled and that walking was difficult for him. They would go slowly, they said. At first, both he and Abdul were shaking with fear and looking over their shoulders all the time to check if anyone was following them. They had heard lots about the drug smugglers in Baramcha but had never thought for one minute that they would end up among them. The four walked through the mountains for what seemed like hours, with Mohmood repeatedly asking the smugglers to stop so he could lean on a rock and rest his legs. The rest of the time he tried to put on a brave face for his uncle, who seemed to be struggling even more than him. It was hot in the afternoon sun, even at this time of year, and he collapsed two or three times. They poured water on his face to keep him going.

As it got dark, they at last stopped on a flat part of the rocky path and lay down for the night. Mohmood's leg was swollen badly and scratched from where they had walked through the bushes. It was getting cold. 'Stay here and I'll go and get some food,' said one of the men, who must have been from the area. He returned with some hot tea, bread and just one blanket for Mohmood and Abdul to share. It barely covered one person, never mind two. There was also nothing to rest their heads on, so they had to make do with the rocks. Neither of them slept. It was too cold, and Mohmood's back was hurting from lying on stones.

It was almost a relief when at six o'clock the following morning they started their journey again. They didn't have to wait long until another two smugglers arrived on motorbikes. The drugs were passed over and tied on to the vehicles. Few words were exchanged. These men had done this many times before. The next stage seemed to go very quickly – a few hours at most. Mohmood was much relieved to see Gulali, who by comparison had had a good night's sleep at the smuggler's house – at least his fears regarding her safety had been unfounded. He shiftily handed over the money he had agreed to pay the smuggler. It wasn't clear what happened to the drugs, but Mohmood was not going to ask any questions. The three of them had no time to waste, so they quickly arranged for a car to take them to Quetta, more than 200 miles to the north-east. From there Mohmood and Gulali would travel on to Islamabad.

But not Abdul. He preferred to wait in Quetta rather than travel all the way to the capital, wasting money on hotels, until he had heard the decision of the British government about his application. The three had been through so much together in the last few days that saying goodbye was harder than any of them could ever had imagined. But Abdul had relatives he could stay with for a couple of days in Quetta while Jamal continued to try and persuade MoD officials in London to give him sanctuary.

Jamal had first applied for sanctuary for Abdul and Shaista's other brother, Anargull, who had also worked as a chef at the base, in September, soon after the Taliban took over. Abdul had worked for the British since 2006 – longer ago even than Shaista – and he had the certificates to prove it. Once he was made redundant in 2013, he continued working with a major contractor in the region as a kitchen assistant until the following year. After that, he joined the police for a short period before becoming a shopkeeper.

As soon as Abdul, Mohmood and Gulali had crossed the border into Pakistan, Jamal had begun emailing the ARAP team on their behalf. From Abdul's email account he told them he had fled Afghanistan and was already in Pakistan. Earlier, Jamal had read a tweet from Ben Wallace, that made him believe that Abdul would be a shoo-in for the scheme. Wallace had written that, as operations had drawn to a close in Afghanistan, the ARAP scheme was accepting people who were in third countries. Officials told Abdul to stay safe and that they would let him know as soon as a decision had been made. Jamal, who was relying on a tiny salary, sent him another 30,000 Pakistani rupees to keep him going. But after a few days Abdul had to move from his relatives' house, which was minute, and into a hotel. It was charging 1,000 Pakistani rupees a day.

Days turned into weeks and still nothing from the MoD. After a month of waiting, Jamal couldn't afford to send him any more money again. 'You'll have to leave, Uncle,' Jamal told him, regretfully. And then they heard the news – he had been rejected. Jamal felt terrible that so many members of the family had made it out of Afghanistan but that his uncle, the person who had helped secure Shaista his gardening job in the first place, had had his application turned down. It didn't make any sense. Feeling hopeless, Abdul turned round to make the long journey back to Lashkar Gah.

As Mohmood and Gulali waited patiently in the hotel in Islamabad, another, even bigger problem arose for the Guls. Jamal had received a disturbing email from the MoD: they were threatening to rescind Mohmood's eligibility on the basis that they had only just been made aware of the fact that he had a wife. Questions were clearly being raised about why he needed to come to England. Could she not take care of him in Lashkar Gah?

Jamal could not bear to tell Mohmood what was happening behind the scenes, aware that to do so would leave him panicked and broken. 'Just be patient,' he told his brother as Mohmood and Gulali waited expectantly for details of their flights to Britain. Jamal told his father instead, saying to withhold the information from his brother. He didn't know at the time but Shaista did tell Mohmood there was a risk he might have his eligibility taken away, believing it was better to be honest with him now rather than crush him later. Mohmood was so anxious he stopped eating. 'If I go back to Afghanistan, what is going to happen to me?' he asked his father.

The MoD asked Shaista to justify why his son should still be eligible for sanctuary in the UK, given his 'new' circumstances. The response would have to be good. Jamal sought advice from his British contacts, who he thought would know how to make a far better case than he could. He explained, on Shaista's behalf, how the original application for Mohmood had been accurate because he had indeed been disabled as a result of gunshot wounds inflicted by the Taliban and that he was therefore unable to work. He was reliant on Shaista's income, which at this point consisted of British handouts, and unable to take care of himself. Under the new Taliban regime, as a woman Gulali was unable to work or to go outside the house without a male escort, so she was limited in what care she could provide. There was certainly no way that she could provide for them financially. Jamal also explained on Shaista's behalf how he had in fact mentioned that Mohmood had a wife in a phone call he had received from an interpreter working for the MoD back in August and believed that, if Mohmood was accepted, then she would also automatically be accepted too. If his eligibility was now rescinded, Mohmood's life would be in grave danger. He had already been imprisoned once by the Taliban. Now Mohmood and his wife had left home with hardly any money or belongings and had risked their lives further to travel through Taliban checkpoints over the border into Pakistan. He begged the MoD to let them both into the UK. It seemed to work. A few weeks later, in November, they were given the MoD's decision. They were both allowed to come to the UK. The whole family was incredibly relieved. But Abdul, who would have to wait until the summer of 2022 for a final response, having made his case further, got only rejection.

Meanwhile, back in Lashkar Gah, life had gone from bad to worse. A few days after Mohmood, Gulali and Abdul left for Baramcha, the Taliban came knocking yet again. Salma and her family had only two days to get out of the family house. If they refused, they would be put in prison. They were not the only ones being forced out of their home, though; the same was happening to families across the city. Anybody who had a reasonably sized house and who had family members who had worked for NATO or the Afghan government became a target. Salma and Faiz did not dare stand up to the Taliban. They took what belongings they could manage and moved into a cramped two-bedroom house on the outskirts of the city. Not long after, a senior Taliban commander moved into their house. They were never given any money in compensation, nor did they expect it. Salma couldn't help wondering what would happen to her parents' precious garden.

Every now and then her younger sisters would visit Salma and her family in their new home, but their trips became less frequent with the ever-tightening Taliban restrictions on their freedoms. It was also impossible for Faiz to get work, and so they found themselves having to rely on the money Shaista was now sending them from England. The house they had moved to was costing 5,000 afghani (about £47) a month in rent – something they would never have been able to afford otherwise – but it had no proper garden, so their two goats spent most of their time inside with them, which made the house feel even more cramped. But the goats were essential to their survival as food was becoming scarce and so Salma had kept them for their milk. Without a job, Faiz was becoming more and more withdrawn. He had also grown a long beard after the Taliban banned barbers in the province from shaving or trimming them, as doing so allegedly broke Islamic law. Their three remaining sons had also stopped going to school because they were too frightened to leave the house, scared that they might suffer the same fate as their brother Shir. They had not heard from him since he had been kidnapped from school nearly six months ago. Not a day went by that Salma did not think of him.

Although his first name was Hazrat, the family had nicknamed him Shir, which translates as 'lion', because of his bravery. However, the Taliban did come and ask more questions about Shir, who was 16 at the time of his disappearance, but refused to say where he had gone. Even more disturbing was that they kept reminding Salma that her father and brothers had worked for the British government and had run away to the UK. She denied it, of course. Another reason for her to avoid leaving the house.

Over time the Taliban tightened their grip. For those who could remember, it was as if the country had gone back to the 1990s, when they controlled Afghanistan for the first time. Rumours circulated in Lashkar Gah that the Taliban had even brought back stoning to death for adultery. It was also not uncommon just to see people being tortured or beaten with cables or rifle butts out in the streets. Men accused of working for the previous Afghan government were taken from their homes in the middle of the night and never came back. One day when Salma was with Faiz buying vegetables at the market they saw three women being beaten with canes on the floor until they bled. Their only crime – not having their faces covered.

The barbarity was ironic, but not surprising. When the Taliban had first taken control of Kabul back in August, they had declared a general amnesty for the population, announcing the news via mosques and social media. And yet since then people who had worked for the previous government had disappeared, especially former members of the police, intelligence agencies and militias. Nobody was ever told where they had gone. At the same time the Taliban continued the hunt for both civilian and military personnel who were affiliated with the former government across Helmand, especially senior commanders.[5] The levels of suspicion among the local Afghan civilians were growing, with no one knowing who they could really trust. If someone was taken, then their loved ones would be left wondering which family member had betrayed them.

Before the war, Salma's sons had had a carefree life. They had been taking private English classes; they sang along to Bollywood music played as loud as the radio would allow. Nowadays they spent their days inside dreaming of a life of freedom in Britain with Shaista and the rest of the family. But dreaming was futile, and deep down they knew that they would have to make do with just each other, and the goats, for company.

15

Enduring Pain: Scotland, 25 July 2022

Jamal, who had finished his shift as a taxi driver in the early hours of the morning, awoke to a string of picture messages from Meena, one of his younger sisters, back in Lashkar Gah. He felt the sudden urge to retch. There was Salma lying slumped on the ground, crying out in agony. The whites of her eyes were blood-red from where a group of Talibs had pummelled her face with a brick. The meat of her left cheek was a mixture of congealed blood and purple bruising. And her top lip had ballooned to more than twice its normal size after they struck her with the butt of an AK-47. Blood trickled from an open gash in her ear.

They had targeted her when Faiz was out in the fields with their three sons. 'They hit me with a brick and I don't know what happened after that. I just closed my eyes,' Salma told her brother as soon as he reached her. The group of four men had turned up when Salma was washing the dishes. The smell of morning coffee still lingered in the air. There was a loud bang at the gate, which nowadays they always kept locked. A few weeks ago rumours had spread that the Taliban were carrying out a systematic search of any houses in Kabul that they believed were linked to Afghans who had worked for the previous government or with coalition forces. They were looking for uniforms or weapons – anything that could be used as evidence of their past. Then they had started looking in Helmand. They first searched Salma's house when Meena and her husband were visiting. Behind a blacked-out window on the ground floor, the two sisters watched in disbelief as armed Talibs dug the fresh soil outside and discovered a pile of tattered documents that Salma had grabbed from her father's old property and buried there several days earlier. The documents included Shaista's and Jamal's papers from the British Army. There were also photographs of Jamal with the soldiers he had worked with. Jamal already had copies of them on his mobile phone so she could have burned them and it wouldn't have mattered. But now, she realized, the Taliban knew everything for certain. Yet, much to her surprise, the men left quietly and she had heard nothing from them since. Abdul and Anargull also had their properties searched, although they had already burned any documents that linked them to the British. They even went to the house of Spozhmai's brother – Naz's husband – who had served in the police. Thankfully, they never discovered where he had hidden his uniform. Salma had heard that they had arrested a local military commander who was well known in Lashkar Gah as having been responsible for killing many Taliban. He was beaten so badly that he died in custody. Most of the men who worked for the previous government were believed to be in hiding.

At the local school, which her three boys were now attending, all they seemed to teach was violence. Of course, all the teachers were men, and Salma assumed that most of them were members of the Taliban. She knew they were trying to change her sons' mentality so they believed in the Taliban way of thinking. The prospect of her sons' future terrified her. The previous government had taught them to be nice to each other. Now the boys were being told that once they grew up they needed to fight for their country against Western values.

'Don't shave' was another lesson. They were also being taught that a woman's place was in the home, cooking, cleaning and looking after the children. Women shouldn't be allowed to study or shop on their own, or do anything related to Western culture. Salma was just grateful that they were not being taught how to use weapons. Under the new Taliban regime, if the children did not study or failed to turn up for a class, they would be hit with cables. The boys had returned home on multiple occasions crying, begging not to be sent back to school again. But to keep them at home would only arouse suspicion.

Since she had witnessed the execution the previous year, Salma had not seen any more public killings, although she was sure they were happening elsewhere. Women were still being hit for not being covered up properly or for walking alone in the streets. Life for everyone was horrible.

So when the bang at the gate came, Salma was more cautious than ever. She crept outside as quietly as she could to take a look through the tiny hole. She could see the men's AK-47s. They had long, scraggly hair and very long beards. It was difficult to make out their faces but it was obvious they were the Taliban. One – a stubby-looking man – and a second, taller one were using radios. She could hear their grunts. It sounded like they were in contact with some Talibs further away from the house. A sound, somewhere between a gasp and a squeal, escaped her mouth. She involuntarily put her hand over it, as if to force herself to be quiet. Salma crept back towards the house as they banged at the gate even louder. Perhaps they heard her. A few minutes later they had jumped over the wall and were inside the compound.

Where was Shaista, they wanted to know. When she told them she was not in touch with her father, they started the beating. One pulled her hair and pushed her to the ground, while another put his foot on her throat. 'Where are your parents?' another shouted, his spit flying on to her face. 'I don't know!' she cried, praying these were not the same Talibs that had searched the property days earlier. Then he got out his phone. Salma gasped in horror. On the phone were a series of pictures showing the hole she had dug and the papers proving Shaista and Jamal had worked with the British troops. They had waited until she was home alone to confront her with the evidence.

'We have all the documents you hid in the property,' said one man, although he didn't need to explain what she was looking at.

'We know it was you. Where are your father and your brothers?' he asked again.

'They are not here. They're in the UK, but I have no communication with them,' she admitted, defeated. She had never been so scared.

'Did your father leave you to be a spy for him?' he snarled.

'No, my husband is a farmer. Look at me, I'm just in the house. I've never worked for any foreigners,' she replied, now crying uncontrollably with the shock of it all.

They were barely listening.

Then they hit her face with the brick. She didn't remember anything after that.

Several hours later Faiz and the boys returned to the house to find her still lying on the floor. She hadn't had the strength to try and find her mobile phone to call for help. They alerted the neighbours and her uncles, Abdul and Anargull, and raced her to the hospital. She was checked over briefly and sent home after spending one night there.

Months later Salma would still suffer from bad headaches and struggle to see through her damaged eye. Even standing seemed like a chore. She also became more nervous about accepting calls from her family in the UK, making sure she did so only when the family were completely alone inside the house.

When Jamal told his father about the attack, Shaista was silent for a long time. Razagulla didn't stop crying. It was now a year since the Taliban had taken over their city, and it seemed as if it were only yesterday that they had been fighting their way through the crowds at Kabul airport. They had been given a council house in Sauchie, a picturesque town in Clackmannanshire, 30 or so miles north-east of Glasgow. Mohmood, who had arrived from Pakistan in January, lived around the corner with his wife. Distressed at the thought of being so far away from them, Jamal and Spozhmai had left Coventry and moved temporarily into Mohmood's house, where they were sleeping on a mattress on the living-room floor – although Mohmood and Gulali had two bedrooms, one of them was too small for any adults to sleep in.

When the couple had first arrived in the UK they had been taken to Glasgow by mistake after their ten days' quarantine in London. They arrived at the hotel in Glasgow only to be told that they were 'not on the list'. They stayed for two nights before being driven back down to Crewe, to stay with Shaista and the others at the Chimney House Hotel. Mohmood had liked the hotel, but the fate of his uncle Abdul was a constant worry. He felt as though he was somehow responsible because he had been the one who had left him back in Pakistan. In the end, Mohmood and Gulali spent only six weeks in Crewe before they were offered the home 250 miles away, in Clackmannanshire. They were lucky because it was around the corner from Shaista and the others.

Now in Scotland, Mohmood was missing his friends and family and was struggling to get used to the weather. He believed his gunshot injuries made him feel the cold more than his siblings – or at least that is what he told them. But he was finally receiving the doctor's care he so badly needed, and they had a teacher coming round to the house once a week to teach both him and Gulali English.

Shaista's younger sons had started at the nearby school, but Esmatullah had been told he would have to wait until September to start college. Although they all liked the scenery in Scotland, with its rolling hills and deep blue lochs, it had been hard to adjust to their new life. Shaista had become withdrawn, refusing to plant any flowers in the garden of his new house despite Jamal's encouragement. Mohammed Sahil, who was normally confident and outgoing, had started putting cream on his face to make himself look white like all the other children in his class. Esmatullah was clearly suffering from serious mental health issues, crying at night and pulling out his hair. When Jamal was staying over at Shaista's one night, he awoke to hear shouting downstairs, where Esmatullah was sleeping.

'Get off me! Why are you doing this to me! Why did you destroy my life?' Jamal heard his little brother shouting. He ran downstairs.

'Fuck off, no,' Esmatullah shouted again.

'What's happening, brother?' said Jamal, shaking him gently.

Esmatullah sat up, as if ready for combat. 'Nothing,' he told him.

'You've been talking to yourself and you're swearing,' Jamal told him.

Esmatullah said that he was fine. But the nightmares got worse and worse. The medication he had been given by the doctor didn't seem to be having any effect and in the end he was referred to a specialist. Then he returned one day from an appointment to tell Jamal that the doctor had asked if he had thought about killing himself, and that he had replied yes.

'Don't say that! They'll put you in hospital,' Jamal had reprimanded him.

But Esmatullah didn't seem to care. 'I'm tired of this life,' was his reply.

Jamal thought his head was broken. He tried his best to lift his brother's spirits, devastated that he could be feeling so low. 'You're going to get better,' he assured him.

Sometimes they would find shattered mugs in his room. Jamal warned Razagulla to keep any knives away from him, believing that one day he would wake up and find his brother dead. The family were living on edge, waiting for the next sign of trouble.

By now Jamal, the only member of the family who could speak good English, had got himself a job as a taxi driver. He was the breadwinner, with his small income being shared across not only the family in Britain but also their relatives in Afghanistan. Aware that so many of them were living in such total destitution, it was hard for him to say no to their requests for help. And yet Jamal himself had his own struggles. He was desperately trying to secure a payout from the British government for the injuries he had suffered when he had been shot on the front line in Helmand. One of his interpreter friends in Glasgow had been awarded £10,000 in compensation after he was shot in the neck. Jamal, who had been shot twice and believed that his injuries were more severe, was sure he would be given similar treatment and had already started spending the money in his head. He had ideas of setting up a business. Yet ten months after sending his medical records to the compensation scheme he had heard nothing. To say he was disappointed would be an understatement.

Yet although he had his frustrations with the UK, Jamal had high hopes for the future. For him, Britain was now his home, but he also wanted to do more to help those who had not managed to escape. He and his old interpreter friend Rafi Hottak, whom he met at a protest outside the Home Office the previous year, had stayed in touch over recent months, discussing over the phone what next steps they could take to ensure more Afghans whose lives were in danger could make it to the UK.

Years after concerns had first been raised about the MoD's scheme for helping those who had served with the British, it seemed there was still huge confusion over who the policy applied to.

One former interpreter, Sajid Naeemi, had waited for months for a decision from the MoD about whether his two-year-old son could join him and his wife in the UK, only to be told that he had applied to the wrong government department and that he would have to go through the whole process again with the Home Office. Sajid, who already found it hard to trust people and could admittedly be short-tempered in far easier circumstances, was so infuriated with the government's response that he said he was now beginning to regret his service with the British army. He couldn't believe that they had brought Pen Farthing's animals into the country but that, when it came to his little boy, it was an ongoing struggle. Granted, his case was more complicated than most. Sajid had come to the UK in 2016 after spending two years working alongside UK troops. He moved to Oldham with his wife at the time and started a job with Amazon. But three years later they divorced and he married his second wife, Mena, on a visit back to Afghanistan. He applied for Mena to come and live with him, and while they waited, their son Yosuf was born. Solicitors advised him that if he restarted the application it would be rejected on the basis that he did not have enough money to support them both. So he waited. And then, in October 2021, two years after Mena first applied for a visa, it was finally granted. Hoping that they could apply for a separate visa for Yosuf later, Mena, who was by then pregnant with their second child, took the heartbreaking decision to board a flight to the UK, leaving her son behind with her sister. In January 2022 the MoD requested copies of Yosuf's passport and birth certificate. However, it took until July 2022, when the case was raised in the press, for the MoD to admit that Sajid had sent them to the wrong department.[1] During that time, his newborn daughter, Aqsa, had died from a heart condition. The couple's fight to be reunited with their son continues and still hasn't been resolved.

There were many cases like Sajid's, of Afghans already in the UK trying and failing to get their relatives into Britain. Indeed, the news of the brutal attack on Salma prompted Jamal to apply for her and her family to be given sanctuary in the UK like her parents and brothers. For Jamal, it was starting to feel as if the threat that the Taliban posed to his family was all-encompassing and never-ending. And Salma's application was just one among thousands.

If Salma were allowed into the UK, that would go some way to alleviating Shaista's worries, but even then there were his other daughters to think about. And thinking was something he did a lot of these days. It might seem strange, but often the family looked back at their time at the Chimney House Hotel with fondness. When they left, four months after they arrived, Shaista felt sad. They had been there so long that he had developed an affection not only for the other Afghan families staying there but also for the hotel staff, who were so kind and helpful. He especially liked a young staff member named Emma, probably in her twenties, who went out of her way to care for them. If he needed any medication or to go to a doctor's appointment, she would drive him there in her car, along with an interpreter. When it came to their departure, Shaista thought he saw her crying. He was truly touched.

Quite a few of the Afghans had left the hotel around the same time as the Guls. Shaista's good friend Hanif had been moved to a house near Aberdeen: even further north than they were and still too far away for regular visits, especially without a car. But sometimes they spoke on the phone, although it was not the same and they missed each other. Otherwise, Hanif, who could speak English, was settling well into his new life. He was still looking for a job – paying weekly visits to the local job centre – but he was sure his time would come. 'It's a nice place. I like British people. I have a good life here. They are providing everything for us,' he would tell his friends.

For Shaista it was much harder. The family had been given a caseworker, whose job it was to check up on them, and he loved his new house, but he knew of no other Afghans in the town. Unable to speak English, life there seemed quite isolated – boring, even, was how he would describe it to

Jamal. He was by no means ungrateful – he was free from the Taliban – but the only real structure he had to his life was to pray five times a day. Even then, the nearest mosque was nearly an hour's walk away. Back in Lashkar Gah there had been a never-ending stream of family and friends coming round to the house to visit them. Sensing their father's loneliness, Mohmood or Jamal made a point of taking him and Razagulla out on day trips. Sometimes they would head into Glasgow, where some other interpreters lived, and they would meet up with them and have a barbecue. They took a tent to shelter from the rain and stayed the night, keeping awake until the early hours of the next morning, laughing and joking.

But it was at moments like this that Shaista would think back to Afghanistan. The attack on Salma truly frightened him. It frightened him because he knew the Taliban could do anything to his family and there was nothing he could do about it. He spoke to her and followed the news regularly, so he had some idea about what she and her family must be going through. They chatted whenever they could. But his dreams were about an Afghanistan in another age, far into the future, when it would be safe enough for him and all his family to live there. He would visit his daughters, his grandchildren and his brothers, and they would sit together, playing cards and drinking tea, and life would be good.

Then reality set in. He couldn't remember the last time he had heard something positive come out of his country. Some days the guilt Shaista felt about those who were left behind was hard to bear. It wasn't just Salma he was worried about but all of his daughters, who had little chance of ever escaping the life they were being forced to endure. Shaista didn't regret his decision to become a gardener at the military base in Lashkar Gah. Quite the opposite. He was proud of what he had achieved there and, given the chance, he would go back in a heartbeat if he thought it would make a difference. But his views on the NATO coalition had changed over the last few months as he saw his country enter into one of its darkest periods. Despite his lack of regret about his own role, he had stopped believing that the British and American combat missions, Operation Herrick and Operation Enduring Freedom respectively, had been for the good. Before they arrived, the Guls may have been poor but at least they were living in peace. Yet families like his were now the enemies of the Taliban and the Taliban were now their enemies. The West's mission, like the other foreign ventures that had come before them, had proved pointless. To Shaista, they had run away, leaving the country in a worse state than when they had first arrived. When Shaista applied to work with the British forces back in 2007, he did so believing the Western troops would make his country a better place. Now he knew it had all been for nothing.

Postscript

The Gul family's story does not end there. In fact, for some of them, such as Shaista's youngest sons, it is only just the beginning. And they are all, like many Afghans, still suffering the consequences of the West's war in Afghanistan and the disastrous withdrawal in August 2021. At the time of writing, more than a year after Operation Pitting, the Taliban continues to drag the country back into the Dark Ages. Women like Salma are especially vulnerable. She still awaits any news from the British government about whether she will be given sanctuary in the UK. The female judges, academics and beauty salon owners whose lives were transformed when the British and American tanks rolled into their towns and villages in 2006 are now in hiding, unable to work or even to leave the house without a male escort. Some women have become so impoverished that they are having to sell their children to survive. Men too are victims, with former government employees and those who worked with NATO in some capacity being hunted down and arrested for their perceived crimes.

After he was made redundant by the British, Sayed, Shaista's cousin who had been the first gardener at Lashkar Gah, ended up joining the Afghan police to make money to survive. He was shot in his leg by the Taliban, leaving him disabled. He currently has no work and is living from hand to mouth. As the Taliban rolled into the city, he burned any documents that proved he had worked with the British. However, without such documentation, his chances of escaping the country for a new life in the UK are next to none.

Abdul, Shaista's brother, returned home from Pakistan to Lashkar Gah hopeless and penniless, unable to feed his family. Some days he cannot even afford bread. Shaista's other daughter, Naz , is inconsolable after her husband, also called Abdul, and who also served in the police, was led away from their house in handcuffs by four men and tortured for two days. When the family went to ask of his whereabouts, the Taliban at the local police station denied knowing where he was. Naz believed she would never hear from him again. But he did return home alive, although with the ghastly red marks of lashings all over his body.

And yet for some of the Guls, life is slowly improving. Jamal and Spozhmai are expecting their first baby, and Spozhmai still dreams of being a nurse. Jamal is considering trying to move back to England, where they will be closer to their Afghan friends. If they do, he will try and take the rest of the family with him. Mohmood is hoping to have the shrapnel removed from his leg, which should make life easier for him and Gulali, who is currently his full-time carer. Esmatullah has started college, where he is learning English, and his nightmares appear to have stopped. After everything he has been through, he seems happier. As for Shaista and Razagulla, they're both now taking English classes, which, over time, should help them to make new friends. Shaista has also started gardening again, this time at his house in Scotland.

At the time of writing, there are still more than 5,000 Afghans who worked alongside the British troops and the UK government, including hundreds of interpreters, who are waiting to be rescued from the country. All have been accepted under the ARAP scheme, yet the way out is getting harder and harder for them. According to the US organization No One Left Behind, between 160,000 and 200,000 Afghans eligible for a Special Immigrant Visa for the USA because of their or their family's work with American troops remain behind in Afghanistan. A survey of friends, family and colleagues found that 182 Afghans are already believed to have been murdered while awaiting a visa. A separate poll of 16,000 eligible applicants found that the vast majority had received threats from the Taliban during a six-month period. Now the Taliban are trying to stop those who worked with coalition forces from leaving Afghanistan at all, and complications with obtaining documents such as passports are making their attempts to get to safety in Britain and America even more difficult. Thousands more Afghans who did not meet the UK government criteria for sanctuary have appealed to the MoD for help and are likely to be in the process of being rejected. Some will remain forever in limbo, fearing for their lives but having nowhere else to go. Others will undoubtedly try to make it to Europe illegally. Mohibullah, whose interpreter brother was killed and who still suffers the consequences, is living in hiding in Kabul, relying on handouts from relatives. Such is the chaos in the ARAP unit back in London that a few months after the fall of Kabul he received an email saying his dead brother had been accepted for sanctuary in Britain. Hanif, who was cruelly rejected for sanctuary by the British government even after he had been given details of his flight and bought new dresses for his little girls, appealed against the decision from his new home in the USA. The Brits admitted that they had the wrong information about him and granted him asylum. He has chosen to stay in San Diego.

Many of the lucky ones, the more than 10,000 Afghans who have so far been relocated to the UK under the MoD's relocation scheme, are struggling to find jobs and homes and to learn English. They also all have family living under constant threat back in Afghanistan. Ahmad, who worked for counter-intelligence at Camp Bastion, managed to flee Kabul for Britain two weeks before the withdrawal. But his brother, a farmer living back in Logar province, is still suffering the consequences of Ahmad's work years later. As a punishment, most of what he earns from the land has to be handed over to the Taliban. Qais, the interpreter who waited outside the airport for four days with his wife and children, eventually got on a flight to the UK. Having spent several months in a hotel in Britain, he was told that the family should pack their belongings and a taxi would pick them up to take them to their new house in Bexley, south-east London. They were so excited. But when they got there, it turned out the house was already occupied by someone else. They were moved to Carlisle, more than 300 miles from their relatives. Although Qais doesn't mind their new home and has found work in a local takeaway, his family, who don't speak any English, are unhappy. His father, who worked with the British embassy for nearly 15 years, is living in Kabul in fear of revenge attacks. Shahwali Habibi, like most of the interpreters, has a long list of skills, including in IT and nursing, but without any UK qualifications he cannot find work. Some of the Afghans would like to work for the MoD or join the police, but under current rules they have to wait five years until they have indefinite leave to remain.

Then there are the thousands of Afghans still stuck in hotels waiting for accommodation because of a lack of housing, exacerbated by Russia's war in Ukraine. Some of them have been waiting for more than a year.

Meanwhile, some British veterans are campaigning to get Afghans like Shaista and Jamal a civilian service medal in formal recognition of their services to the British army during the war.

There is no doubt that Britain's efforts in Afghanistan, however futile they may now seem, would not have been possible without the support of the brave interpreters – their 'eyes and ears' – and that of other locally employed staff. Some soldiers would not be alive today if it wasn't for their interpreter translating messages from the Taliban about incoming fire. Not only has there always been a strong moral argument for bringing such loyal people to safety, but there is also a practical one. How will it look to other foreign employees, whom we are likely to need in future military campaigns, if the UK fails to protect the Afghans from the threat of reprisals at the hands of our enemies? Yet over the last eight years of campaigning I have been struck by the reluctance of politicians and civil servants to bring about any meaningful change so as to ensure these people's safety, and by the callous way in which families were kept apart for years even when one of them had been flown to the UK. Nonsensical government policies existed for far too long. It took Ben Wallace, a former soldier himself who became Defence Secretary in July 2019, to fully grasp the absurdity of the status quo and dramatically increase the number of Afghans who were eligible for sanctuary in the UK. One of those was Shaista. Operation Pitting, the UK military operation to evacuate both British nationals and Afghan nationals in August 2021, saved the lives of thousands of people. But for others it was too little, too late. And even at that point, some of the most deserving cases were ignored or wrong decisions made that were based on incomplete information. If someone had listened to the journalists, politicians, military personnel, war heroes and more than 176,000 members of the public who signed a petition in 2015 for the government to help them earlier, there would be far more Afghans living in safety in Britain today.

This book cannot tell every story, nor can it tell any of them in their entirety. It merely tries to provide an insight into the lives of one family, the Guls, so that the sacrifices of the Afghan people are not forgotten.

Acknowledgements

Thank you to the many former interpreters and other locally employed staff, including Abdullah Abdul, Ahmed, Dawari, Sayed Wafa, Mohammed Hares, Rafi Hottak, Shahwali Habibi, Tokhi, Niz, Ahmad, Basheer and Sharif, who made this book possible. And to those who did not want to be named: you know who you are.

David Williams, my former colleague, shone a light on the Afghan interpreters and the dangers they faced as a result of their work with the British military. Without his commitment and dedication, many of them would still be left in Afghanistan. I will also never forget the veterans, serving personnel, politicians and other campaigners who dedicated hours of their time over the years to helping persuade the government to bring vulnerable Afghans to safety. As far back as 2015, James Driscoll, a former major who served three tours of Afghanistan, started a petition calling for Afghan interpreters to be allowed into the UK. It was signed by more than 176,000 people. Dr Julian Lewis, who was chairman of the defence select committee when our Betrayal of the Brave campaign began, was one of the first politicians to listen to their stories. The inquiry he launched in 2017 that looked into the policies that existed at the time was damning. Colonel (ret.) Simon Diggins, former defence attaché in Kabul, and Ed Aitken, a former army captain who co-founded the Sulha Alliance to help interpreters, provided a crucial voice to the cause.

For this book, in particular, I want to thank Bayard Barron for putting up with my endless questions and Lieutenant-General (ret.) Sir John Lorimer, Major-General (ret.) Charlie Herbert, Major James Bolter and Major Malcolm Dalzel-Job for providing an insight into what life was like at MOB Lashkar Gah and elsewhere in Afghanistan. A special thank you to my parents, Helga and Simon, who read early versions of the book and came up with vital changes, my husband, Paul, for his support and encouragement and my two baby sons, Leonidas and Arthur, who stayed in my belly until I finished the first draft.

My sincere thanks also go to my brilliant agent Sally Holloway at Felicity Bryan Associates and to the team at Bloomsbury Continuum, especially publisher Tomasz Hoskins and assistant editor Fahmida Ahmed.

Finally, thank you to Jamal and the Gul family for sharing their story.

Notes

PREFACE

1 https://www.dailymail.co.uk/news/article-8749127/Brave-translators-worked-troops-Afghanistan-given-sanctuary-Britain.html

CHAPTER 1

1 https://www.refworld.org/docid/46f2580dc.html
2 https://www.hqmc.marines.mil/Portals/134/Docs/CCM%20Docs/Monthly%20PowerPoints/120708%20COMCAM%20Imagery.pdf
3 https://www.washingtonpost.com/opinions/in-afghanistan-the-rise-and-fall-of-little-america/2011/08/02/gIQAWHfqwI_story.html
4 https://www.gov.uk/government/fatalities/lance-corporal-david-leslie-kirkness-and-rifleman-james-stephen-brown-killed-in-afghanistan
5 https://www.theguardian.com/world/2012/jul/03/us-army-battles-british-afghanistan
6 https://www.independent.co.uk/news/world/asia/the-british-base-called-stalingrad-1804764.html
7 https://www.theguardian.com/world/2012/jul/03/us-army-battles-british-afghanistan
8 https://www.independent.co.uk/news/world/asia/the-british-base-called-stalingrad-1804764.html

CHAPTER 2

1 https://www.theguardian.com/world/2008/aug/12/afghanistan.military
2 https://www.thetimes.co.uk/article/mod-discloses-that-21-interpreters-have-been-killed-in-afghanistan-dkgj3w6f2k8
3 https://www.thetimes.co.uk/article/200th-british-soldier-to-die-in-afghanistan-named-as-private-richard-hunt-pr3d78k6gn9

CHAPTER 3

1 https://www.bbc.co.uk/news/10263713
2 https://www.theguardian.com/world/2009/jun/03/afghanistan-us
   -airstrikes-errors
3 https://www.bbc.co.uk/news/world-asia-63554941
4 *The Independent*, 'Rift with Karzai worsens as Nato air strike kills
   95', 5 September 2009.
5 https://www.theguardian.com/world/2009/jun/03/afghanistan-us
   -airstrikes-errors
6 https://www.nytimes.com/2009/06/22/world/asia/22airstrikes.html
7 https://www.theguardian.com/uk/2009/jan/23/military-afghanistan

CHAPTER 4

1 https://www.dailymail.co.uk/news/article-3427348/Our-troops-
   forced-free-prisoners-war-human-rights-Soldiers-face-lethal-Catch-
   22-hold-fighters-hand-case-tortured.html
2 https://www.afghanistan-analysts.org/en/reports/international
   -engagement/secret-nato-jails-that-arent-secret-ambush-and-drama
   -over-detainees/

CHAPTER 5

1 https://drb.ie/articles/war-death-and-hubris/
2 https://www.npr.org/2010/06/24/128058825/in-kandahar-it-will
   -take-a-village-to-oust-taliban

CHAPTER 6

1 https://www.dailymail.co.uk/news/article-3201503/Translator
   -abandoned-UK-executed-tries-flee-Taliban-Interpreter-killed
   -captured-Iran-amid-fears-four-suffered-fate.html
2 https://www.thetimes.co.uk/article/two-british-soldiers-killed-in
   -24-hours-in-town-where-150-afghans-voted-kbngrv877r5
3 https://www.brookings.edu/research/blood-and-hope-in
   -afghanistan-a-june-2015-update/

CHAPTER 7

1 https://pulitzercenter.org/stories/something-nothing-us-strategy
   -afghanistan

2 https://www.msf.ie/article/afghanistan-ten-years-msf-support
    -boost-hospital-lashkar-gah
3 https://www.dailymail.co.uk/news/article-6896711/None-50
    -Afghan-translators-promised-sanctuary-UK-arrived-yet.html
4 https://publications.parliament.uk/pa/cm201719/cmselect/
    cmdfence/572/572.pdf
5 https://bakhtarnews.af/en/local-journalist-wounded-in-bomb
    -attack-in-helmand/

CHAPTER 8

1 https://www.dailymail.co.uk/news/article-6780301/Afghan
    -translators-win-right-bring-loved-ones-Britain.html
2 https://www.dailymail.co.uk/news/article-5691123/Afghan
    -interpreters-SPARED-fees-right-remain-UK.html
3 https://www.itv.com/news/2021-07-22/my-kids-lives-are-in-danger
    -the-afghan-gardener-fearing-taliban-revenge-for-helping-the-british
4 https://www.itv.com/news/2021-07-22/my-kids-lives-are-in-danger
    -the-afghan-gardener-fearing-taliban-revenge-for-helping-the-british
5 https://www.france24.com/en/asia-pacific/20210812-taliban
    -capture-tenth-afghan-provincial-capital-over-weeklong-blitz
6 https://www.rferl.org/a/Pay_Hike_Brings_Surge_In_Afghan
    _Army_Recruits/1900916.html
7 https://www.thetimes.co.uk/article/afghanistan-female-soldier-
    who-trained-with-british-is-stranded-and-terrified-qtrcrv6hp
8 https://www.theguardian.com/world/2021/aug/16/kabul-airport
    -chaos-and-panic-as-afghans-and-foreigners-attempt-to-flee-the
    -capital#:~:text=Desperate%20Afghans%20clung%20to%20the
    ,the%20undercarriage%20immediately%20after%20takeoff.
9 https://www.forces.net/news/afghanistan-extra-uk-troops-and
    -aircraft-supporting-kabul-evacuation-mission
10 https://www.thetimes.co.uk/article/popular-afghan-comedian-has
    -throat-cut-by-taliban-kktfh7p3w

CHAPTER 9

1 https://2001-2009.state.gov/p/sca/rls/rm/27320.htm
2 https://www.thetimes.co.uk/article/my-daughter-fell-unconscious
    -while-waiting-for-flight-to-uk-8lo7l6p2k
3 https://www.thetimes.co.uk/article/banks-told-to-reopen-but
    -afghans-fear-ruin-awaits-g7b3hd9r9

CHAPTER 10

1 https://committees.parliament.uk/publications/22344/documents/165210/default/
2 https://www.thetimes.co.uk/article/planes-leaving-half-empty-after-taliban-set-up-ring-of-steel-6rdvp2wdb
3 https://www.thetimes.co.uk/article/afghan-interpreter-to-move-to-britain-after-rules-change-9h8586pob
4 https://www.propublica.org/article/hell-at-abbey-gate-chaos-confusion-and-death-in-the-final-days-of-the-war-in-afghanistan

CHAPTER 11

1 https://www.independent.co.uk/news/uk/politics/ben-wallace-afghanistan-pen-farthing-b1907749.html
2 https://www.thetimes.co.uk/article/i-will-destroy-you-pen-farthing-warned-defence-aide-over-afghanistan-pet-airlift-z7h30j2ws
3 https://committees.parliament.uk/writtenevidence/42679/pdf/

CHAPTER 12

1 https://www.dailymail.co.uk/news/article-10097661/Afghan-translators-families-forced-flee-borders-finally-whisked-safety.html

CHAPTER 14

1 https://www.independent.co.uk/asia/south-asia/afghanistan-taliban-humanitarian-crisis-warnings-b1955282.html
2 https://www.nytimes.com/2012/10/21/magazine/the-corner-where-afghanistan-iran-and-pakistan-meet.html
3 https://www.dawn.com/news/1399981
4 https://reliefweb.int/report/afghanistan/unseen-and-unheard-afghan-baloch-people-speak
5 https://www.hrw.org/report/2021/11/30/no-forgiveness-people-you/executions-and-enforced-disappearances-afghanistan

CHAPTER 15

1 https://www.thetimes.co.uk/article/visa-backlog-leaves-interpreters-baby-son-stranded-in-afghanistan-zzmqrq2bz

Index

269